IMAGES
of America

DOUGLAS

On the Cover: Ayres Natural Bridge west of Douglas is one of the area's favorite spots for tourists and locals alike. From the mid-1800s to now, people of all ages have had their picture taken under the arch over LaPrele Creek, making it the most-photographed area in Converse County. Pictured in this early 1900s photograph are, from left to right, Albert Sims, Stewart Horr, Miriam Browning, Elsie Cross, Bessie Horr, unidentified, Mary Cross, unidentified, Mabel Rice, and Edith Fizzell. (Courtesy Wyoming Pioneer Memorial Museum.)

IMAGES
of America

DOUGLAS

Linda Graves Fabian, Carol Price Tripp, Arlene Ekland-Earnst,
and the Wyoming Pioneer Memorial Museum

ARCADIA
PUBLISHING

ISBN 978-0-7385-8059-3

Published by Arcadia Publishing
Charleston, South Carolina

Printed in the United States of America

Library of Congress Control Number: 2009940063

For all general information contact Arcadia Publishing at:
Telephone 843-853-2070
Fax 843-853-0044
E-mail sales@arcadiapublishing.com
For customer service and orders:
Toll-Free 1-888-313-2665

Visit us on the Internet at www.arcadiapublishing.com

This book is dedicated to the families of Linda Graves Fabian and Carol Price Tripp for instilling in us a love of history, a sense of community, and a spirit of giving!

Contents

Acknowledgments

First and foremost we owe a debt of gratitude to the Wyoming Pioneer Memorial Museum for allowing us total access to its vast photographic and research collections. A big thank you to Marie Claudia Goodin, Carrie Prell, Gail Kirkland, and Noni Crain for always making us feel welcome in the "back room" and for bringing us whatever data we asked for. Many people before us have gathered and compiled information about Douglas's history, especially for the Diamond Jubilee Days in 1962. We gleaned a lot of particulars from those early works for this book, and we thank those unidentified authors for their contributions. Also to fellow classmate, author, and historian, Tom Lindmier for his personal opinions, advice, and willingness to write the Foreword. To Wyoming's renowned historians and good friends Dave Kathka, Mark Junge, Rick Ewig, Larry Brown, Phil Roberts, and Cindy Brown for teaching us to love and value history, and for their constant encouragement. To Richard Collier, who has gained an excellent reputation by photographing all areas of Wyoming, and for always being there to advise us. A personal note of thanks to Aunt Gladys and to our parents (Mark and Georgia Graves and Roy and Ethel Price) for making sure we grew up in such a wonderful community. To all the previous authors (specifically Russ Tanner, Lynn Houze, Nancy Weidel, and Starley Talbott) of the Images of America series for their words of advice and encouragement. To all the members of the Wyoming State Historical Society and the chapters for continuing to make the legacy of Wyoming known to others, and for constantly working to make sure the goals of the society are met. And, finally, to our patient husbands. All photographs are from the collections of the Wyoming Pioneer Memorial Museum in Douglas unless otherwise noted.

FOREWORD

Until the latter half of the 19th century, the territory containing central Wyoming was virtually an unoccupied wilderness, excepting the Native American peoples, a few mountain men, and traders. For centuries, the Platte River Valley had been hunting grounds for Native American peoples, and sadly, also their field of combat. Different bands had vied for possession of these lands, which was necessary to support their nomadic existence. Spanish explorers sought riches in gold and silver throughout this region but never established settlements.

Later trappers sought another form of wealth in the form of animal furs. These men coexisted with the local Native Americans, often marrying into a tribe for companionship and protection. Annually these fur trappers and Native American peoples gathered in large camps, called rendezvous, to sell their furs, purchase supplies, and socialize. Eventually the rendezvous system gave way to trading posts and provided the Native Americans and trappers with a more permanent supply base.

With the Louisiana Purchase, the region became a territory of the United States. Through this region the Oregon Trail became the major highway connecting the Eastern states with the West. Throughout the 1840s and 1850s, thousands of emigrants passed over this road, seeking new lives and fortunes along the Pacific coast. Tension developed between the indigenous peoples and these travelers with occasional violence. In the 1850s and 1860s, violence escalated as traffic on the road increased and stage lines, telegraph lines, and ultimately the railroads made their appearance. But still this vast area along the Platte River remained sparsely settled.

During this migration, the U.S. Government directed the military to establish small isolated garrisons to provide peace along the Oregon Road. New forts were developed along the route with Fort Laramie becoming the primary bastion in the upper Platte River Valley. Settler protection became more important, and efforts were made to keep the native peoples away from the major routes of travel. Treaties were negotiated, only to be dashed by acts of human indifference or racial bigotry on both sides.

By the late 1860s, a new form of white incursion on Native American lands began as settlers began to fill the river and stream valleys in south-central Wyoming. To protect travelers, settlers, and Native Americans alike, the military was called upon to establish more military posts. One of these new posts was Fort Fetterman. This post was established in 1867 on the south side of the Platte River and near the intersection of the Oregon and infamous Bozeman Roads. In 1868, a treaty was signed at Fort Laramie giving the area north of the Platte River and east of the Big Horn mountains to the Native Americans as a hunting ground. The Bozeman Road and all the military establishments north of the Platte River were abandoned. Fort Fetterman became the last military bastion in the area. The fort's existence was critical to the military during the next decade, but ultimately the Native Americans were forced onto reservations and the fort was closed in 1882.

From the buildings of the old fort, a town arose. This small community served the needs of the newly created cattle ranches and the cowboys they employed. In 1885, news circulated that a railroad would pass near the small community of Fetterman. Within two years, Fetterman's population exploded to over 200. The citizens who occupied buildings should have removed them from the military reservation as a condition of the sale. Had the buildings been removed, the military would later abandon the reservation and place it open for sale. For some reason, the abandonment of the reservation didn't transpire. The military ignored the "squatters," learning the responsibility of law enforcement to the local civilian government. Despite the law enforcement officers' best efforts, this new town became notorious for its murders and debauchery while its citizens awaited the railroad's arrival.

The tracks of the Fremont, Elkhorn, and Missouri Valley Railroad halted 10 miles east of Fetterman, at the edge of the still-active military reservation. It was then announced that the railroad company would establish a new town at this end of track. Immediately after this announcement, many citizens of Fetterman rushed to the area indicated by the railroad company as their new town site. New legislation in the U.S. Congress permitted the railroad to continue in 1887.

These enterprising citizens established a tent town on the banks of Antelope Creek, but the railroad town site company had other intentions and surveyed their new town south of Antelope Creek, where they sold lots for businesses and homes. Debates immediately commenced on the name of the new town among local residents. Many wanted to name the town "Fetterman," but the Illinois-based railroad town site company dubbed their town "Douglas," in honor of famed Illinois senator and presidential candidate Stephen A. Douglas. With the matter settled, Douglas became the region's commercial center and the towns of Antelope and Fetterman rapidly ceased to exist. Douglas sat within the boundaries of Albany County with a population of 805 in 1886, and in March of the following year, the community was incorporated. The town's growth slackened temporarily when the end of the railroad moved westward to Casper in 1888.

Converse County was established March 9, 1888, and Douglas was named its county seat. The young village gained additional stature when it welcomed the establishment of the Wyoming State Fair and grounds in 1905. Through energy and a firm faith in itself, Douglas thrived, and its population increased to almost 2,000 by 1907. In 1914, a second railroad was established through town: The Burlington Route. Now two railroads had stations in town with scheduled passenger service. Douglas became primarily an agricultural community throughout the first half of the 20th century, with a steady population of approximately 2,500.

Douglas thrived as a small town until the early 1970s when the oil and gas rich region created a population influx. Through the last three decades of the 20th century, the Wyoming Law Enforcement Academy was established in the area, along with additional coal mines and more oil and gas developments. Today Douglas is not only an important agricultural community, but also a major mineral community.

—Thomas Lindmier

One

The Military

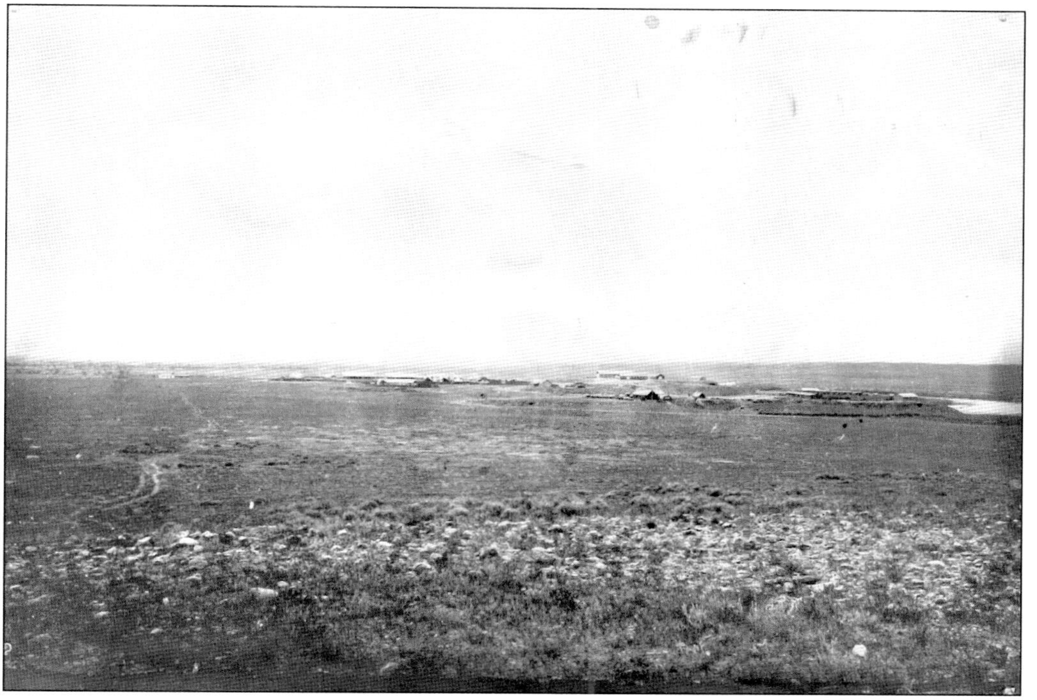

Fort Fetterman was built by Maj. William McEntyre Dye in 1867 to provide protection and supplies to emigrants along the Bozeman and Oregon Trails. This distant view of Fort Fetterman was taken in 1872 by William Henry Jackson. In a letter to the adjutant general, Major Dye described the post as "situated on a plateau above the valley of the Platte, being neither so low as to be seriously affected by the rains or snow; nor so high and unprotected as to suffer from the winter winds."

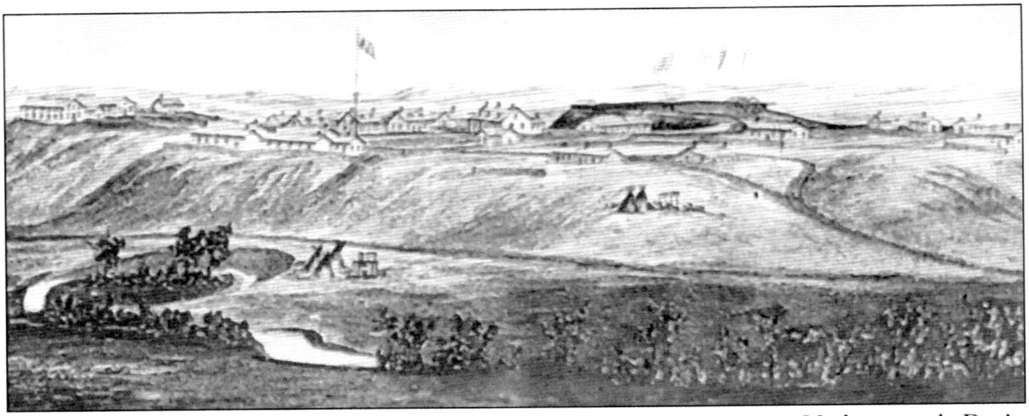

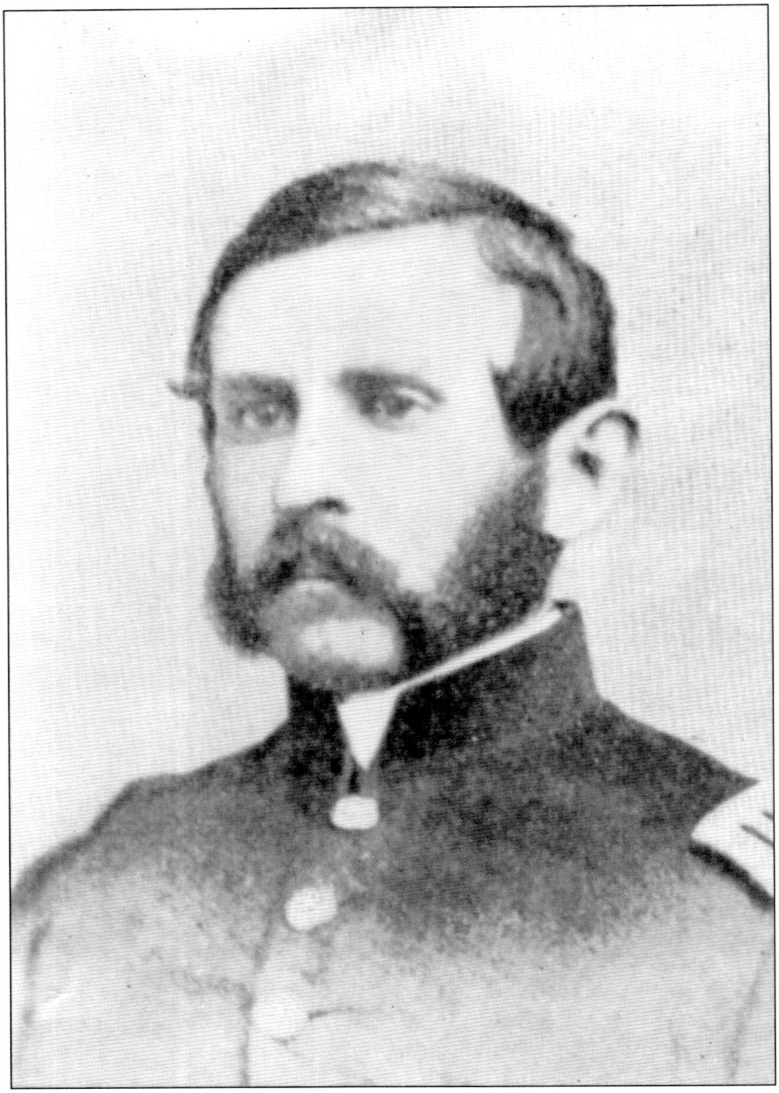

Unfortunately Dye's optimistic view didn't hold true, and Fort Fetterman was soon considered a hardship post by those stationed there. Dye's successor, Brig. Gen. H. W. Wessells, reported finding "officers and men . . . under canvas exposed on a bleak plain to violent and almost constant gales and very uncomfortable." (Courtesy Wyoming Trails and Tales Web site.)

The post was named Fort Fetterman in honor of Capt. William J. Fetterman, killed in a fight with Native Americans near Fort Phil Kearny on December 21, 1866.

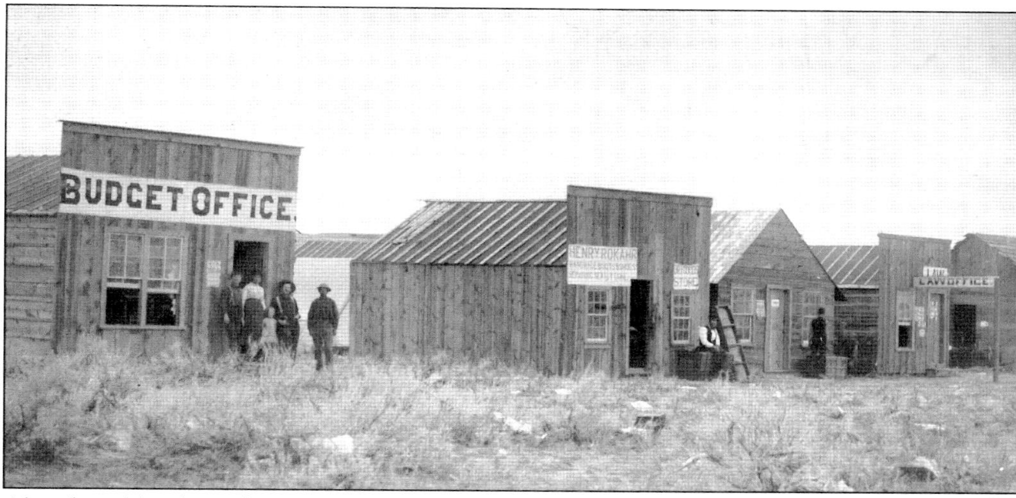

Abandoned by the military in 1882, the community of Fort Fetterman flourished and boasted numerous services for those living in the area. The town's newspaper, the *Douglas Budget*, was established in 1886, first in a tent and later in the building shown above. Editor Merris Clark Barrow (pen name "Bill Barlow") was born in Pennsylvania. Upon arriving at Fort Fetterman, he established the newspaper, which is still in existence today. A very witty and forward-thinking fellow, Barrow went on to serve two terms as mayor of Douglas and was elected to serve in the Wyoming State Legislature.

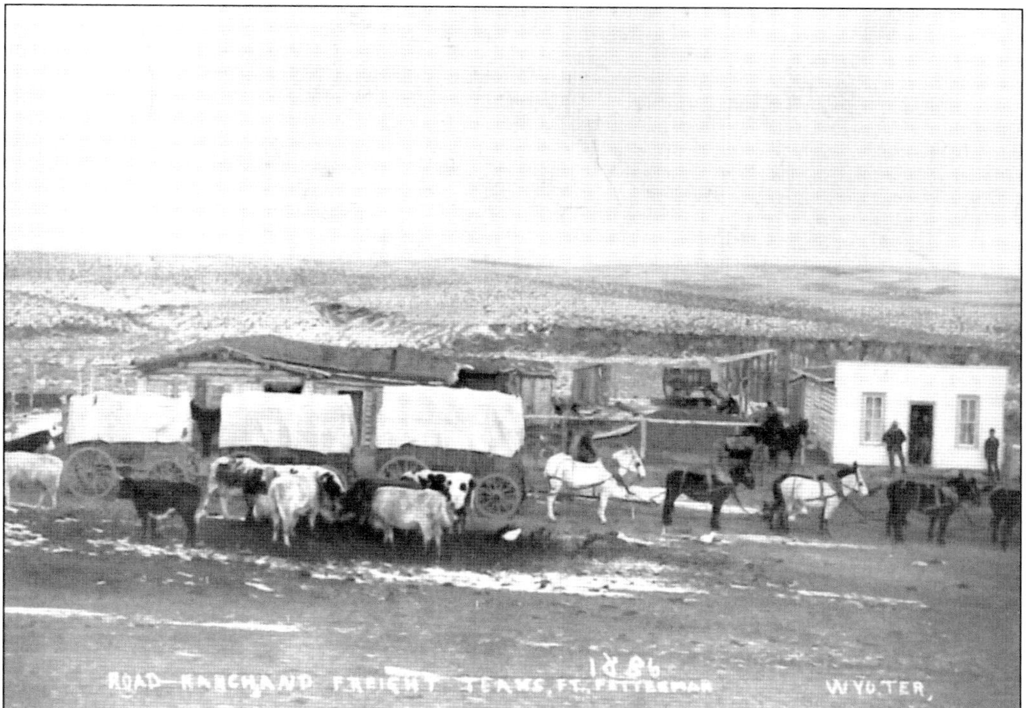

Though abandoned by the military, Fort Fetterman remained an important community for travelers on the emigrant trails. As depicted in this 1886 photograph, area ranchers received their supplies in Fetterman, delivered on a regular basis by freight teams.

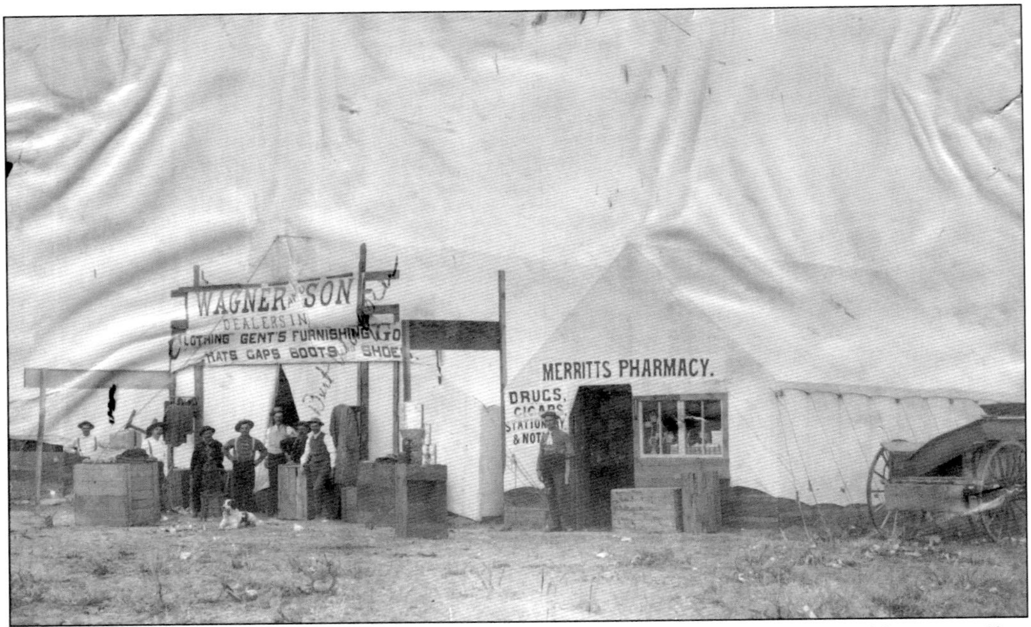

Canvas structures were the norm in "Tent Town," and businesses sprang up quickly in an effort to provide much-needed goods and services to its citizens. The images above demonstrate that many brave entrepreneurs were prosperous: it didn't take long for tents to be replaced by wooden structures.

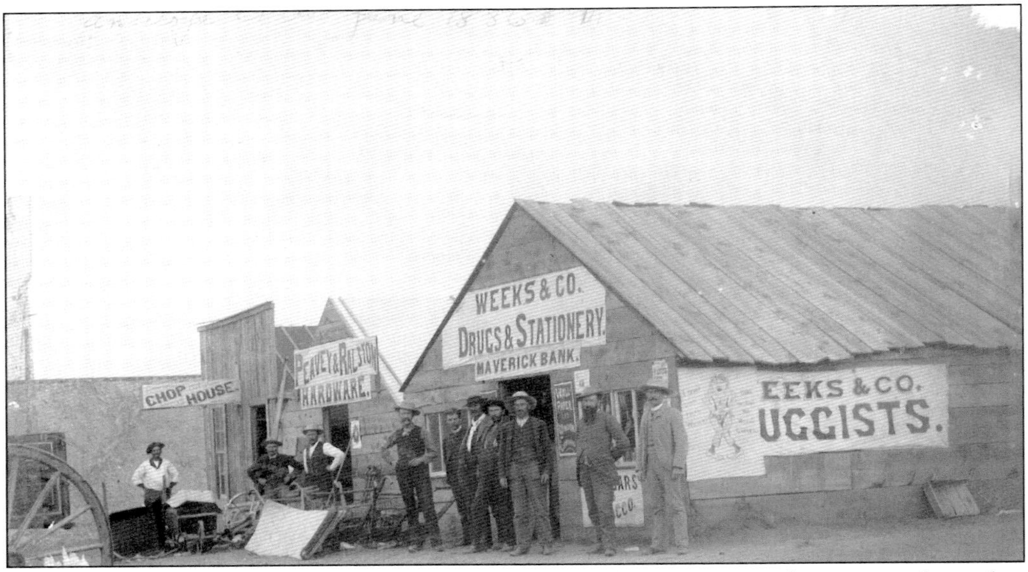

Merchandise of all types was plentiful, and ranchers in outlying areas soon began to trade in what was now called "Antelope." They traveled many miles to purchase goods, and it wasn't uncommon for businesses to make hundreds of dollars before breakfast. Notice the caricature advertisement on the side of the building. It says, "I don't like this water! Give Oh Give me Week's Ginger!" Apparently the druggist was adept at mixing up his own concoctions.

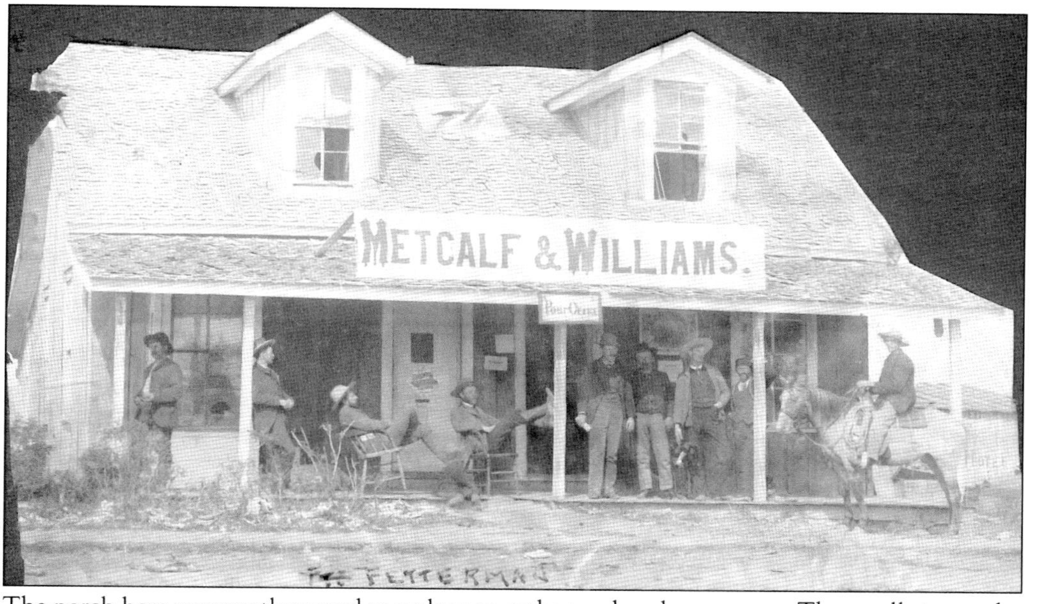

The porch here apparently served as a place to gather and exchange news. The small sign under Metcalf and Williams suggests that the store was also the local post office. Even today in most Wyoming towns, the post office is the place to see and be seen.

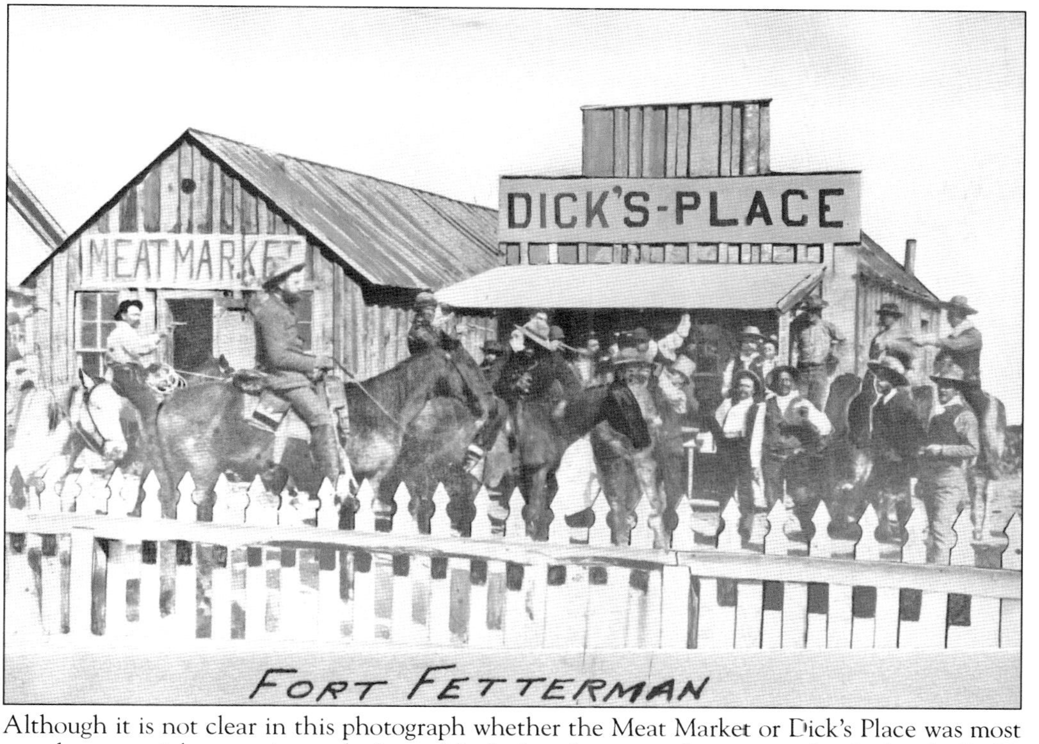

Although it is not clear in this photograph whether the Meat Market or Dick's Place was most popular, one might guess it was the latter. No doubt a favorite gathering spot for the locals, Dick's Place was only one of several saloons.

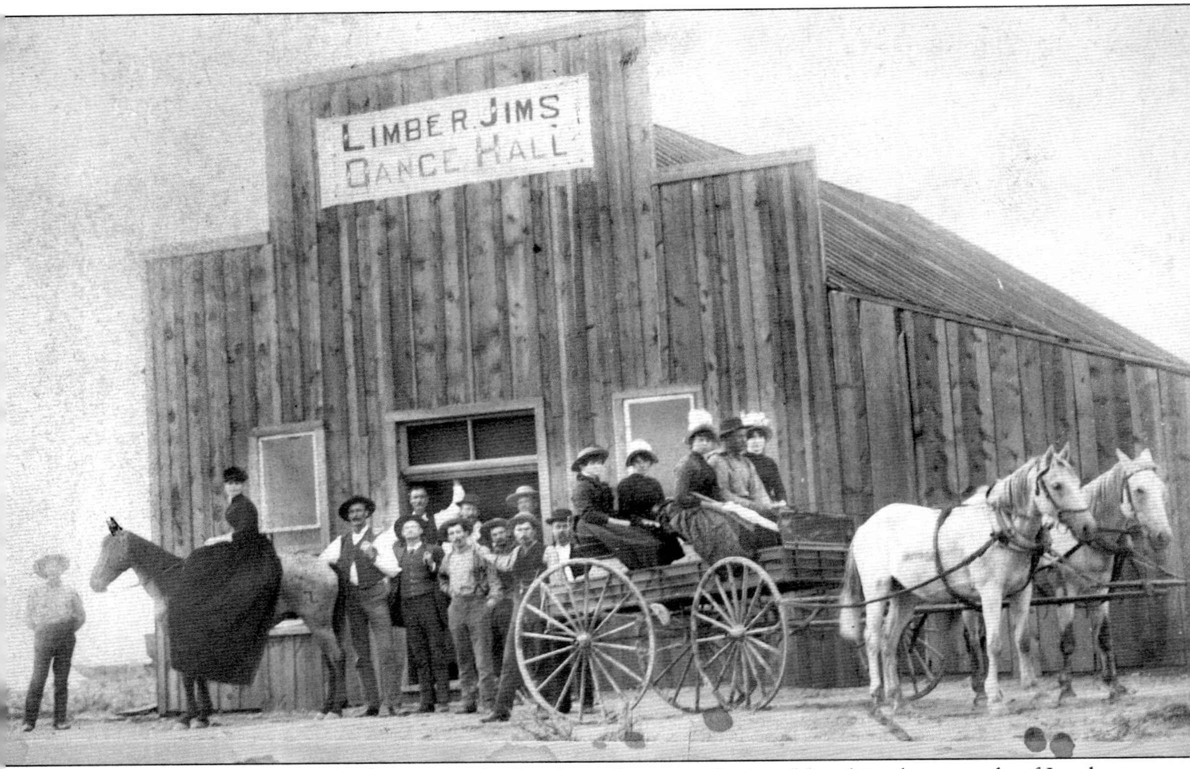

Entertainment was a high priority for local residents, as depicted by this photograph of Limber Jim's Dance Hall. One must wonder if the people in the photograph were locals or had been imported for the patrons' enjoyment.

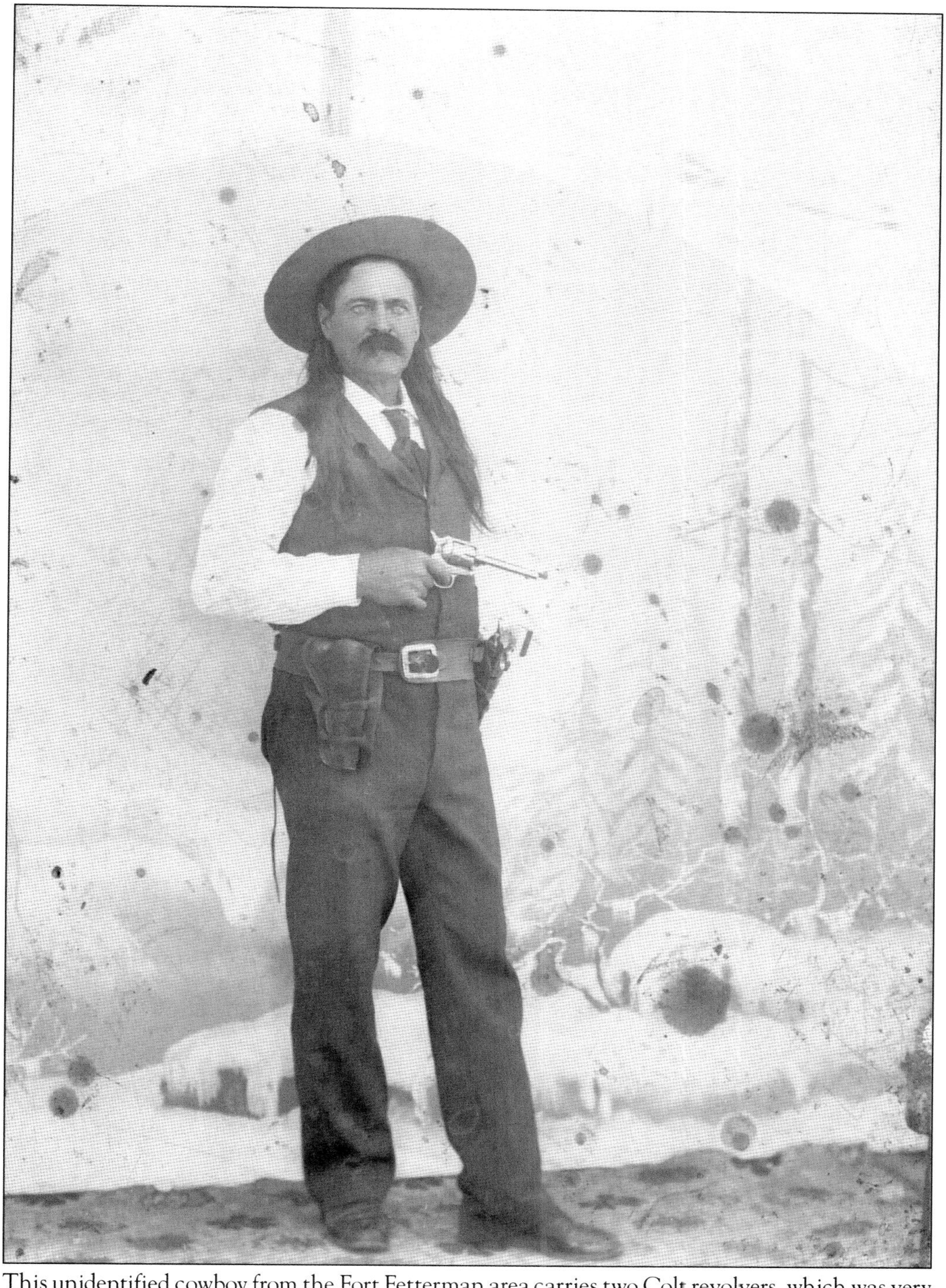

This unidentified cowboy from the Fort Fetterman area carries two Colt revolvers, which was very uncommon in the late 1880s—unless looking for trouble. The background in the mural (though difficult to see) depicts a barren wintery scene, suggesting that the photograph was taken by a professional photographer.

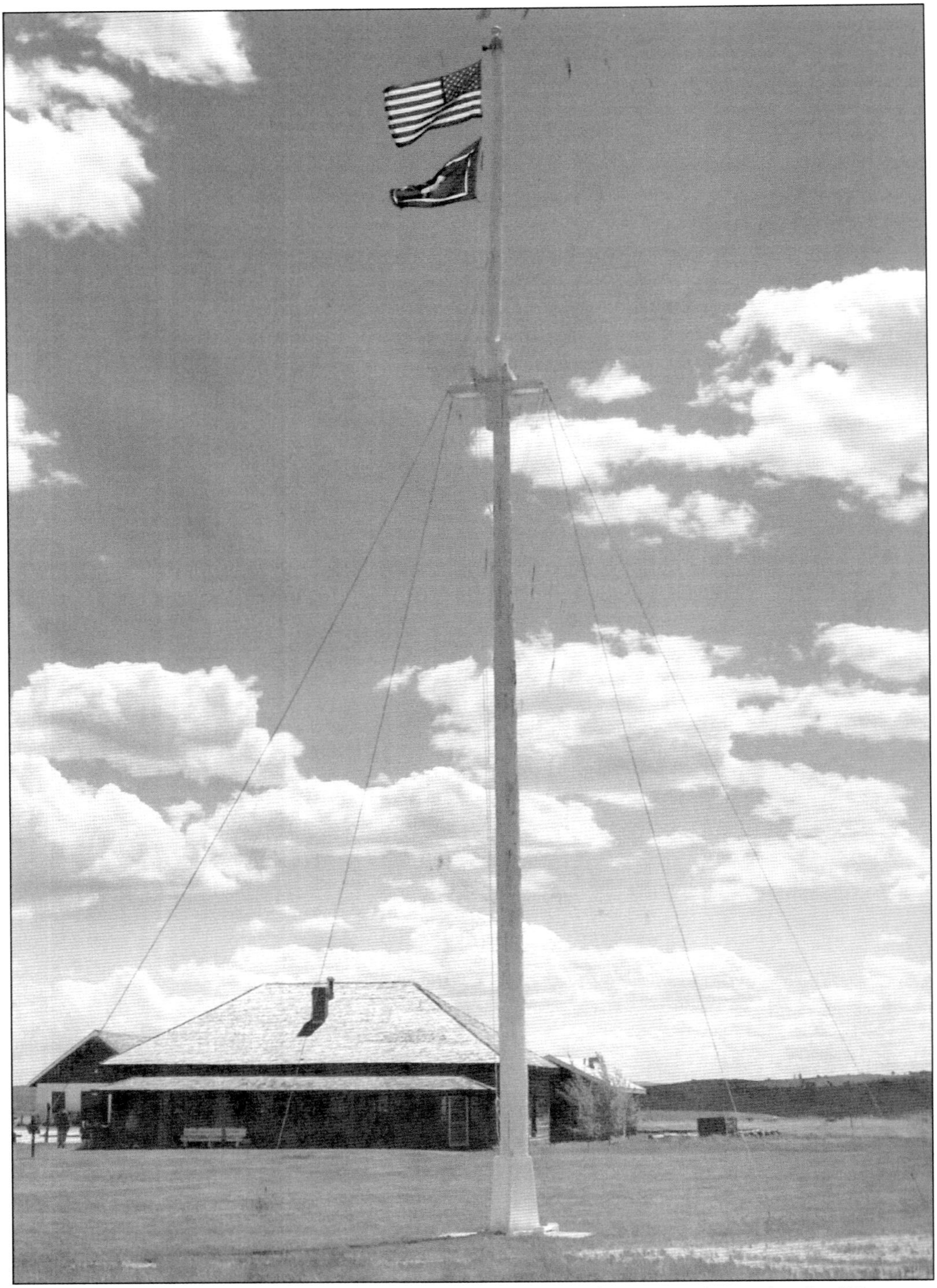

Fort Fetterman was named a state historic site in 1962, and is presently run by the Wyoming Department of State Parks and Cultural Resources. Every summer, volunteers and staff host Fort Fetterman Days, a celebration of those who served and lived there. (Courtesy Joni Goodwin.)

Two

The Iron Horse

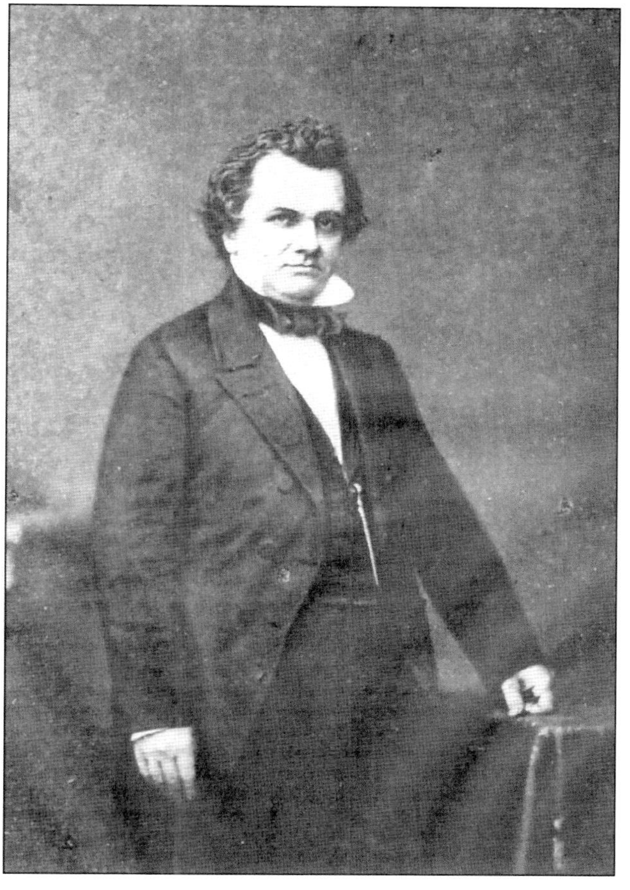

As word of an impending railroad construction effort loomed, it became clear that the tracks would not be near Fort Fetterman or the newly established town of "Antelope," but rather about ten miles to the east. Working out of their Chicago headquarters, representatives of the Fremont, Elkhorn, and Missouri Valley Railroad had secretly determined where they were going to lay tracks, and it was nowhere near the former military post. They then proceeded to name the town after the great orator and Illinois senator Stephen A. Douglas, a hearty advocate of westward expansion. Newspaper editor Bill Barlow was not in favor of the name. Resignedly, however, he encouraged citizens to wholeheartedly support their new town.

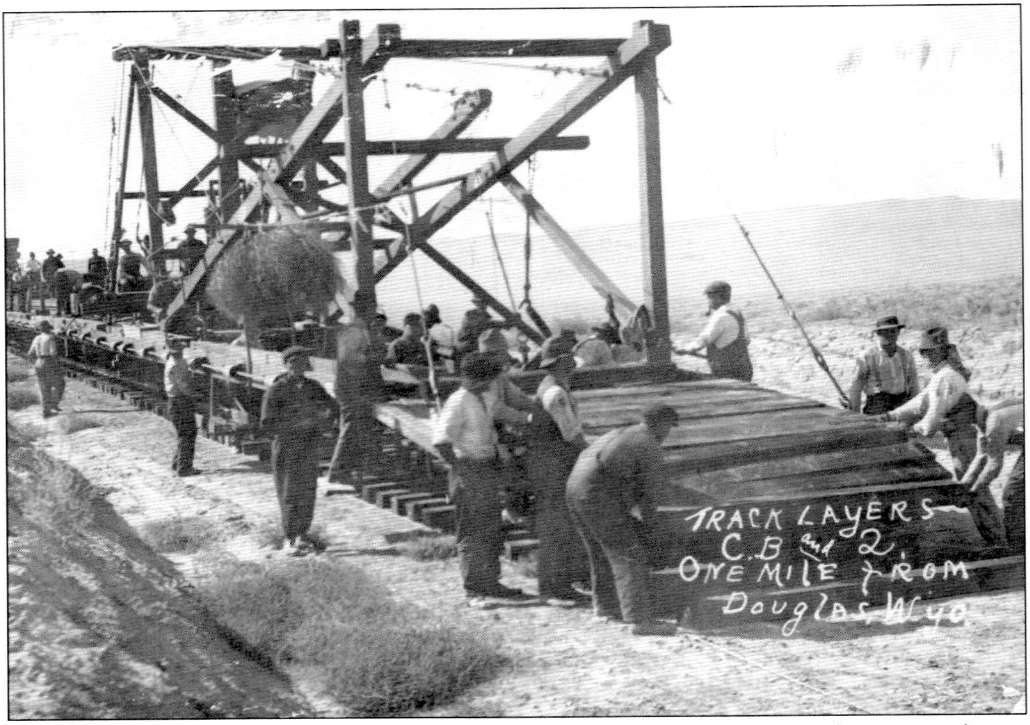

This image depicts workers employed by the Chicago and Northwestern Rail Company laying track outside the new town of Douglas. The Chicago and Northwestern Rail Company was the parent company for the Fremont, Elkhorn, and Missouri Valley Railroad, which built track to Douglas from Fremont, Nebraska, in 1886.

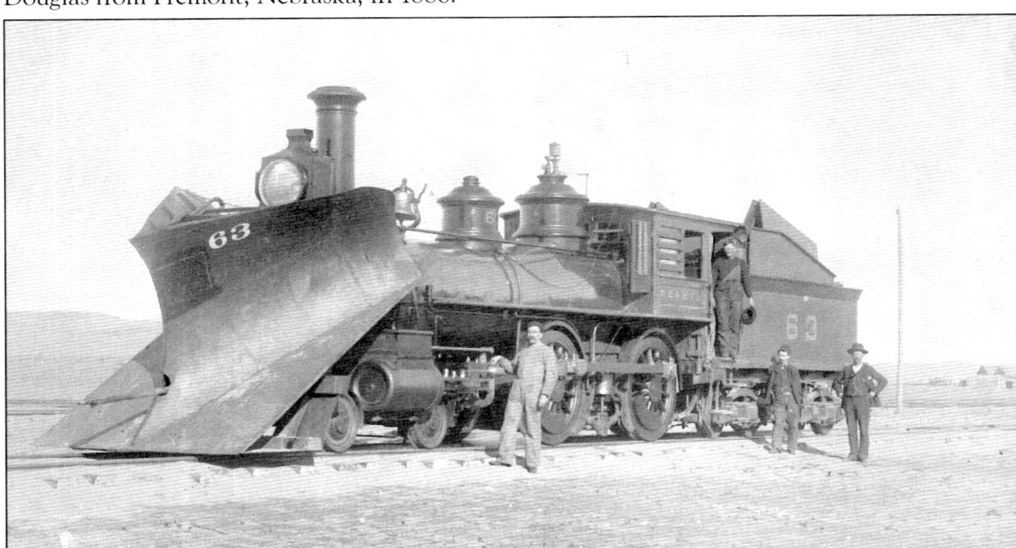

Engine No. 63, belonging to the Fremont, Elkhorn, and Missouri Valley Railroad, made its way to the new town on rails owned by the Chicago and Northwestern, which was blazing a trail across the southern expanse of Wyoming Territory. According to the Douglas Railroad Interpretive Center, no one knows where Engine No. 63 is now, but in 1886, it hissed to a stop in Douglas.

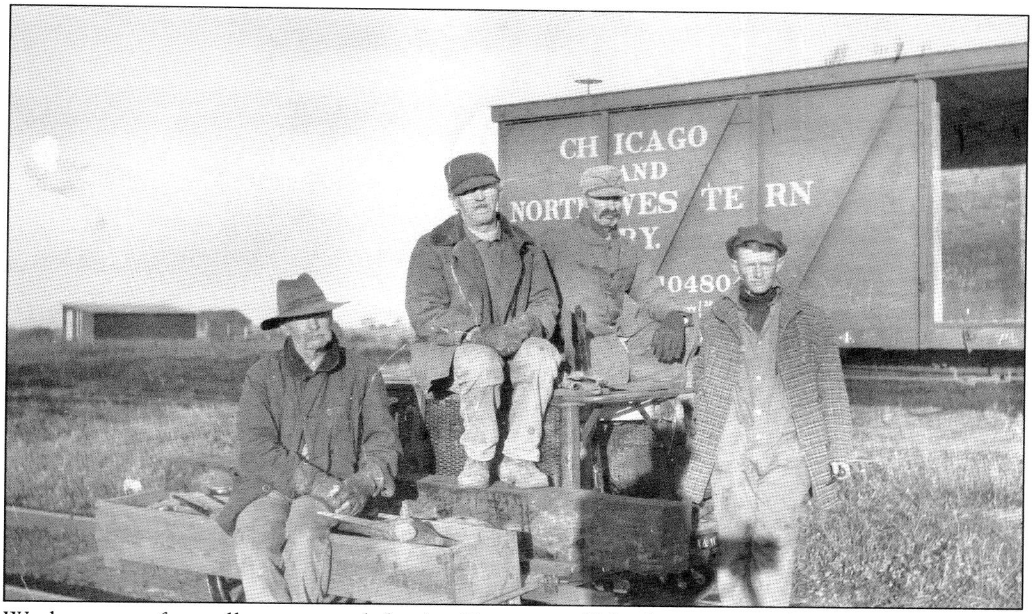

Workers came from all over to work for the Chicago and Northwestern Railroad. Martin R. Price, on the left, came to Wyoming from Pennsylvania because he hoped that working for the railroad would promise a good future for his family.

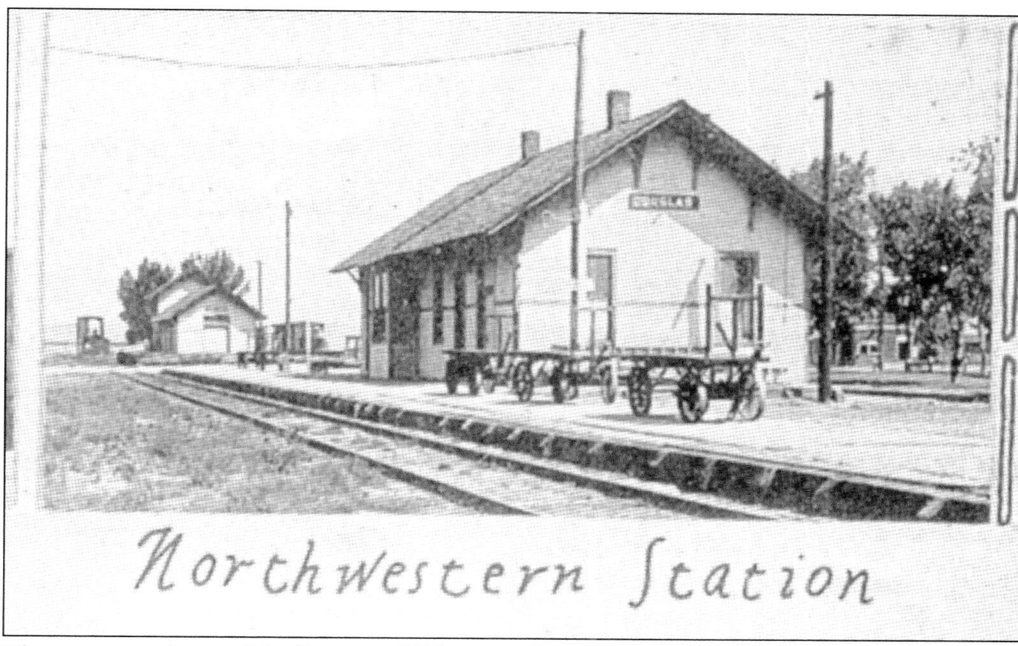

The passenger depot of the Fremont, Elkhorn, and Missouri Valley Railroad was built according to standardized plans and included a waiting room, a ticket office, two restrooms, and a freight room. In 1994, the depot was listed on the National Register of Historic Places. Restored by the City of Douglas, it reopened to the public in 1995.

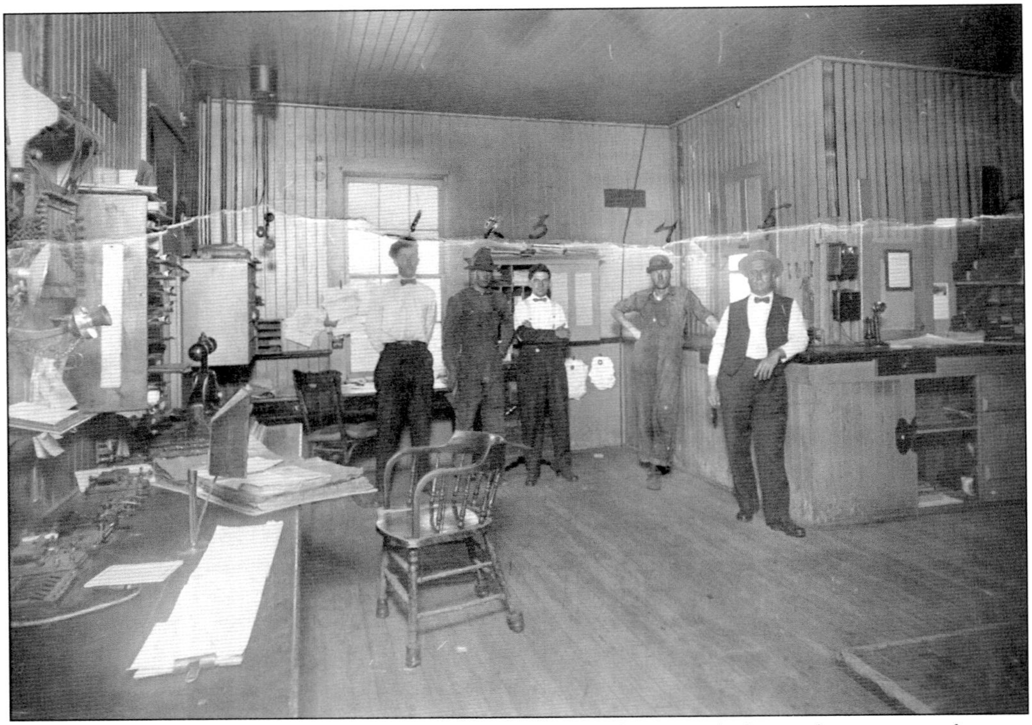

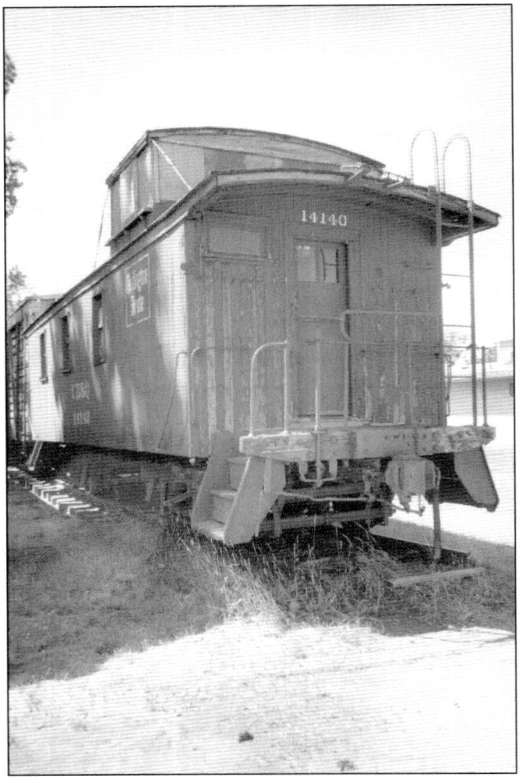

This photograph shows the interior of the Chicago and Northwestern Railroad passenger depot. Three of the people in the photograph are identified (left to right) as Frank Logan, Dick Anthony, and Earl M. Criss, the telegraph operator. Over the years, the building has been a flour mill and later a wool warehouse. Today it has been restored to its appearance during its depot era and is home to the Douglas Chamber of Commerce.

Caboose No. 14140 served as an office and living quarters for a train's brakeman, flagman, and conductor. Although called many things throughout the years, the name "caboose" stuck. It most likely derives from the Dutch word for a ship's galley, *kabuis*. This particular caboose is now on display at Douglas's Railroad Interpretive Center, one of the most popular attractions in Converse County.

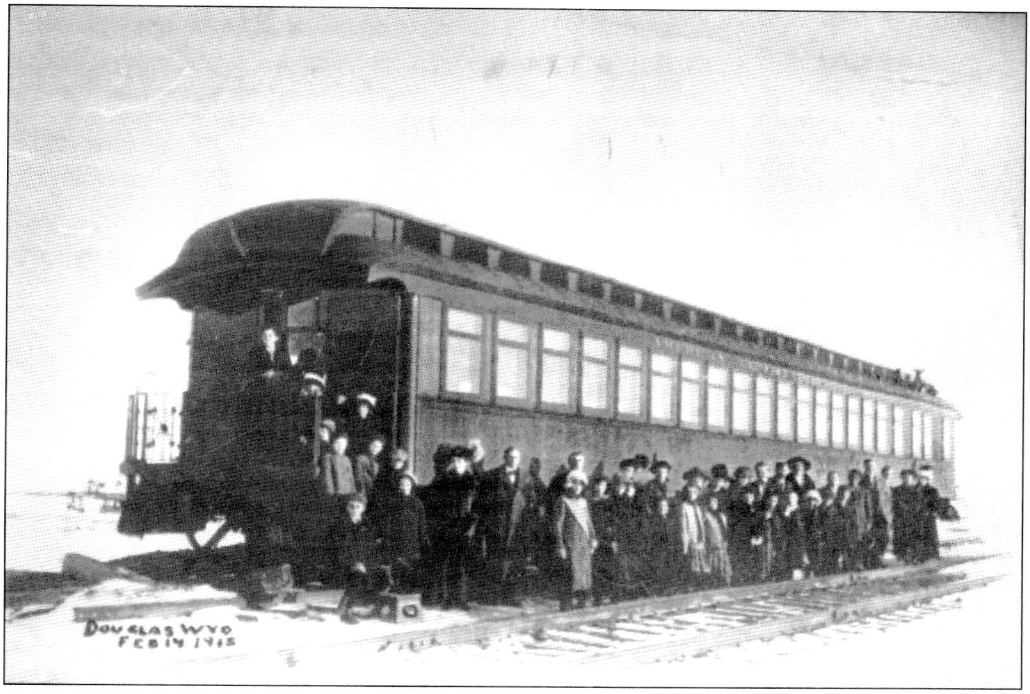

In January 1915, the First Baptist Church of Douglas held services in a "chapel car" called "Glad Tidings." Apparently there were seven chapel cars in existence, serving various places in the West. The brainchild of Baptist preacher Dr. Wayland Holt, the chapel cars would pull into a town, and the traveling evangelist would spend his days going house to house, encouraging people to attend a service in the chapel car.

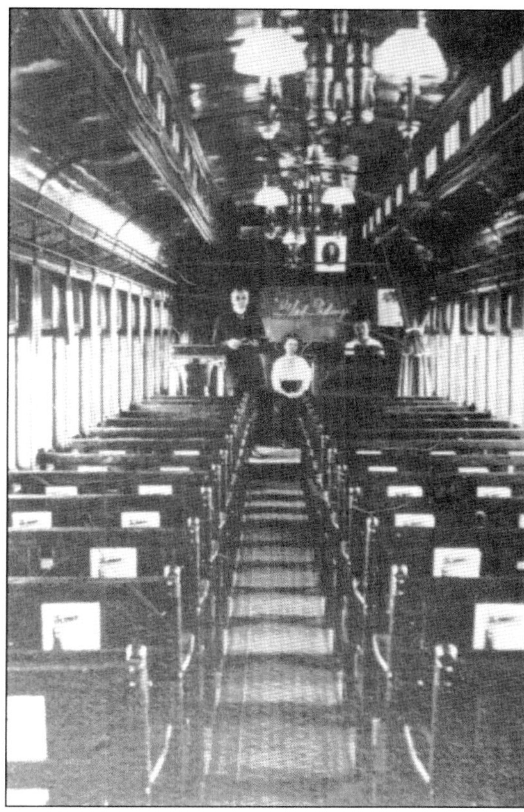

Dr. Holt mentioned the idea of railcar chapels to his brother, railroad executive Colgate Holt. Colgate organized a "Chapel Car Syndicate" to raise money to build the cars. Inside Glad Tidings, the parishioners could enjoy a sanctuary, pews for about 125 people, and an organ. One end of the car served as a parsonage for the missionary and his wife, complete with a living room, kitchenette, and sleeping quarters.

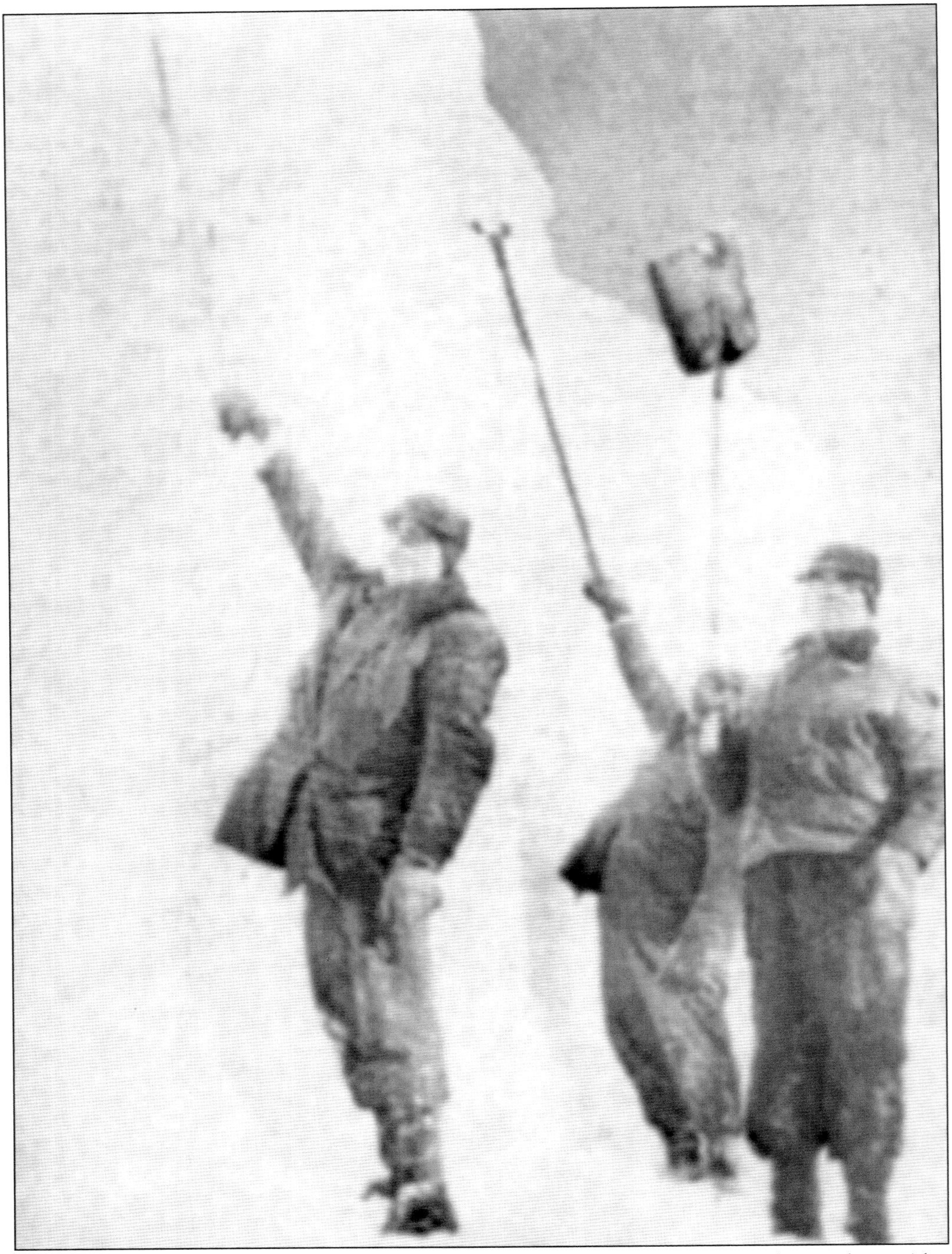

Albeit 61 years ago, the Blizzard of 1949 is still fresh in the minds of many Douglas residents. Also known as "The Great White Death," the blizzard was a series of storms that lasted for several weeks, spreading its misery over Wyoming, Colorado, and Nebraska. The U.S. Air Force dropped thousands of tons of hay to save cattle and sheep. Many people died, and more than a million head of livestock were killed in the tristate area by this blizzard.

Three

MERCHANTS AND MERCANTILISM

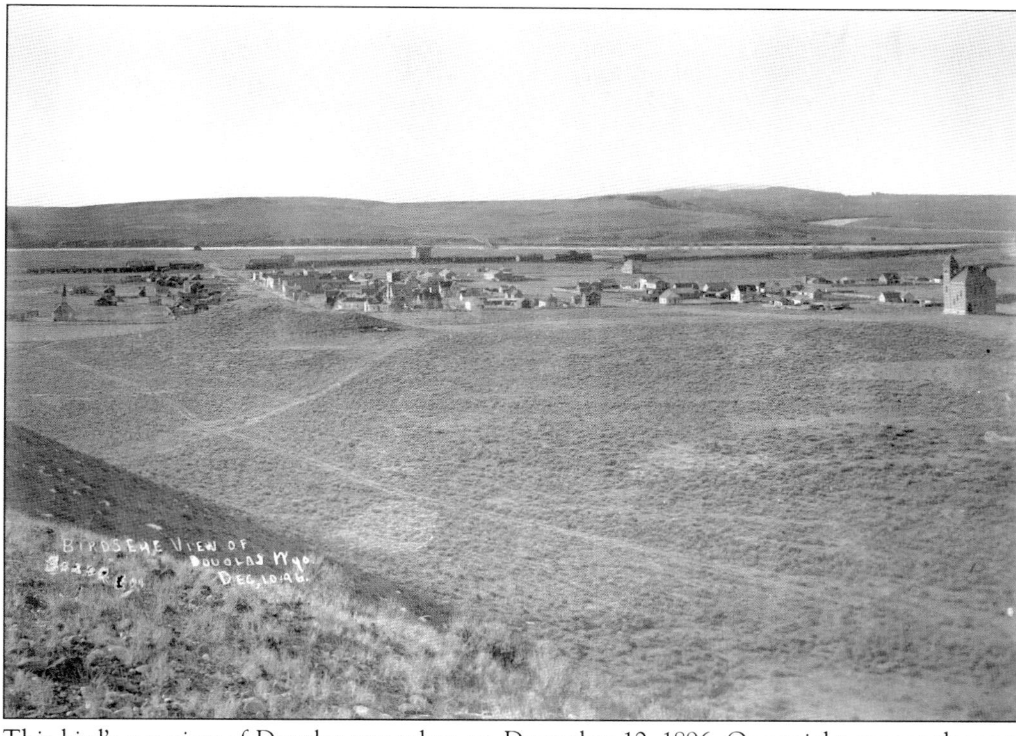

This bird's-eye view of Douglas was taken on December 10, 1896. One might expect the vast plains to be covered by snow, but it appears the day was dry and the winds calm. Upon close examination, the train tracks just behind the town can be seen. The curve of the North Platte River can be seen in the background.

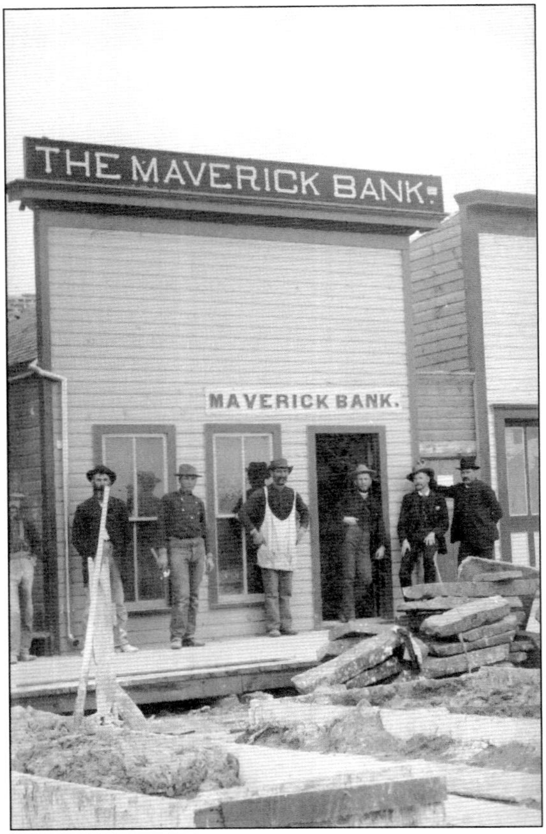

While the Maverick Bank was among the first buildings in Douglas, heavy street work was progressing slowly. The bank was originally located on the corner of North Second and Center Streets. The man in the doorway has been identified as H. T. Blackburn.

The luxurious Valley House Hotel was home to many a traveler. Built in 1898, it was the first such lodging in Douglas. The hotel was located between the railroad tracks, north of the Gene L. Payne Company. Apparently, the Valley House Hotel was cut in half in 1914 to make way for the Burlington tracks, and as rumor has it, was moved under dark of night.

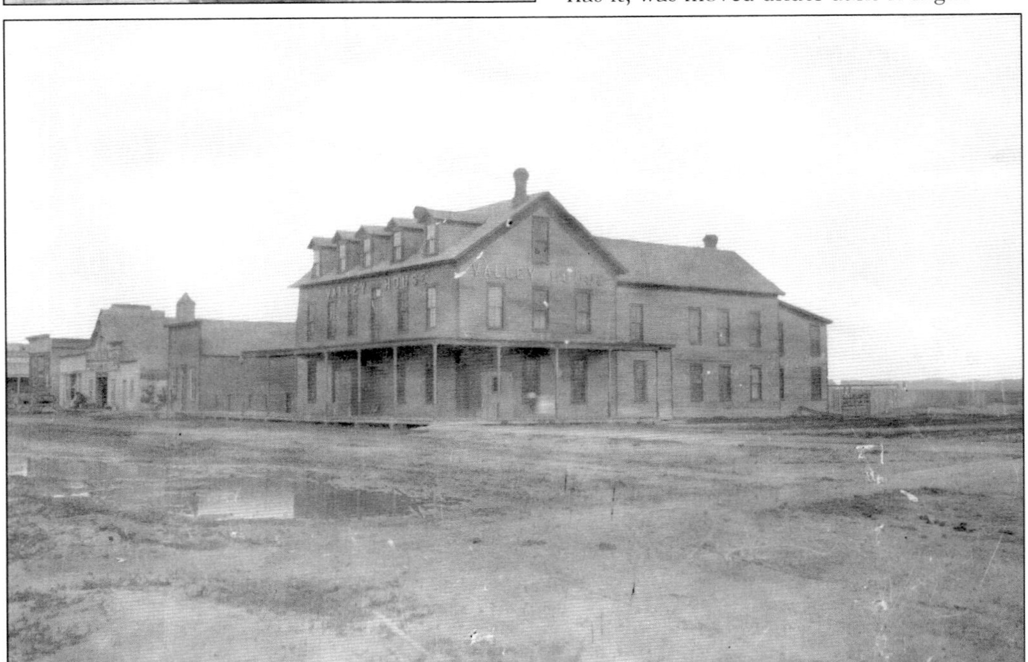

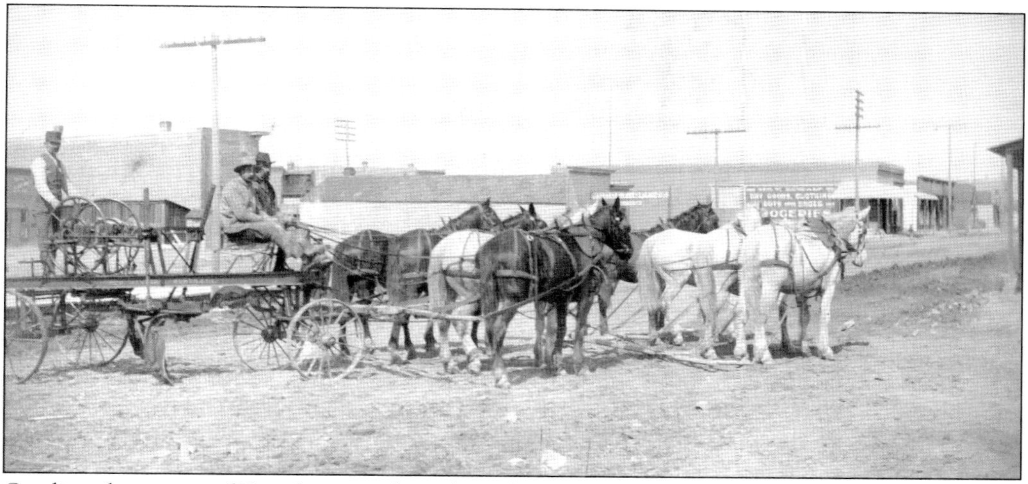

Grading the streets of Douglas was a big job made easier with a team of sturdy horses. John Snow is identified as the man standing on the rig. From the photograph it appears that the town had electricity as early as 1900.

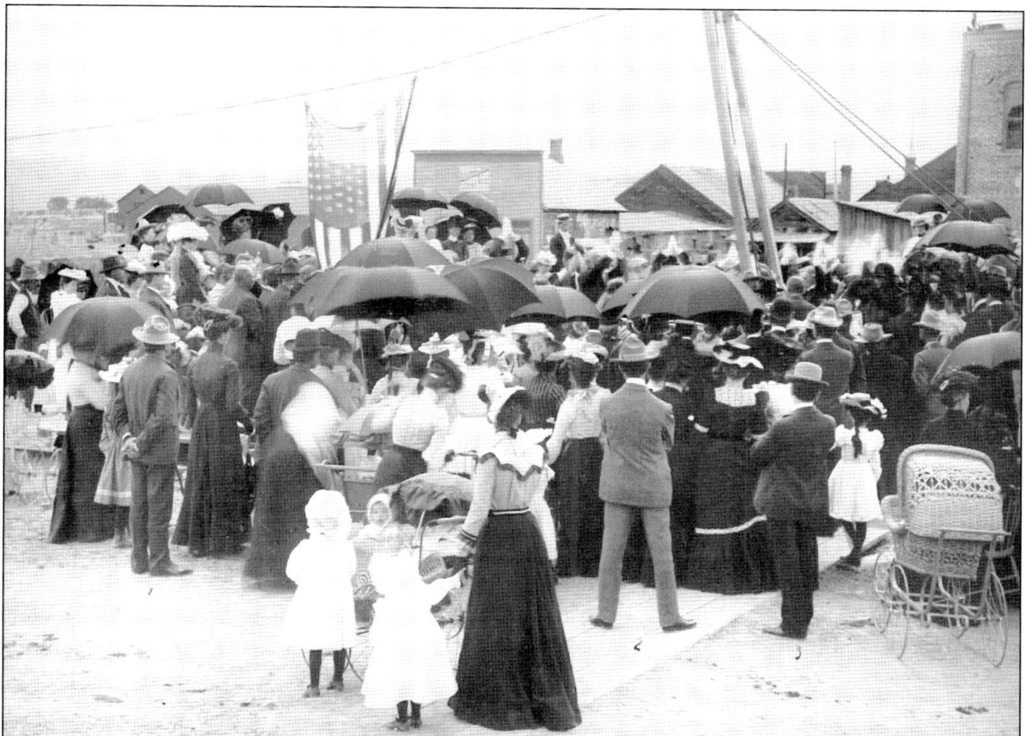

In 1902, the cornerstone was laid at the Unity Temple Building at the corner of Third and Center Streets, a fine day in the history of the community. Although all the people seen here cannot be identified, a notation on the photograph (unfortunately without corresponding numbers on the image) lists "1. Frank York, 2. Bob Potter, 3. O. P Witt, 4. Fred McDermott, 5. Otto Bolln." The many umbrellas held by women in attendance at the big event no doubt provided welcome relief from the hot sun.

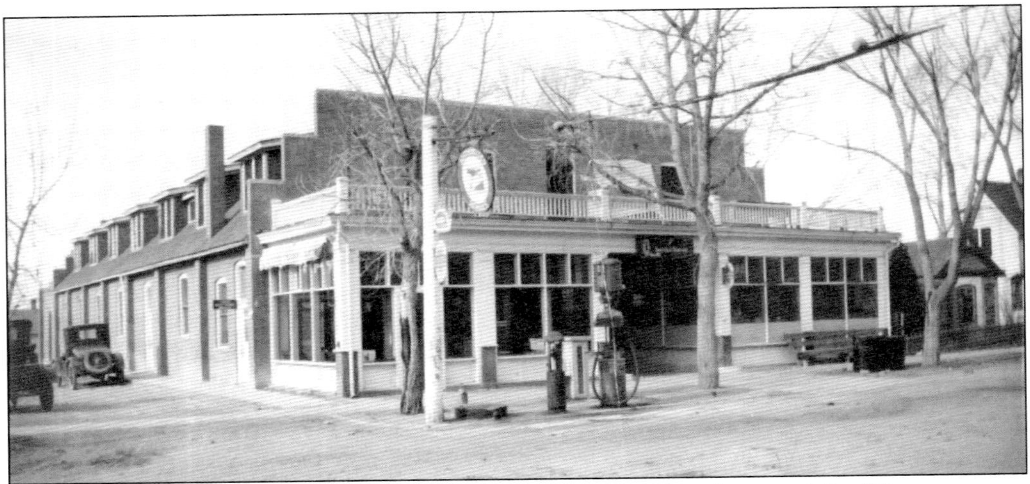

In 1910, the Morsch Garage provided services to the few who owned automobiles. The garage was located at 114 North Fourth Street. From an inventory of historical buildings, survey conducted in 1994, the building was described with "arched window openings with radiating brick voussior lintels and equipped with double-hung, wood-sash windows." Morsch was president of the Good Roads Club from 1911 to 1915. The club functioned much like today's Adopt a Highway program, in that everyone riding in a member's car had to agree to get out and throw ten rocks off the unpaved Yellowstone Highway. (No word as to where all those rocks ended up.)

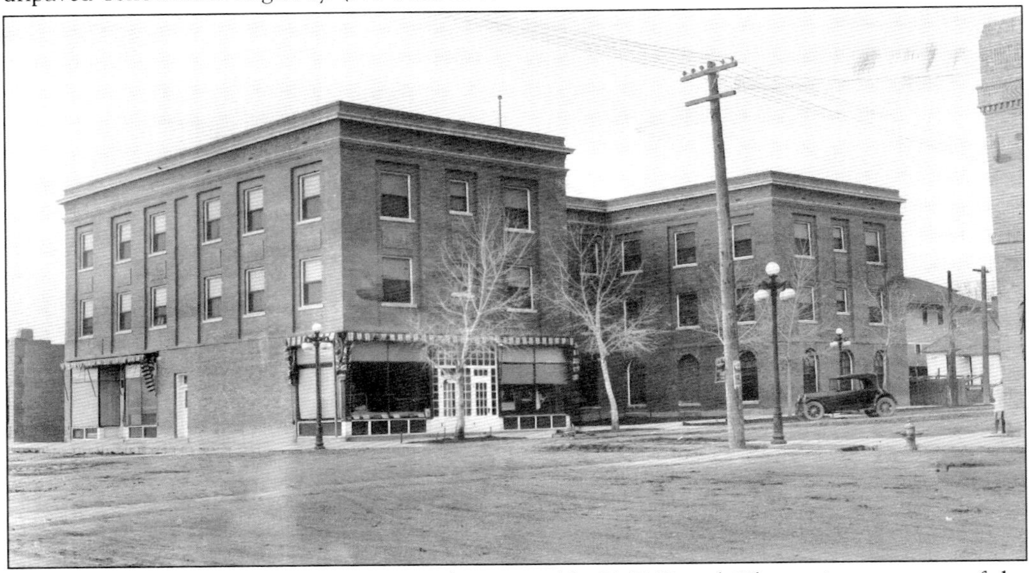

The LaBonte Hotel was built in 1913 on lots owned by E. T. David. The project was part of the expansion and remaking of downtown Douglas during the 1910s, and financed by investors E. T. David, Alva Rice, Otto Bolln, George Cross, and George Smith. The building of the hotel expressed the optimism of Douglas residents. Strategically located close to the railroad depot and the heart of the community, the hotel became one of the town's most popular gathering places, not only for those seeking lodging, but for the locals who enjoyed its distinctive architecture and lovely restaurant. The hotel's popular motto was "Tell Um I'll Meet Ya at the LaBonte." Although the hotel has seen many owners and endured a number of physical changes, it still stands today. In 2009, it was listed on the National Register of Historic Places.

The Steffen Drugstore was owned and operated from 1890 to 1937 by Lorraine Steffen, John J. Steffen, and Ben Steffen. Merchandise included a wide assortment of tonics, sure to fix whatever ailed you. Pharmacist Henry Saul can be seen behind the counter on the left. John J. Steffen served as mayor of Douglas in the early 1900s.

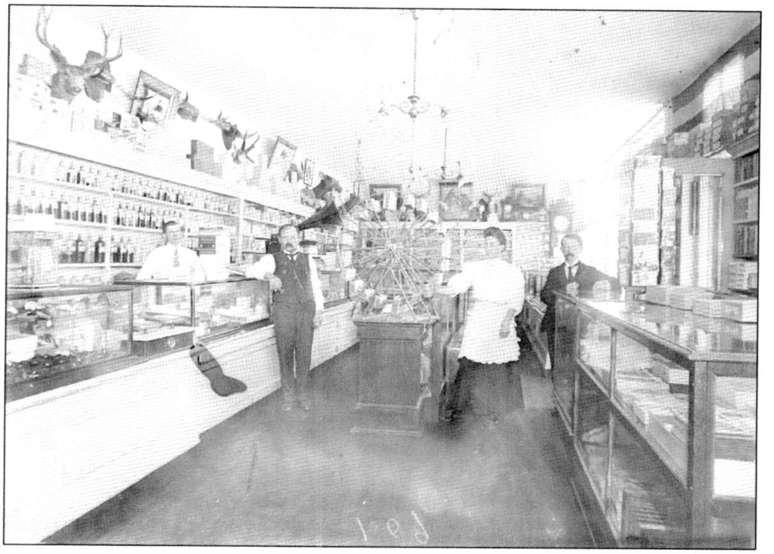

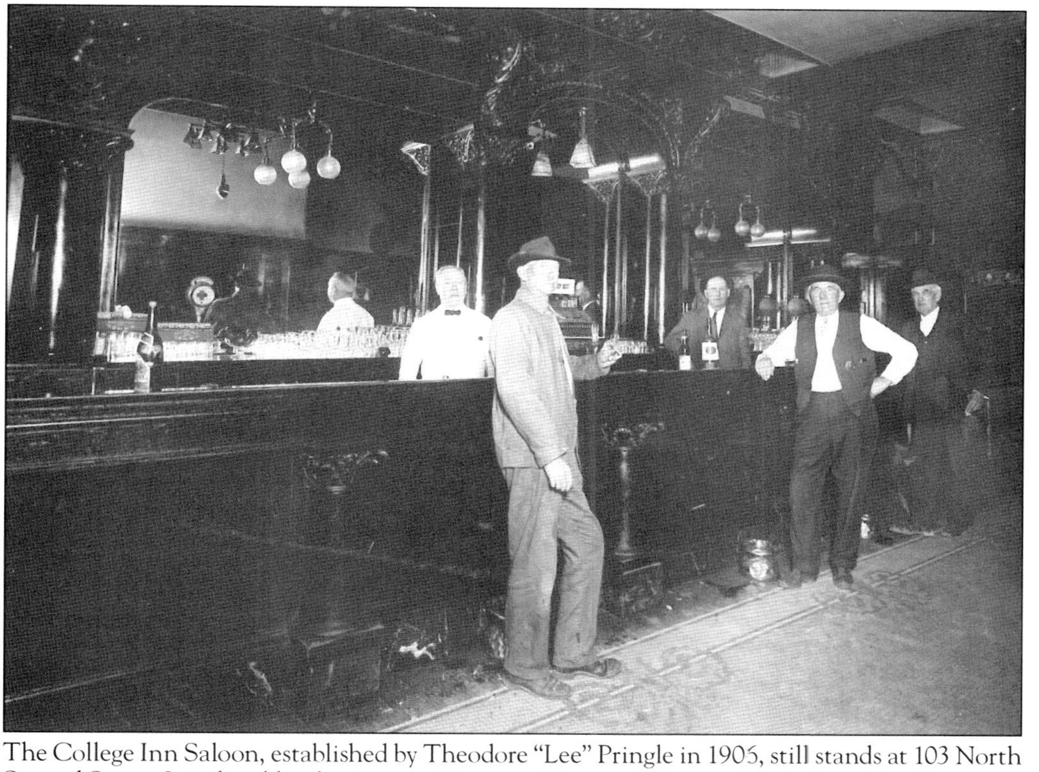

The College Inn Saloon, established by Theodore "Lee" Pringle in 1905, still stands at 103 North Second Street. It is the oldest business in Converse County still operating in its original location. The saloon's owners purchased its exotic bar in 1906 from the Brunswick-Balke-Collender Company of Chicago. The tile mosaic floor is typical of its time. For over 100 years, the saloon has provided Douglas residents with a place to gather, enjoying one another's company, and relax. It survived Prohibition and World War II alcohol-rationing. The saloon was placed on the National Register of Historic Places in the early 1980s.

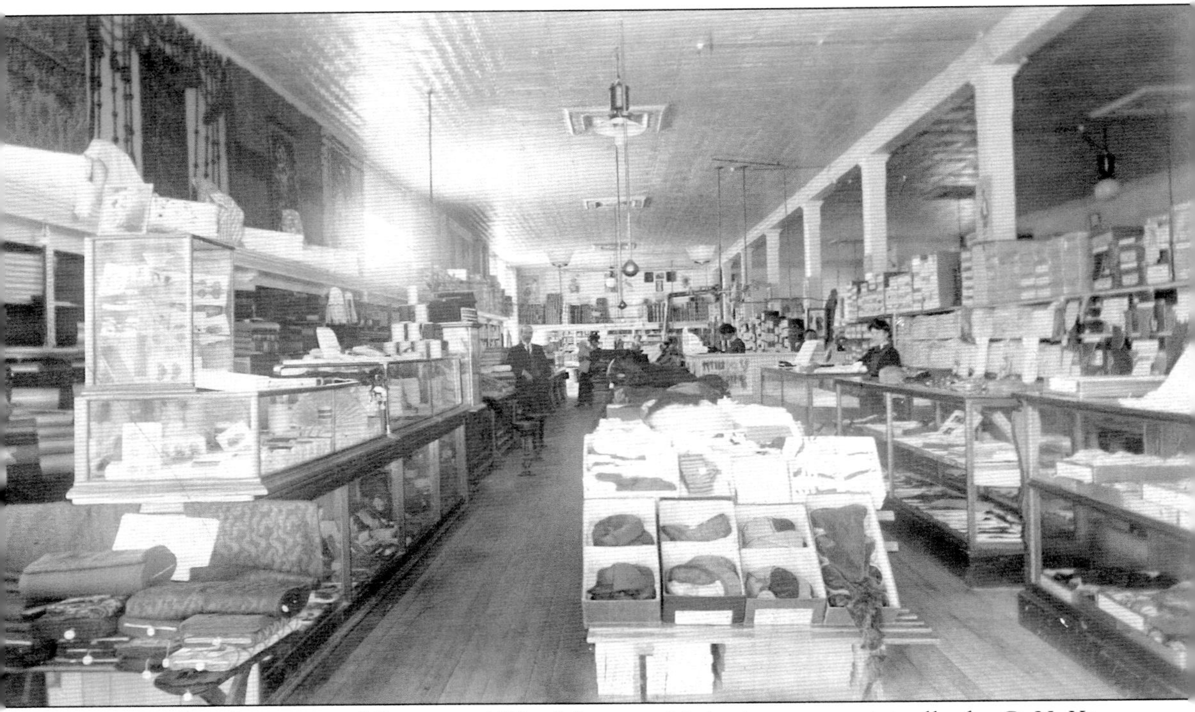

Located at the corner of Center and Third Streets, this business was originally the C. H. King Store, but by the time of this photograph, was known as the George Metcalf Store. While it is difficult to see the people in the photograph, they are identified from left to right as May Eskew, Margaret Ferguson, and George W. Metcalf. The mercantile offered residents some of the finest fabrics and blankets available, along with everything needed by the well-dressed Wyomingite. Metcalf was one of the town's earliest and most successful entrepreneurs. In 1915, Bob Gentle opened the Golden Rule in this same location. Interviewed for the newspaper shortly after the grand opening, Gentle said, "Our opening exceeded our expectations, we have few regrets." He added, "We expect to take pride in this store and believe that the people of Douglas will too." The Gentle family owned and operated the store continually for more than eight decades. The building is now occupied by the Douglas Business Center.

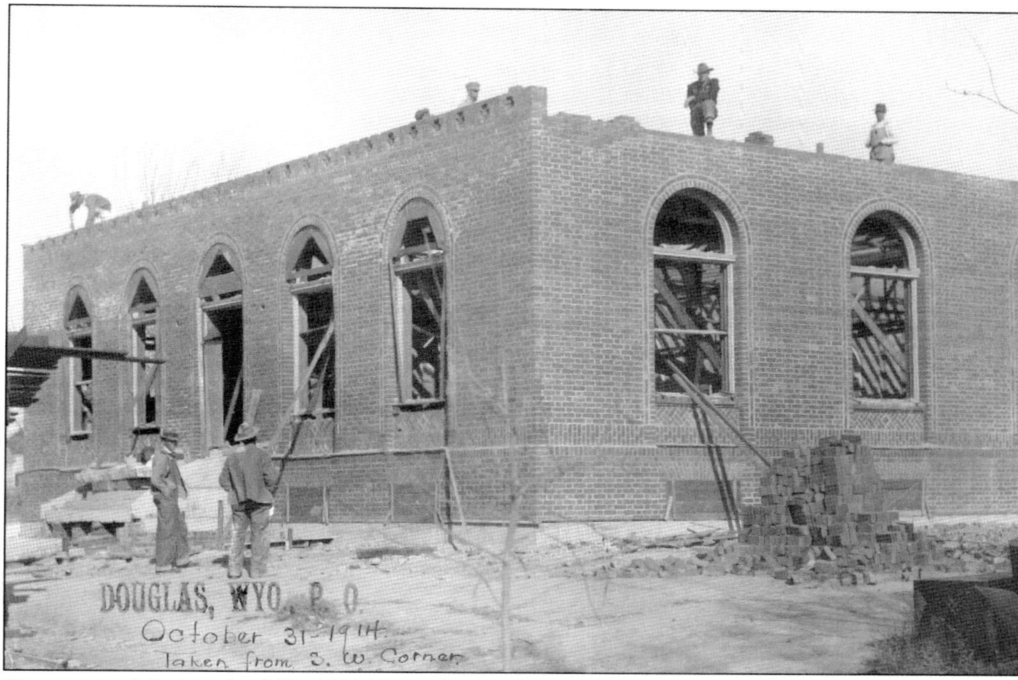

Constructed during the fall of 1914 by architect Oscar Wenderoth, the Douglas Federal Building is one of the finest edifices ever erected in Douglas. Built under the supervision of the Office of the Supervising Architect in the U.S. Treasury Department, it reflects the neoclassical design common among federal buildings. It has always served as a post office and still operates in the same location, maintaining its original look, despite interior upgrades and renovations over the years. The building was listed on the National Register of Historic Places in 1987.

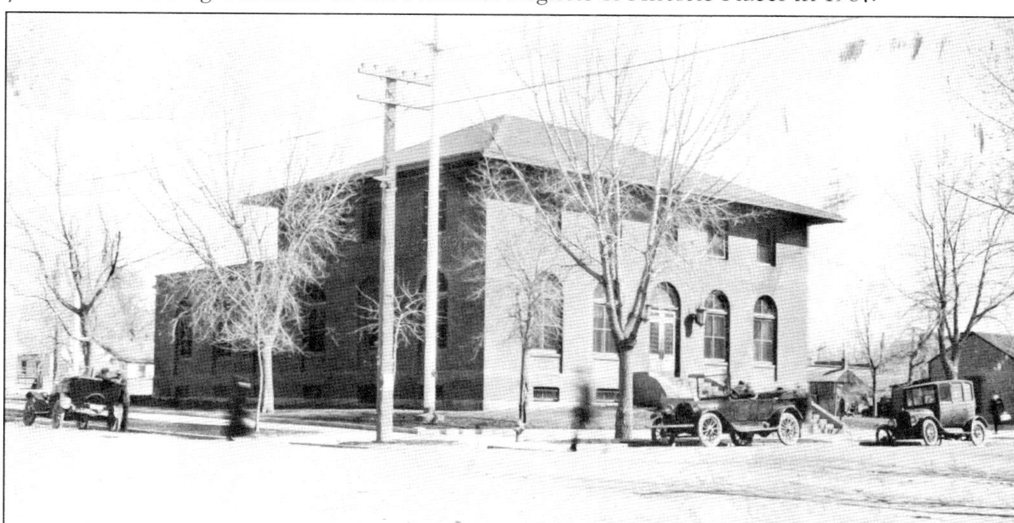

This photograph shows the post office in its finished state a few years after its construction in 1914. For nearly 100 years, the structure has escaped major renovations to the exterior.

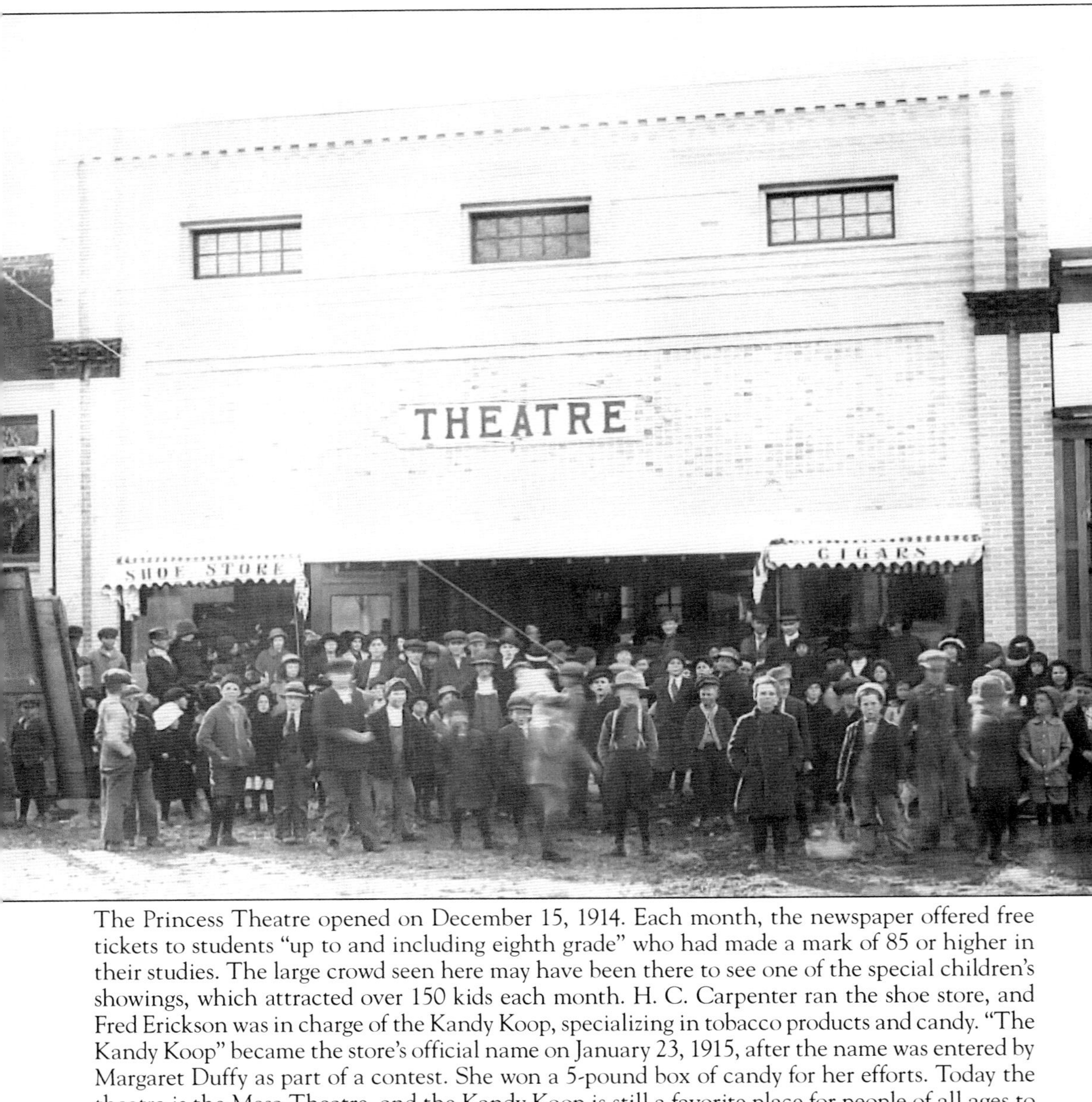

The Princess Theatre opened on December 15, 1914. Each month, the newspaper offered free tickets to students "up to and including eighth grade" who had made a mark of 85 or higher in their studies. The large crowd seen here may have been there to see one of the special children's showings, which attracted over 150 kids each month. H. C. Carpenter ran the shoe store, and Fred Erickson was in charge of the Kandy Koop, specializing in tobacco products and candy. "The Kandy Koop" became the store's official name on January 23, 1915, after the name was entered by Margaret Duffy as part of a contest. She won a 5-pound box of candy for her efforts. Today the theatre is the Mesa Theatre, and the Kandy Koop is still a favorite place for people of all ages to gather. For decades, the Kandy Koop has been known for its "curly fries."

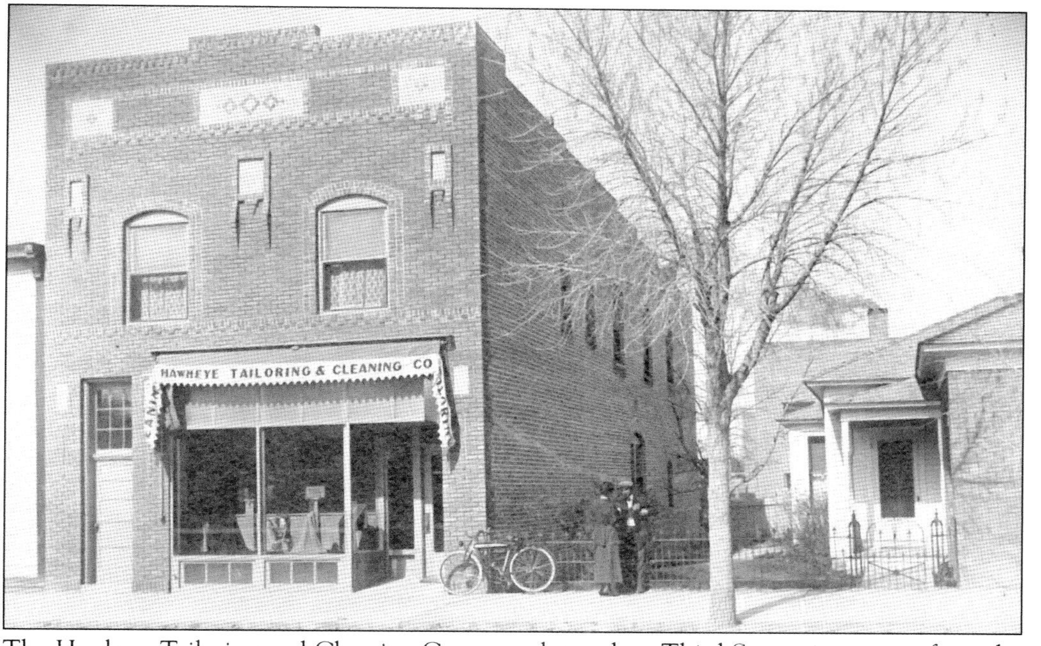

The Hawkeye Tailoring and Cleaning Company, located on Third Street, just across from the post office, was originally located in the LaBonte Hotel. It moved to this location in 1918 after being purchased by Gretta and Everette Smith.

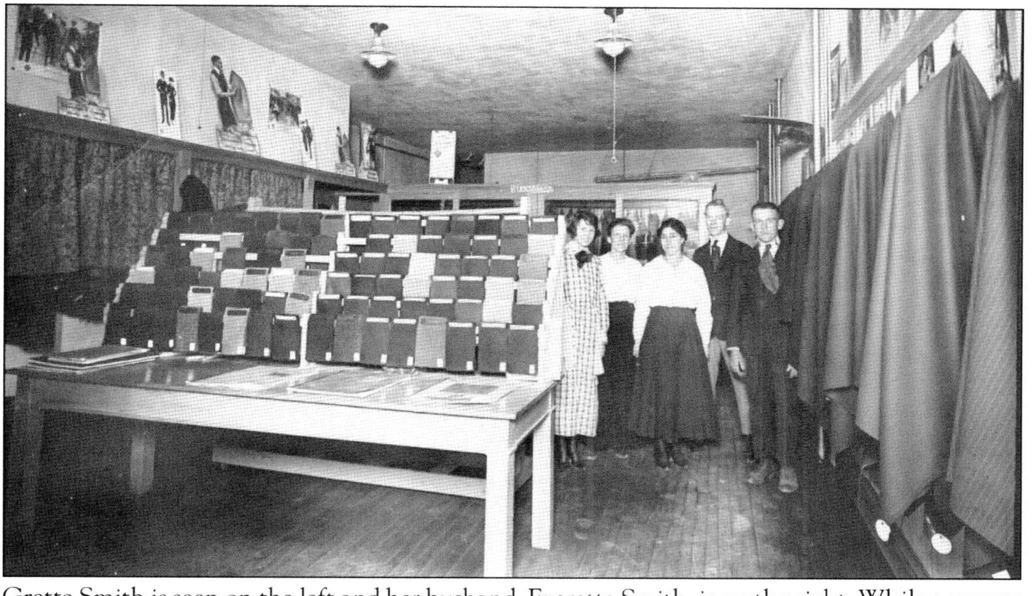

Gretta Smith is seen on the left and her husband, Everette Smith, is on the right. While a presser was on location, the rest of the equipment was housed in a building two blocks away. The Hawkeye was the only cleaning shop in Douglas. In those years it cost 25¢ to press a pair of pants. The Smiths lived in an apartment above their store. The Smiths retired in 1944, selling the business to Iris Thurston. The Hawkeye later relocated to 119 North Second Street. The Third Street building was made part of the Ben Franklin store in the mid-1970s. Both buildings were destroyed by fire in the 1980s. Today it has been rebuilt and includes the town's mini-mall.

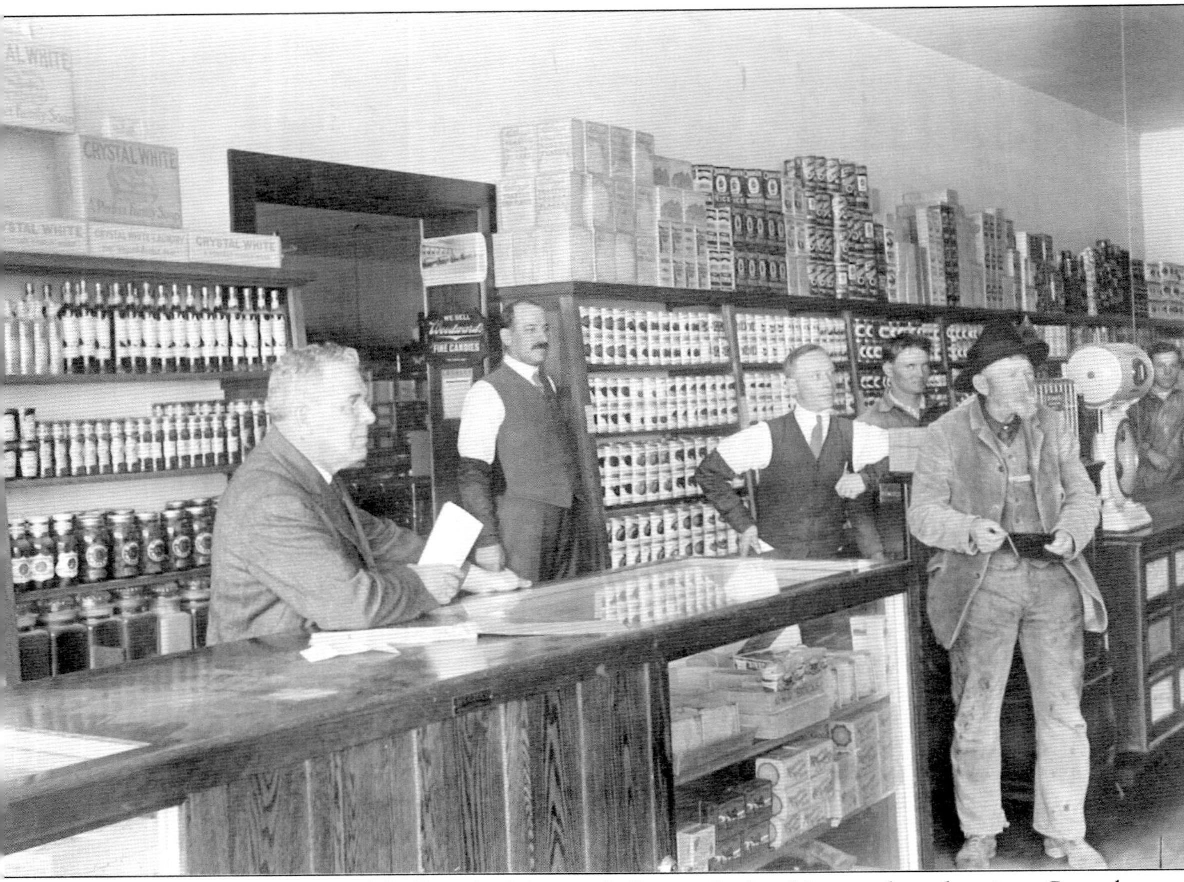

This is an interior view of the Douglas Mercantile Store, which sold canned goods, spices, Crystal White Family Soap, and Kellogg's Toasted Corn Flakes (top shelf in the center of the photograph). The clerks clearly took a great deal of pride in presenting their products. Unfortunately, the mercantile burned to the ground in 1925. The colorful-looking fellow in the foreground is Al Ayres, the bullwhacker for whom the Ayres Natural Bridge is named. He purchased the bridge and the surrounding land in the early 1880s for his freight-shipping business.

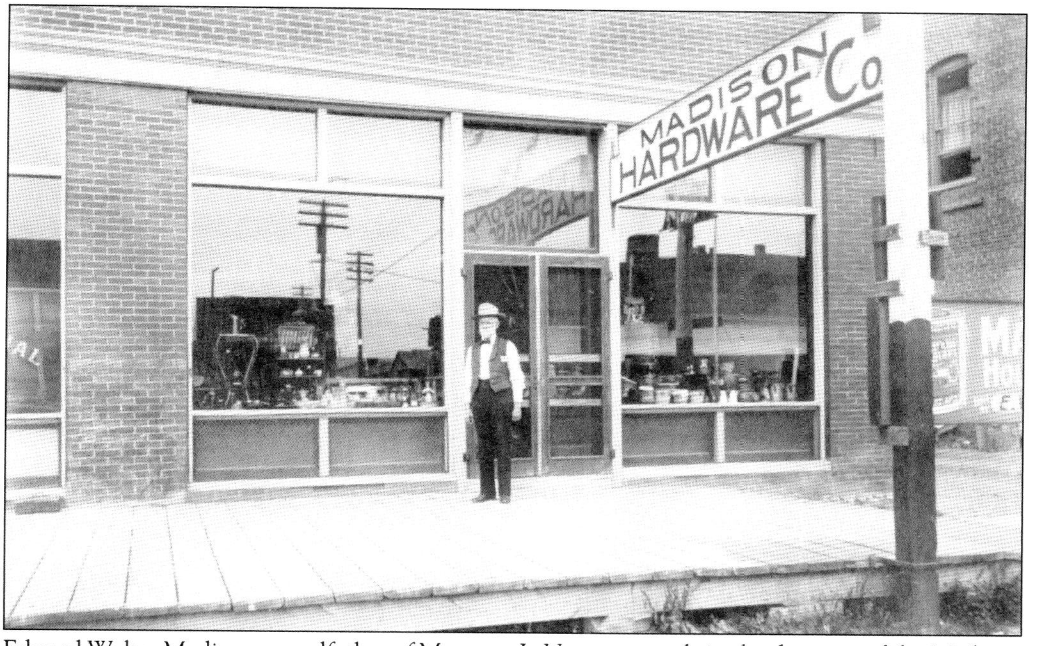

Edward Walter Madison, grandfather of Margaret LeVasseur, stands in the doorway of the Madison Hardware Company. The sidewalks are still made of wood, but from the reflection in the window it is clear that Douglas already had electricity when this photograph was taken.

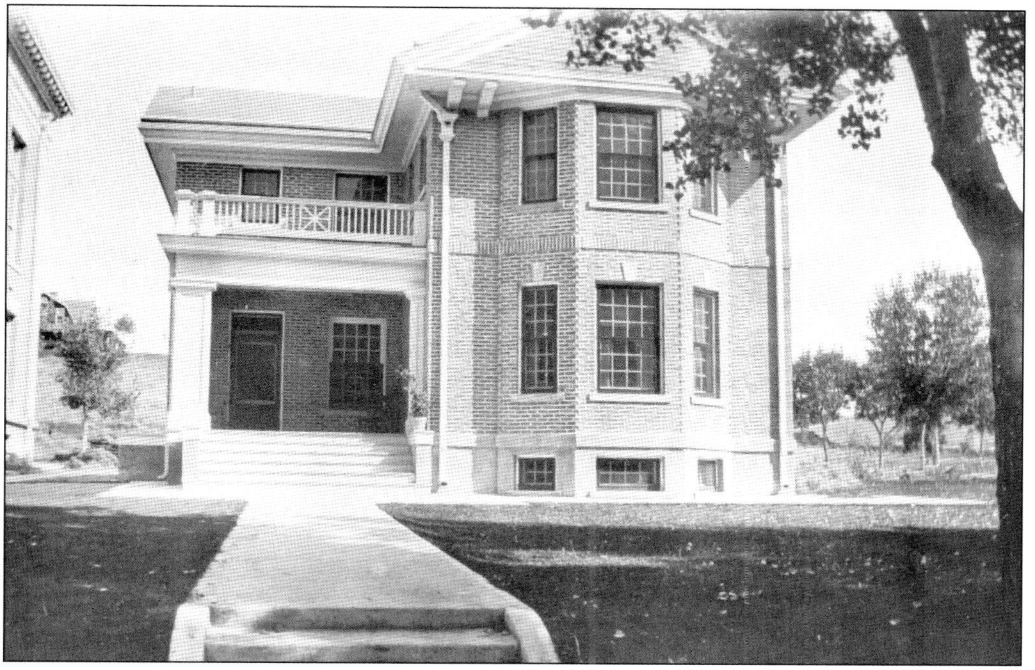

In 1916, this newly constructed penal facility (adjacent to the new Converse County Courthouse at the corner of Center and South Fifth Streets) replaced the former jail located at 118 North Third Street. The new jail included residential space for Sheriff Charles Messenger and his family. The jail and the courthouse were both razed in the 1970s to make room for a newly expanded hospital.

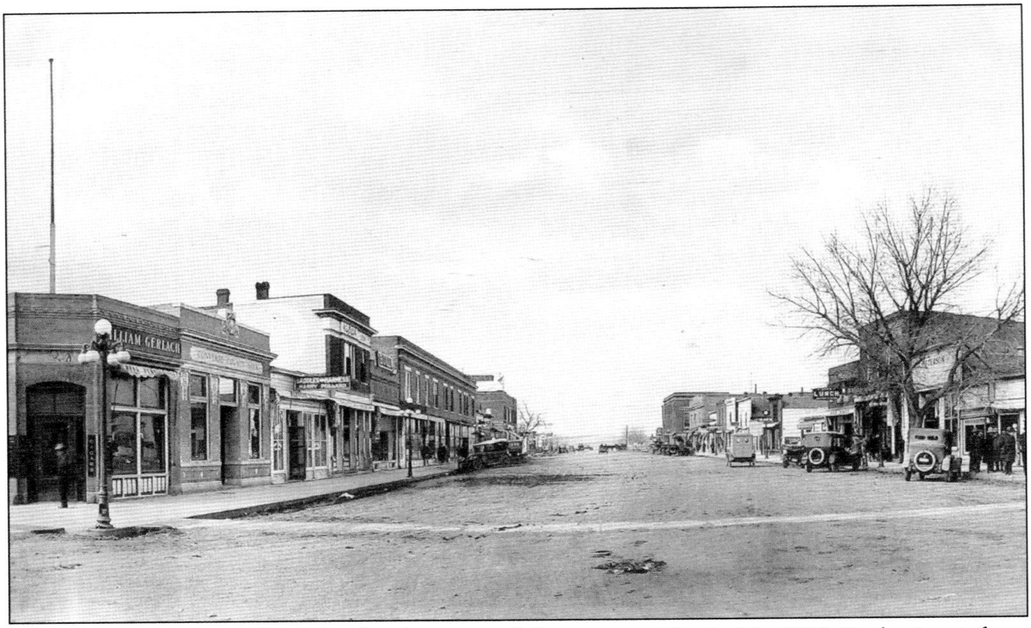

These next few images show the development of the town as it looked in 1920. Each view is from a different direction on Center Street. From the first settlement with its rudimentary buildings and shacks, to a street lined with fine permanent buildings and enthusiastic entrepreneurs, the town was well on its way to serving its residents. Looking north on Second Street from Center Street shows tremendous progress in the town's development from 1902 to 1920. Note the pothole at the front of the photograph; it appears the streets were not yet to paved.

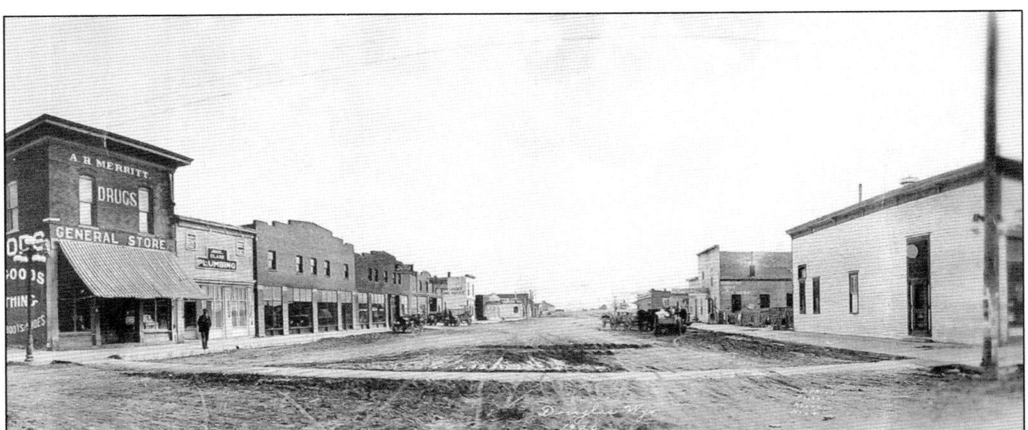

This view looks south on Second Street from Center Street.

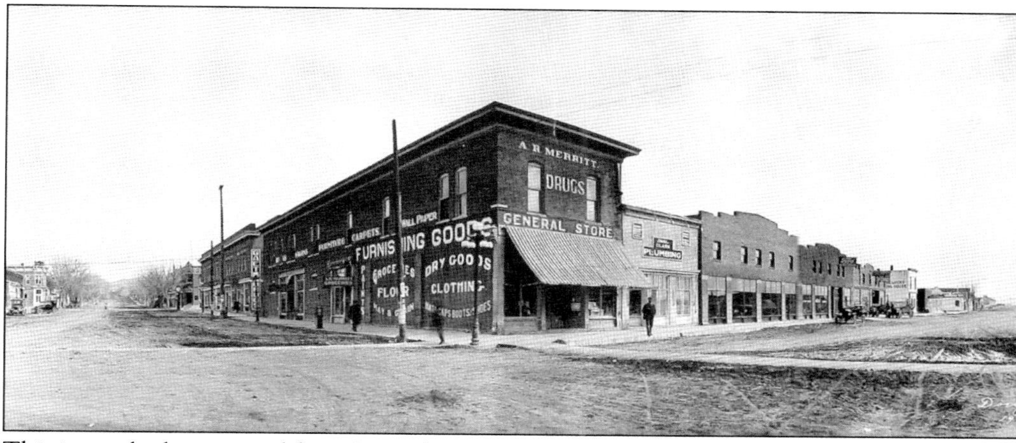

This image looks eastward from Second Street, down the south side of Center Street.

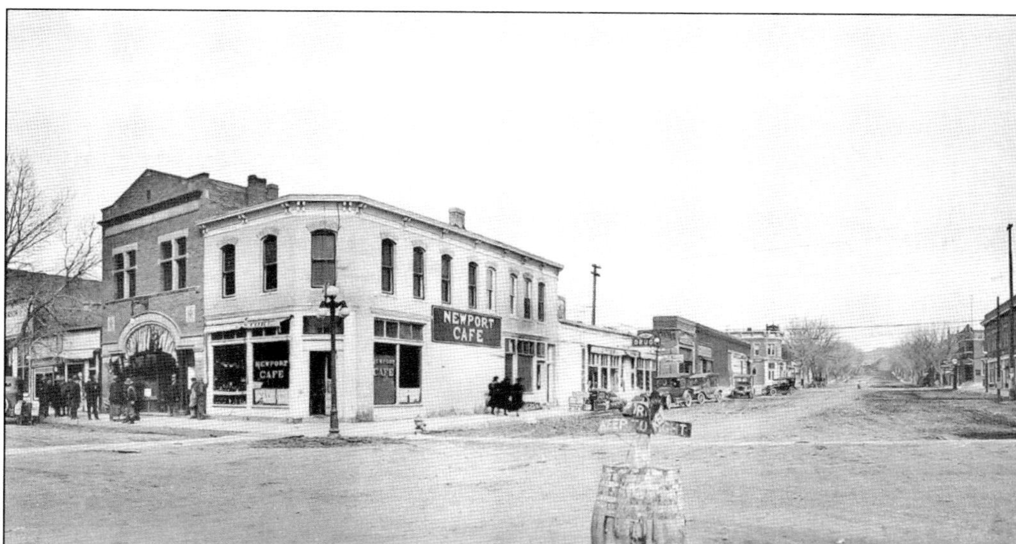

This photograph looks west on Second Street from Center Street. While a beautiful lamppost can be seen in front of the Newport Cafe, stop signs and stoplights to control traffic were still a long way off.

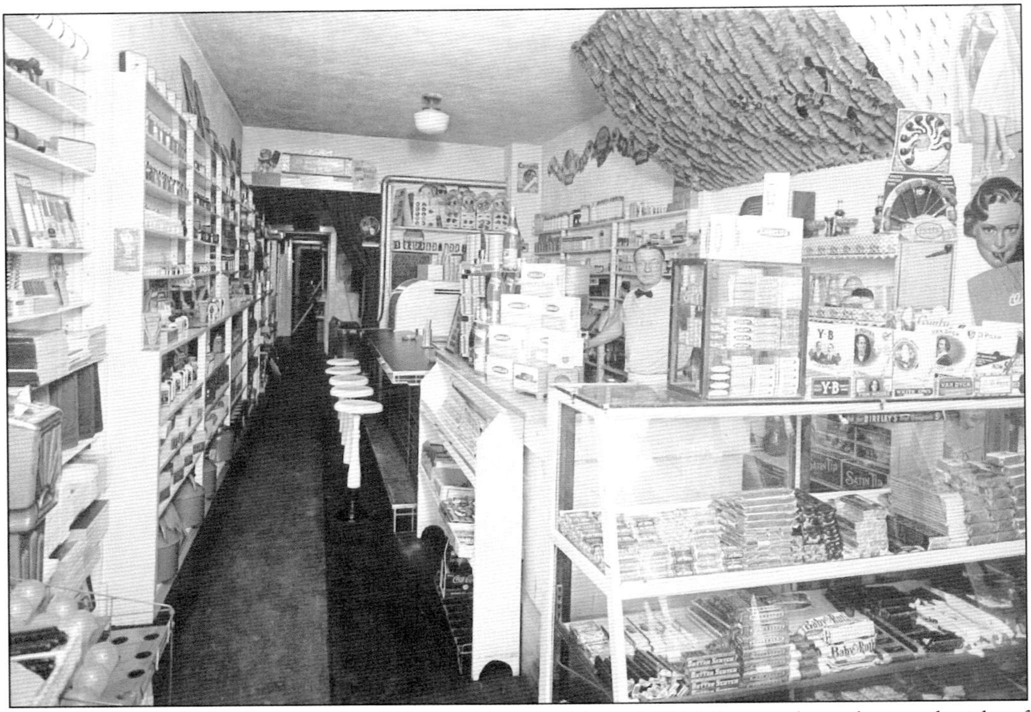

Owner Jim Brady opened Brady's White Palace in May of 1936. Located on the south side of Center Street, it was the best place in town to get a flavored malt and penny candy. The store also sold tobacco products, books, and various sundries.

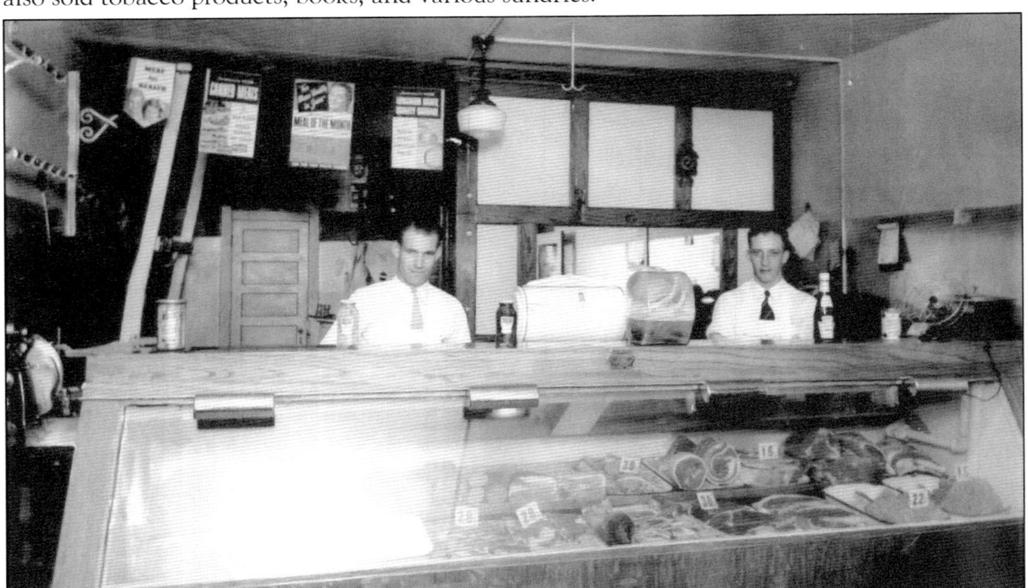

Dick McCormick, pictured on the left, owned and operated the Sanitary Market from 1935 to 1936. The prices of various cuts of beef in the display case are quite different from prices today, but relative to the income of customers at the time. The store later became the first Safeway Store in downtown Douglas. Today the site is home to Ranchero Lanes.

Four

Eking Out a Living

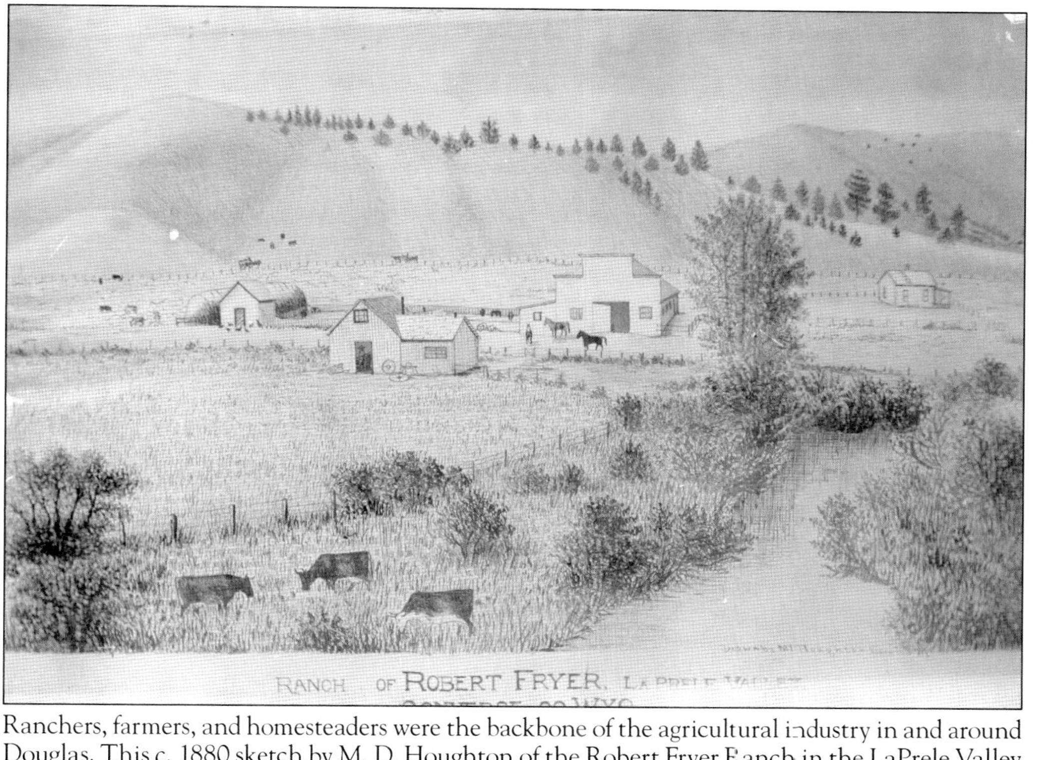

Ranchers, farmers, and homesteaders were the backbone of the agricultural industry in and around Douglas. This c. 1880 sketch by M. D. Houghton of the Robert Fryer Ranch in the LaPrele Valley near Douglas depicts the lush landscape that provided a good living to those in the livestock industry. The abundance of irrigated water and native grasses was crucial to raising livestock of all kinds. Gradually, however, land around Douglas was taken up by homesteads, which brought fences, forcing the larger cattle ranches and sheep outfits to seek more open range.

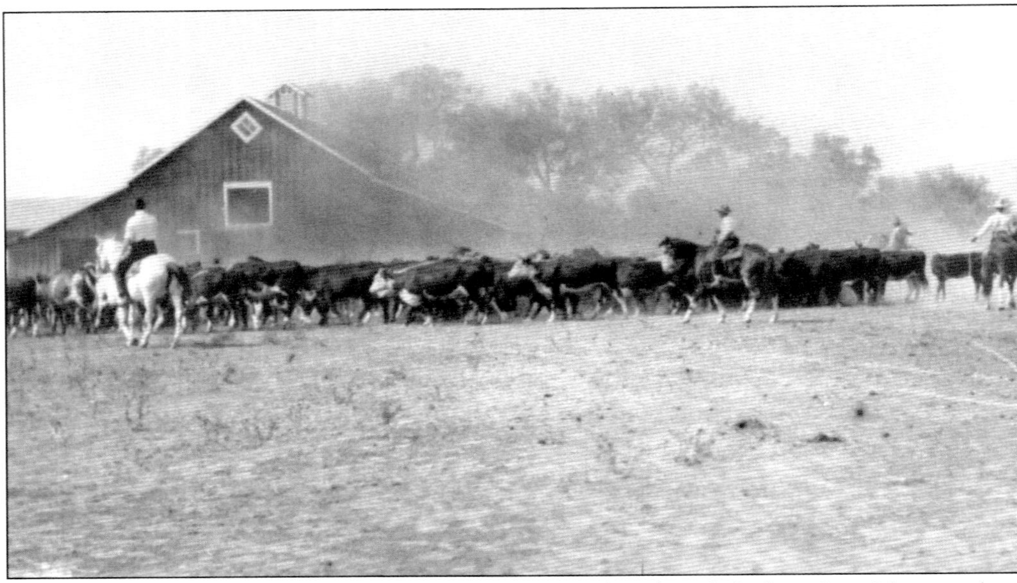

Roundups moved livestock from pasture to pasture, or gathered cattle for branding. Many cowboys are required for a successful roundup; each one was responsible for making sure that the herd stayed together and arrived safely at their destination. Moving the cattle stirred up lots of dust, as is evident in this photograph.

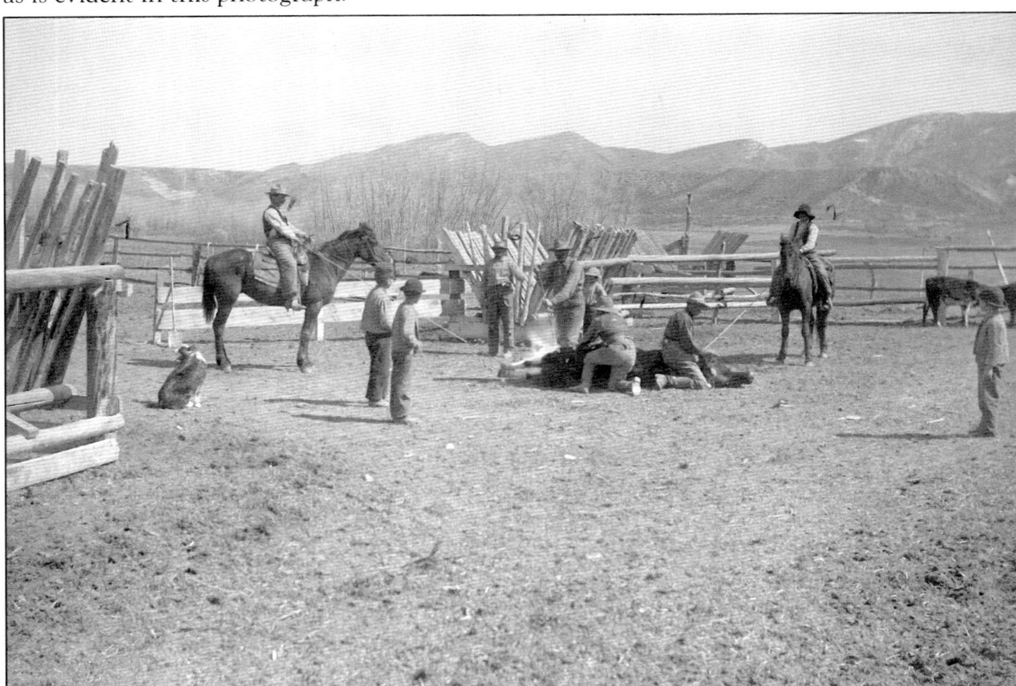

Cattle brands were necessary to identify ownership. Brandings were an opportunity to make "light work" with the help of many hands, but they served as social occasions, too. This branding in the spring of 1897 took place at the Ayres ranch. From left to right, the three young men watching and learning are Jim Ayres, Clement Ayres, and Warren Powell.

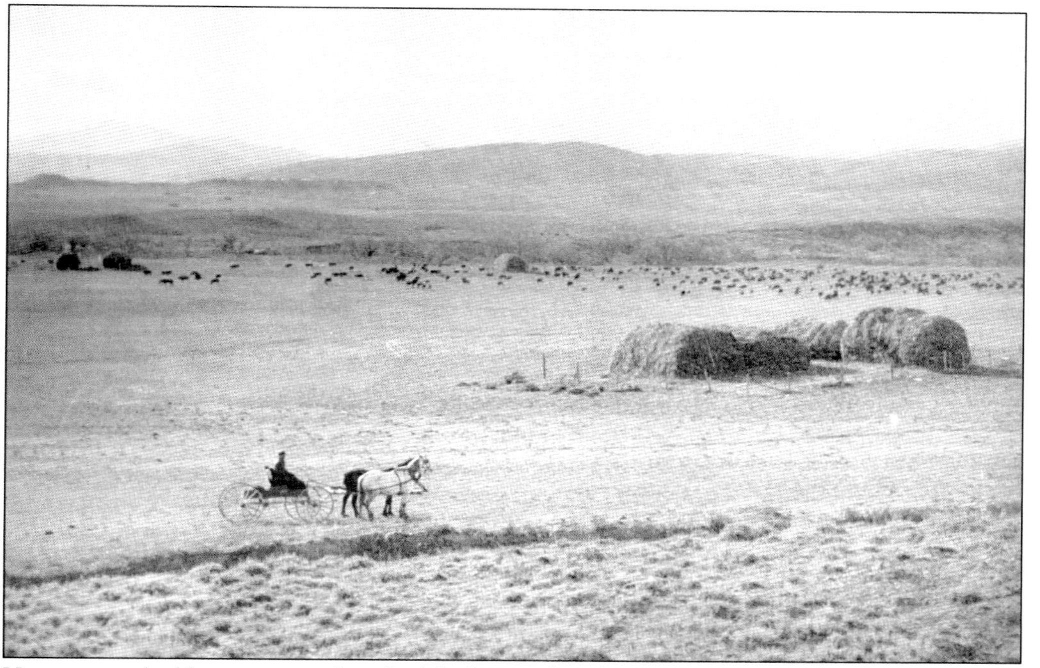

Hay was a valuable crop, providing feed for livestock at least two months out of every year. The non-tillable land and large open spaces, valuable only for grazing, made hay a viable farm market crop. Each aspect of ranching is depicted in this image, with grazing cattle in the background, stacks of hay, and the rancher surveying his livelihood.

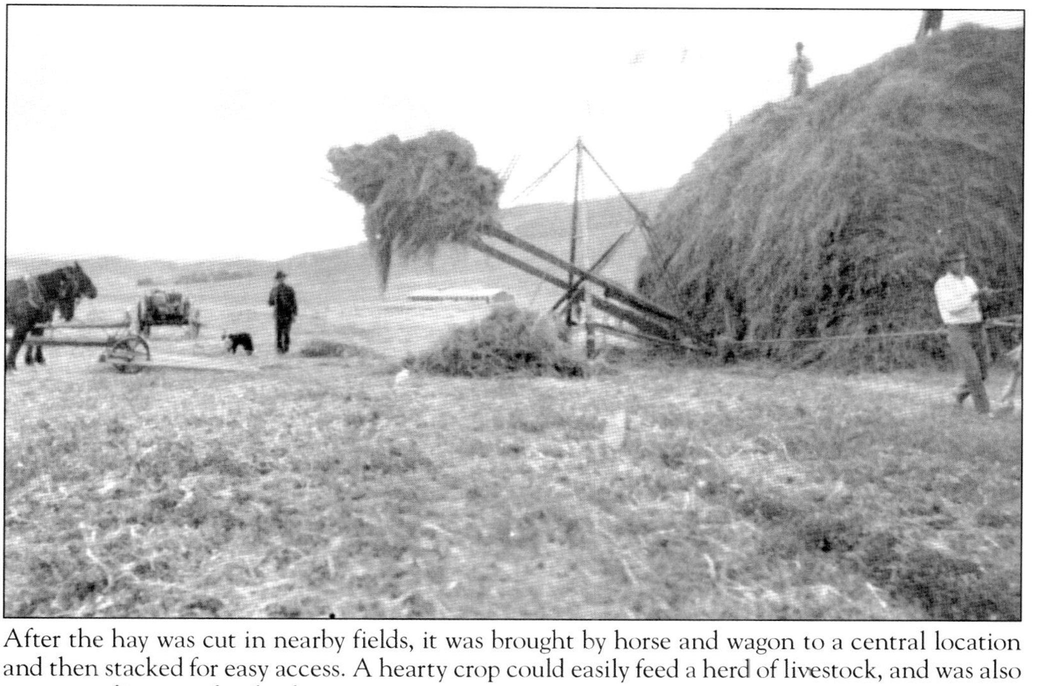

After the hay was cut in nearby fields, it was brought by horse and wagon to a central location and then stacked for easy access. A hearty crop could easily feed a herd of livestock, and was also a source of income for the farmer.

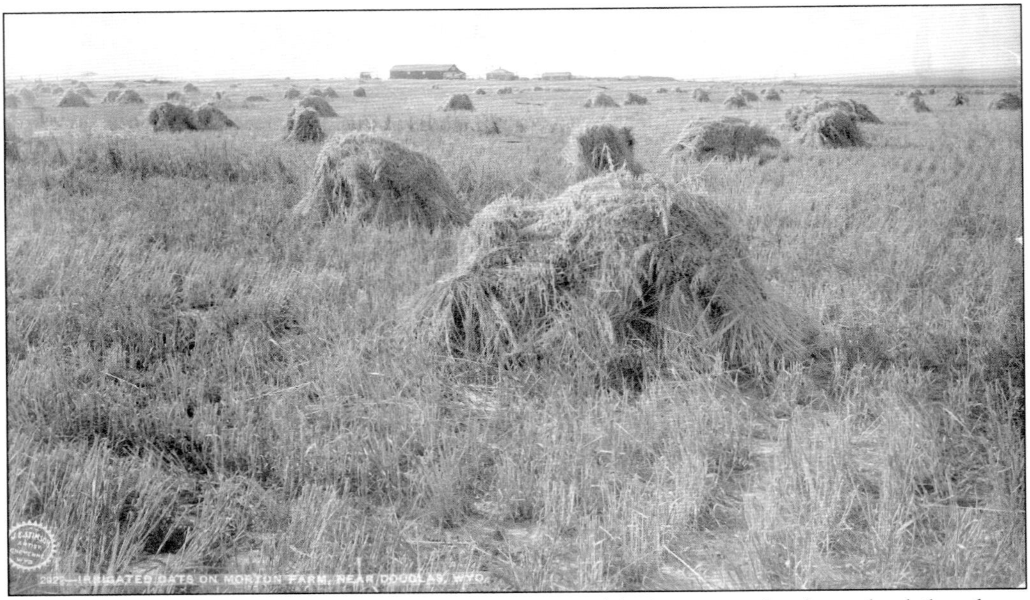

The land yielded many different kinds of crops. Some, like hay, were dry-farmed, while others, such as oats, required irrigation. Here, mounds of oats from the Morton farm near Douglas wait to be gathered and stacked for later use.

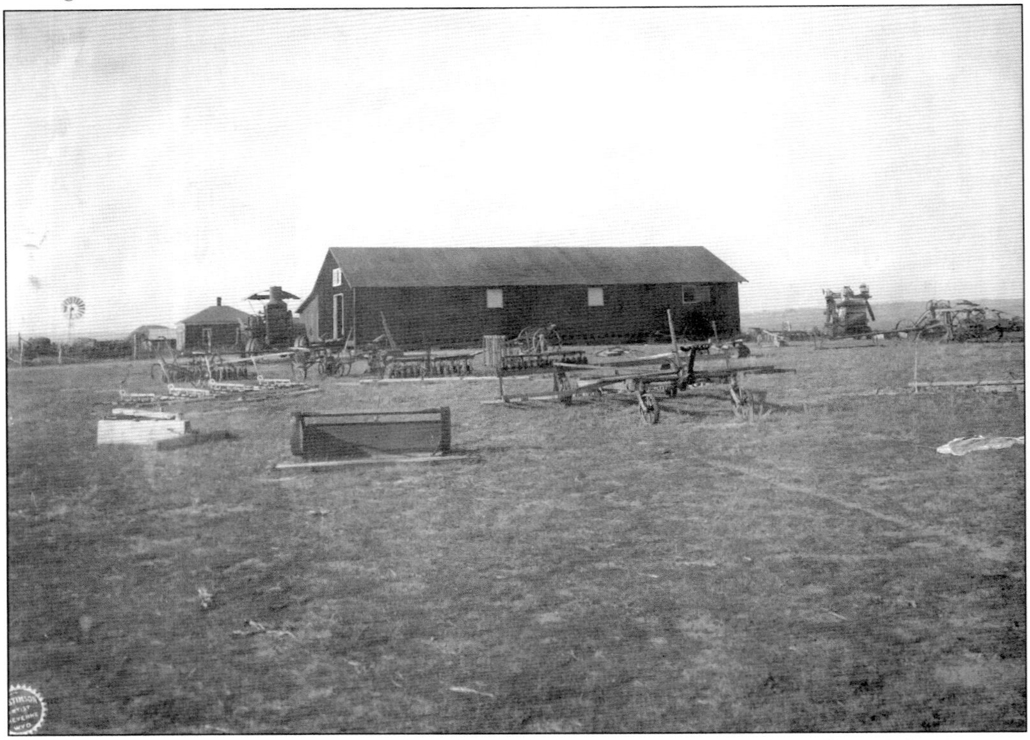

All the implements used in farming can be seen strewn about the Morton farm. John Morton was born in Germany and came to Converse County in 1892. He purchased the Morton Home Ranch from John T. Williams. Morton went on to acquire numerous ranches in his lifetime.

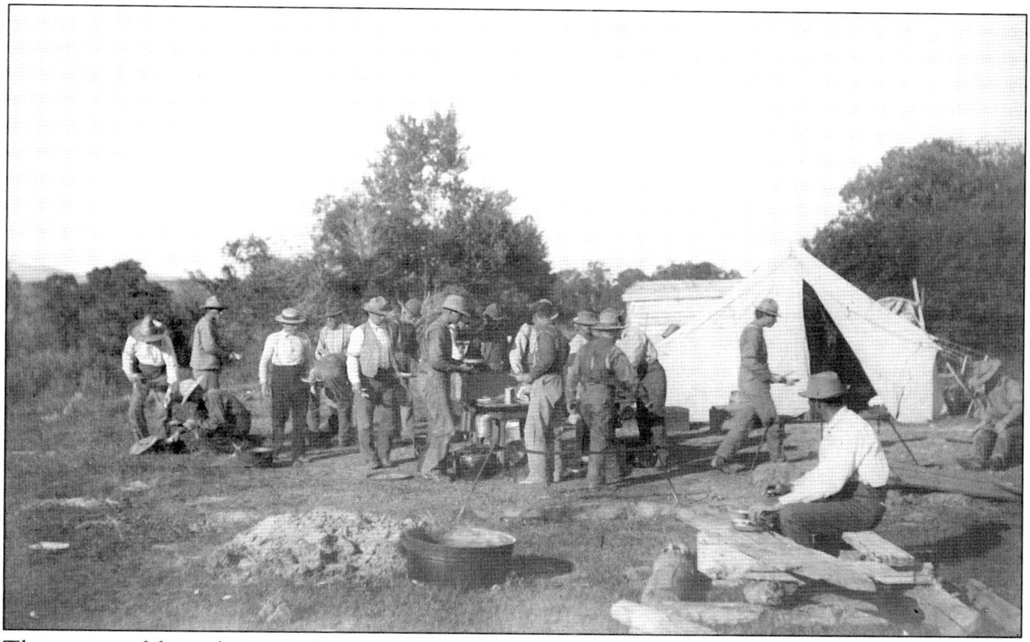

This series of four photographs are of a very large haying crew hired by the V. R. Dude Ranch in the Medicine Bow National Forest, just outside of Douglas. It is difficult to know if the crew was made up of local cowboys, or those who went from ranch to ranch looking for work. Most likely, it was a mixture of both.

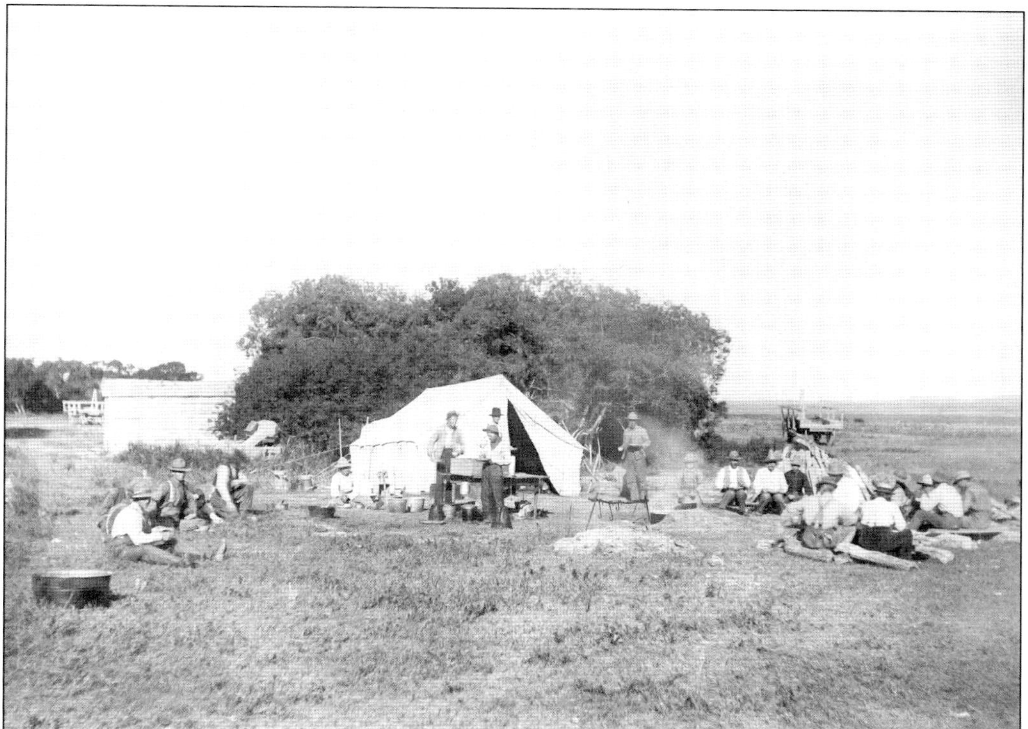

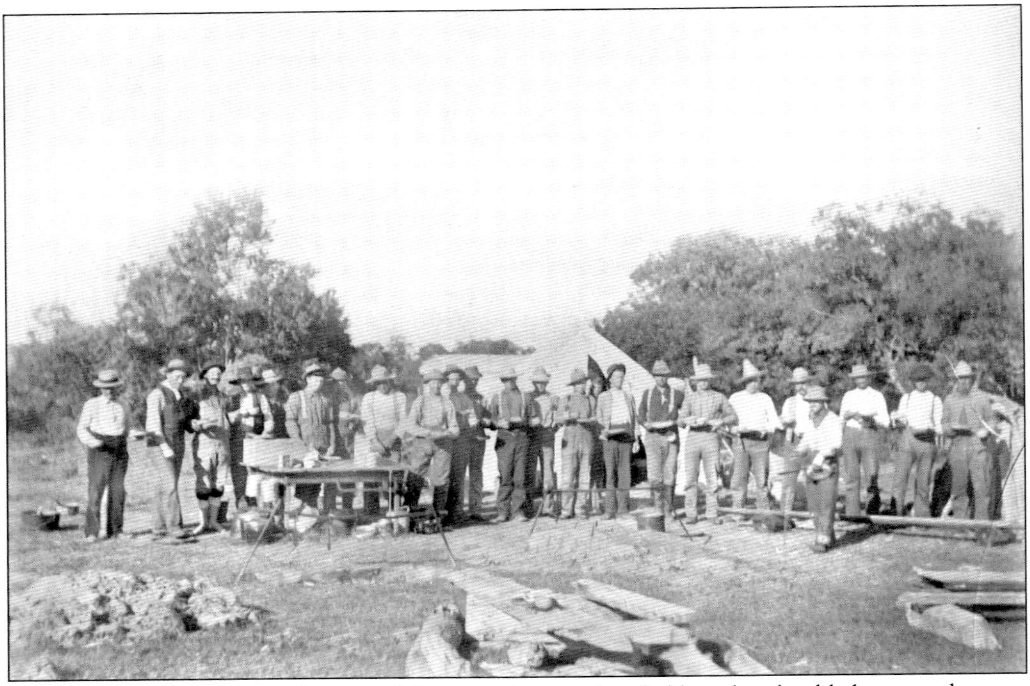

The crew's camp was home for several days at a time, and probably only tolerable because the men knew the cook was close at hand after a hard day's work. The cook's supplies had to be loaded and unloaded after each move.

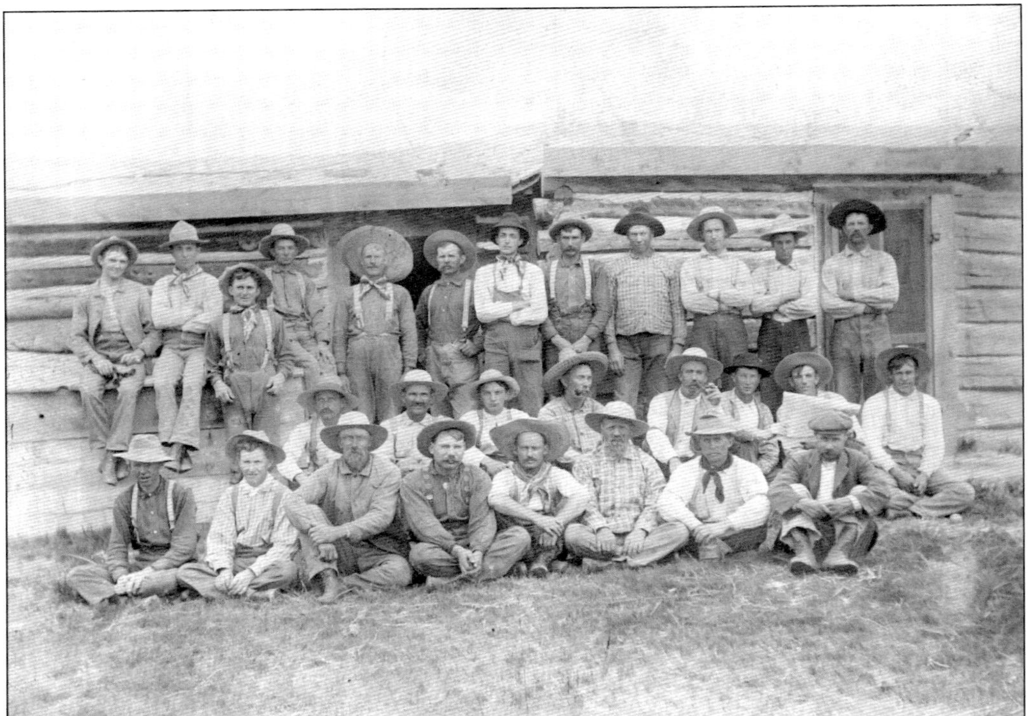

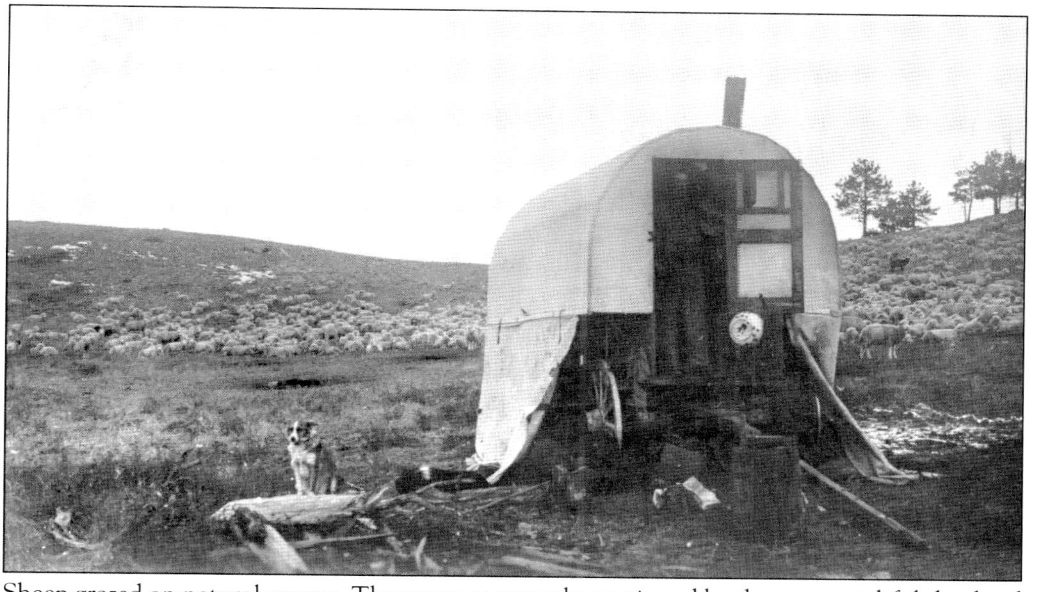

Sheep grazed on natural grasses. They were constantly monitored by the ever-watchful shepherd and his faithful dog. The sheep wagon was the nomadic sheepherder's home, containing a bed, a stove used for cooking and warmth, a table, and many convenient nooks and crannies.

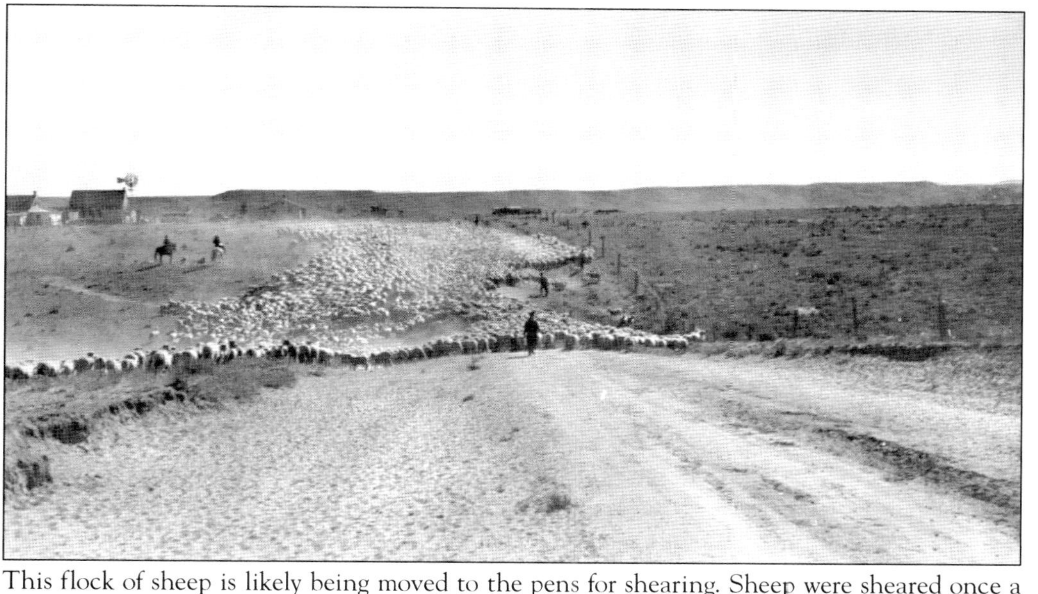

This flock of sheep is likely being moved to the pens for shearing. Sheep were sheared once a year, usually before lambing or in the spring before the weather got too warm. A flock this large would have required a large amount of land for grazing.

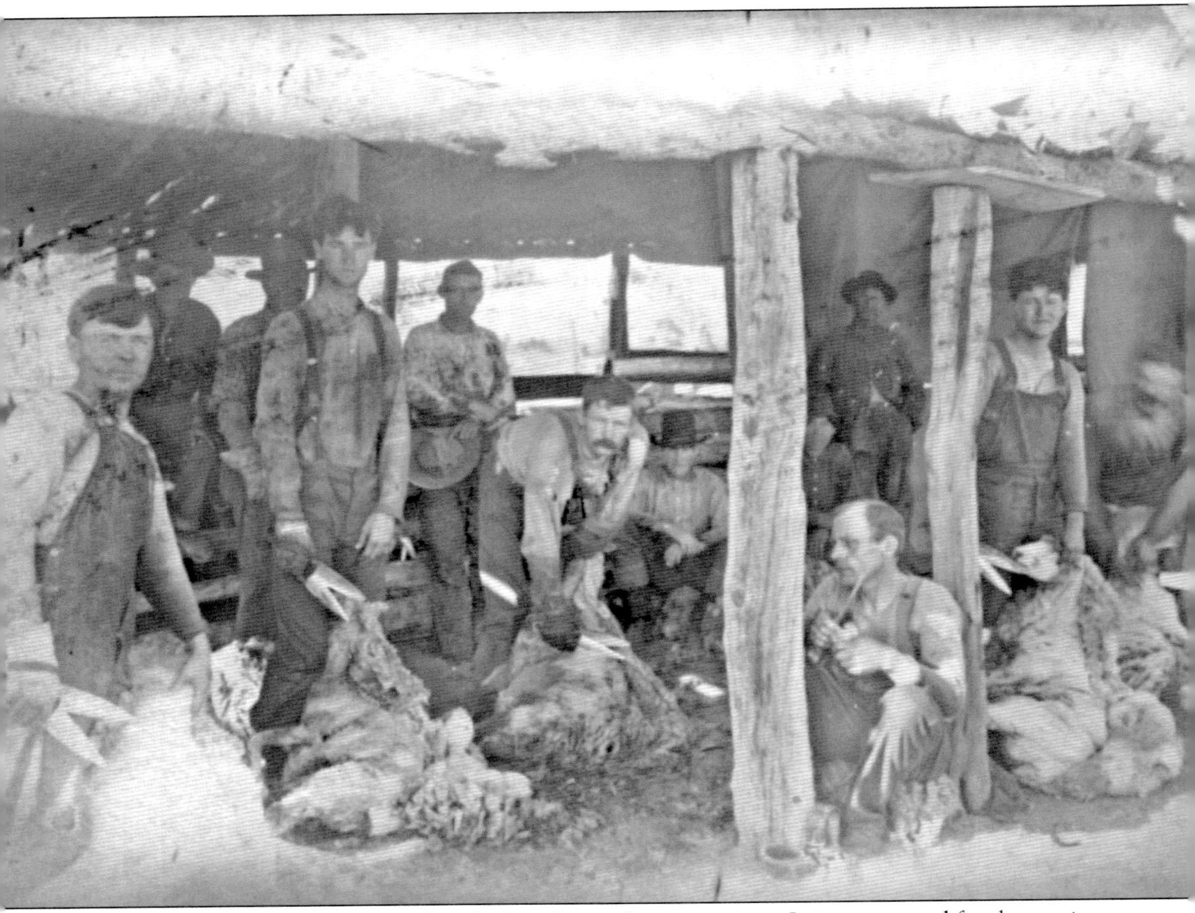

Even today, sheep shearing is done by hand, one sheep at a time. It is an art, and fast becoming a lost art at that. Shearers are often paid by the number of sheep they shear, but they must be careful not to cut or injure the sheep. Removing a sheep's wool not only can boost a rancher's income, but it makes the animals more comfortable during the hot summer months. Most shearers in the late 1800s and early 1900s didn't go from ranch to ranch, but used a central shearing corral. Sheep would be trailed in, sheared, and then taken back to their owner's ranch while another bunch was brought in.

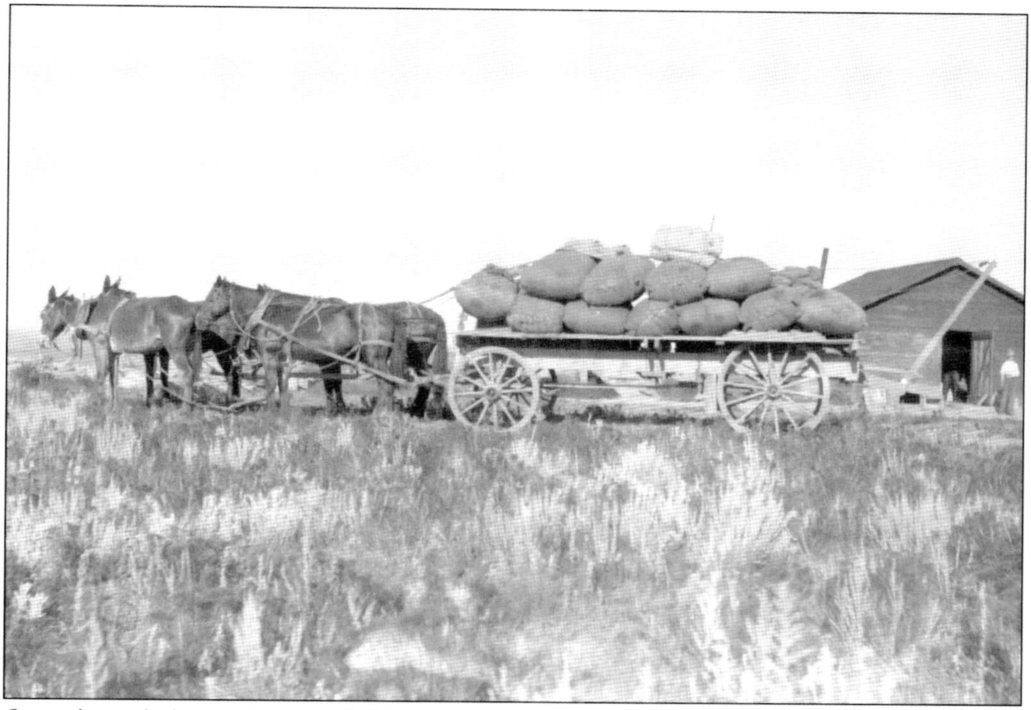

Once sheared, the wool was stuffed into huge gunnysacks, loaded onto wagons, and taken to the local wool warehouse. From there the wool was moved out on railroad cars, most likely to the wool mills where it was made into clothing, blankets, hats, mittens, and more.

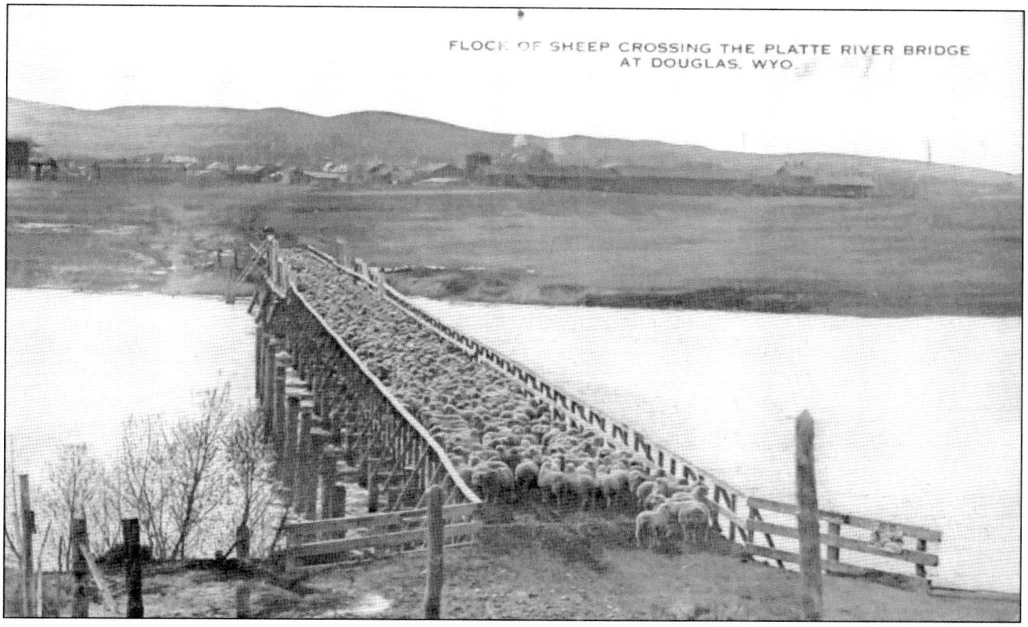

Just look at this massive flock of sheep crossing the North Platte River Bridge. Their return trip, sans wool, would have provided much less stress on the bridge.

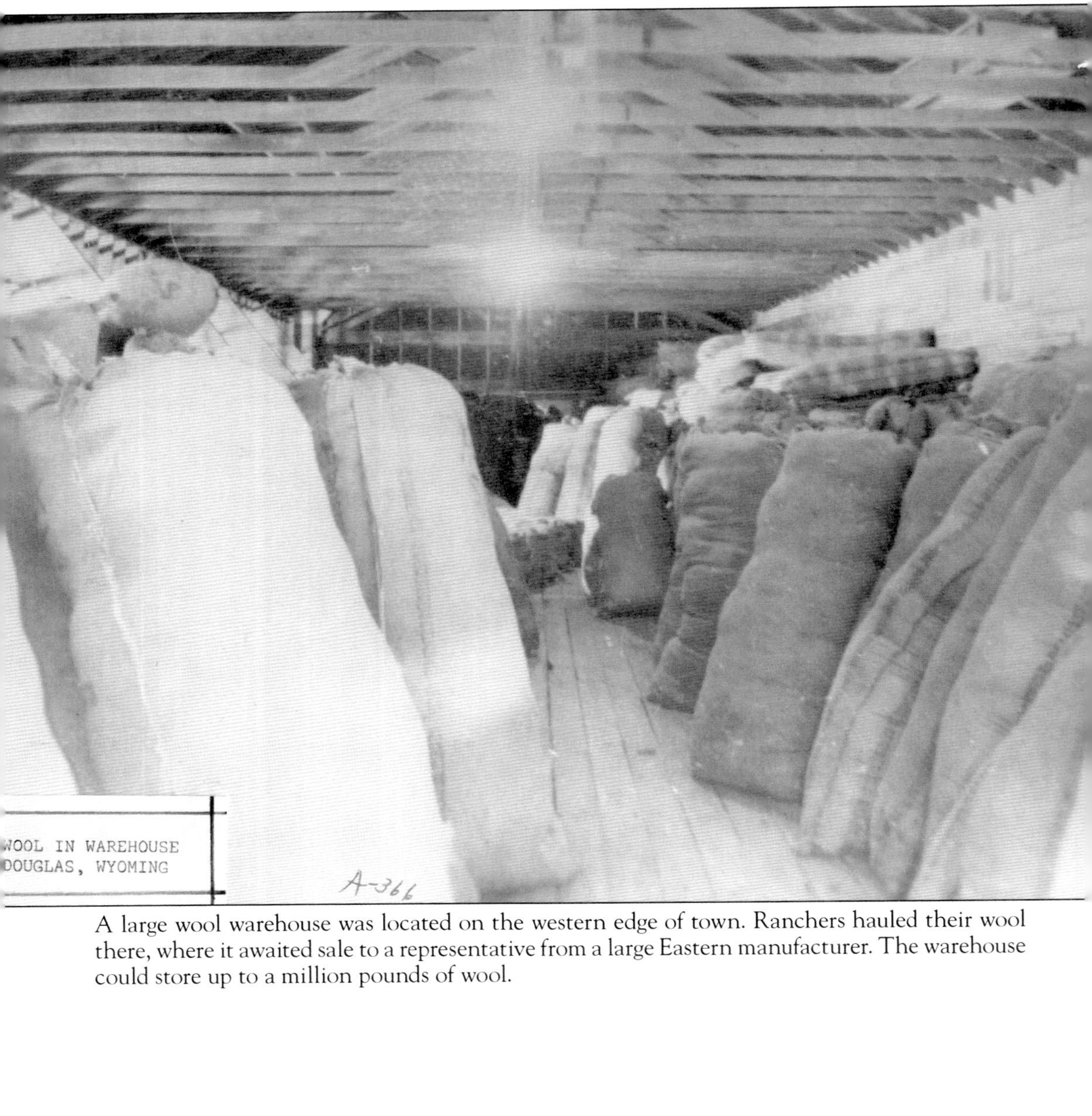

A large wool warehouse was located on the western edge of town. Ranchers hauled their wool there, where it awaited sale to a representative from a large Eastern manufacturer. The warehouse could store up to a million pounds of wool.

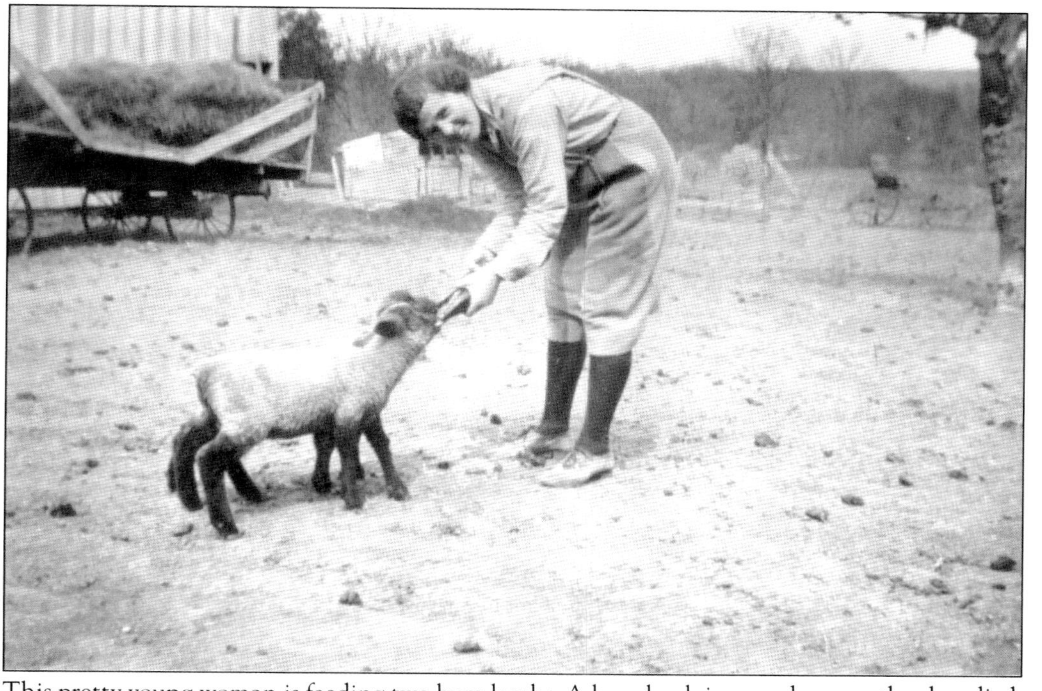

This pretty young woman is feeding two bum lambs. A bum lamb is one whose mother has died, or has rejected or abandoned her offspring. Hand-feeding bum lambs was the only way to increase their chance of survival.

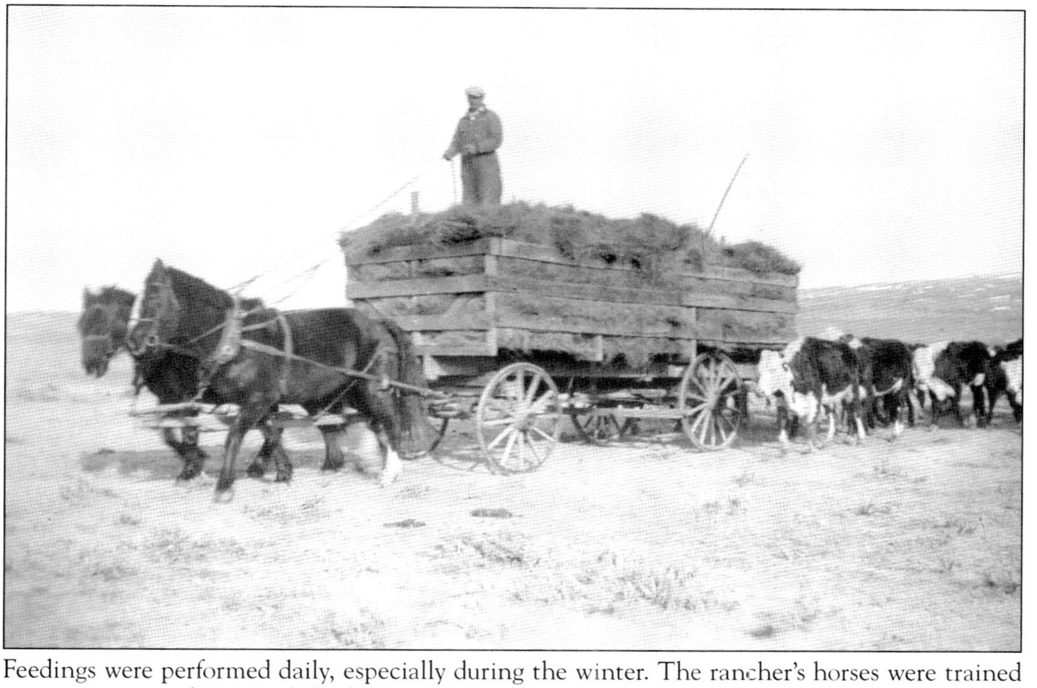

Feedings were performed daily, especially during the winter. The rancher's horses were trained to move at a snail's pace while the rancher tossed hay to the livestock. It was a one-person job most of the time.

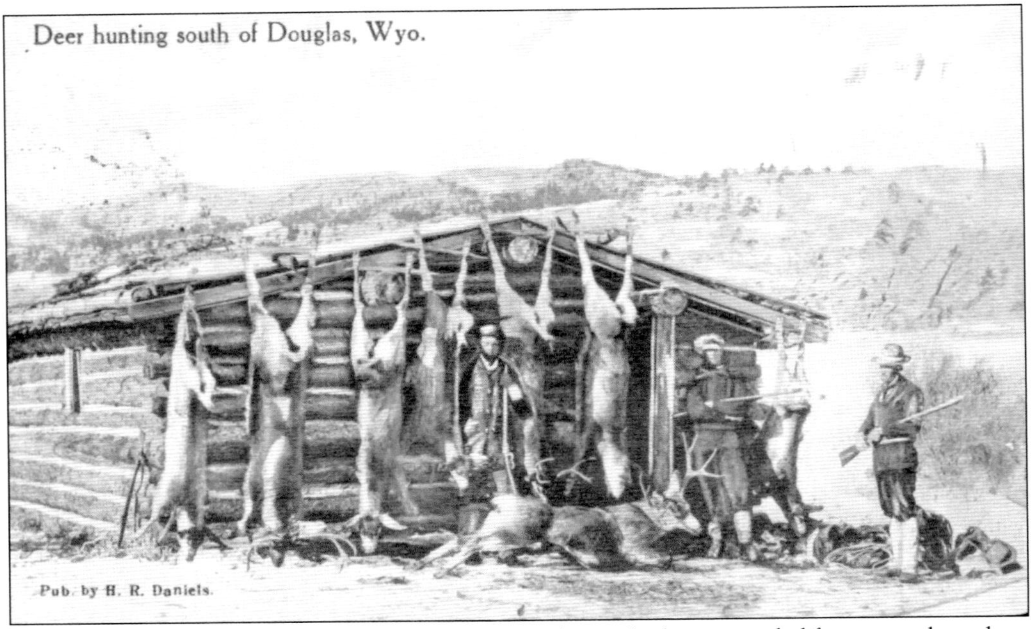

The hunting of ducks, rabbits, elk, deer, antelope, and sage chickens provided farmers and ranchers with food, and the hunting of coyotes protected their livestock. The hugely successful deer hunt pictured here put food on the table for a long time.

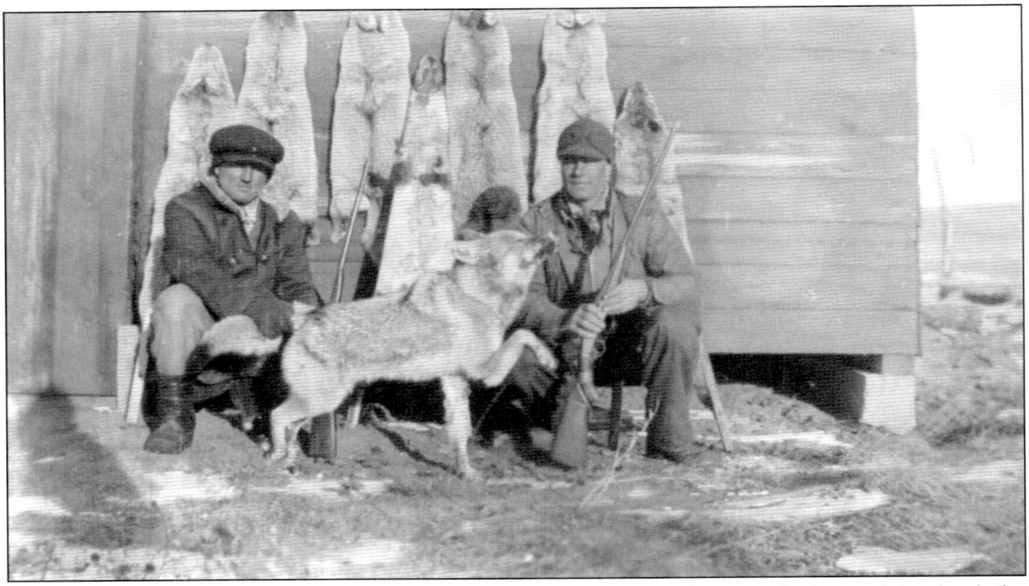

Hunting helped families survive during the long winter months. People hunted for food, for saleable pelts, and as a matter of self-defense against the four-footed predators that savaged their livestock. Here, Roy Price (right) and an unidentified companion proudly display the fruits of their successful coyote hunt.

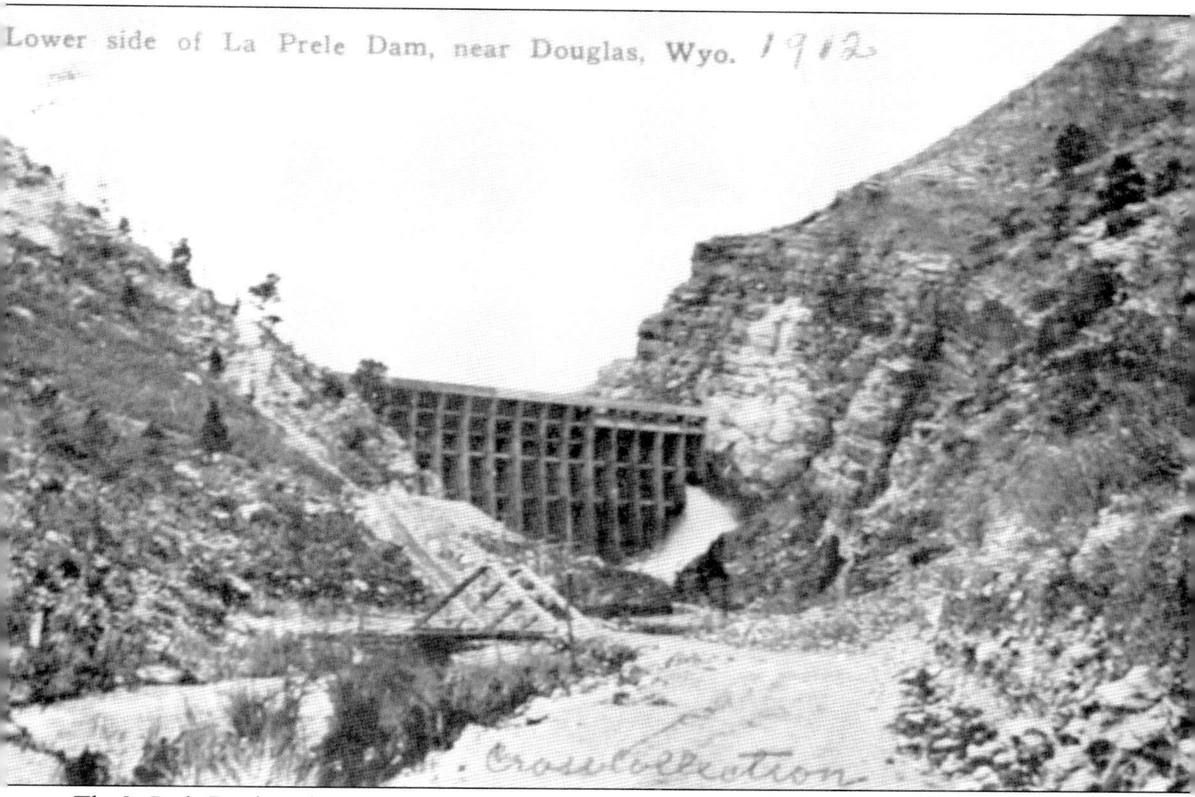

The LaPrele Ditch and Reservoir Company organized in January 1906 to develop local irrigation. In May 1908, the *Cheyenne Daily Leader* reported that the Ambursen Company of Boston had been hired as contractors for the LaPrele Dam. "The dam," the reporter explained, "will be 295 feet in length, 135 feet in height, and will create a reservoir covering nearly 500 acres."

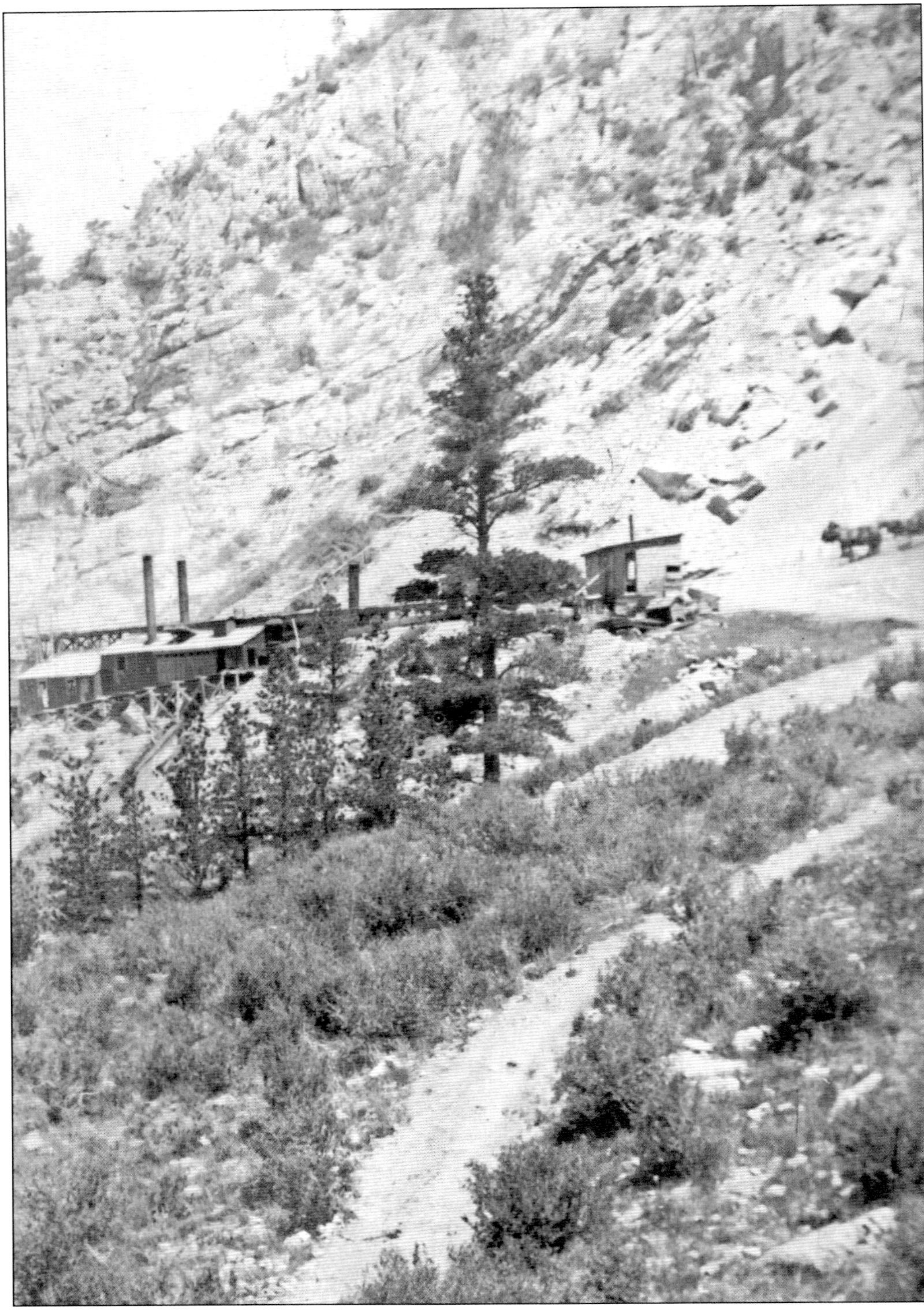

Engineers and workers set up camps below the site of construction in the canyon of LaPrele Creek. They lived and worked there while building the dam.

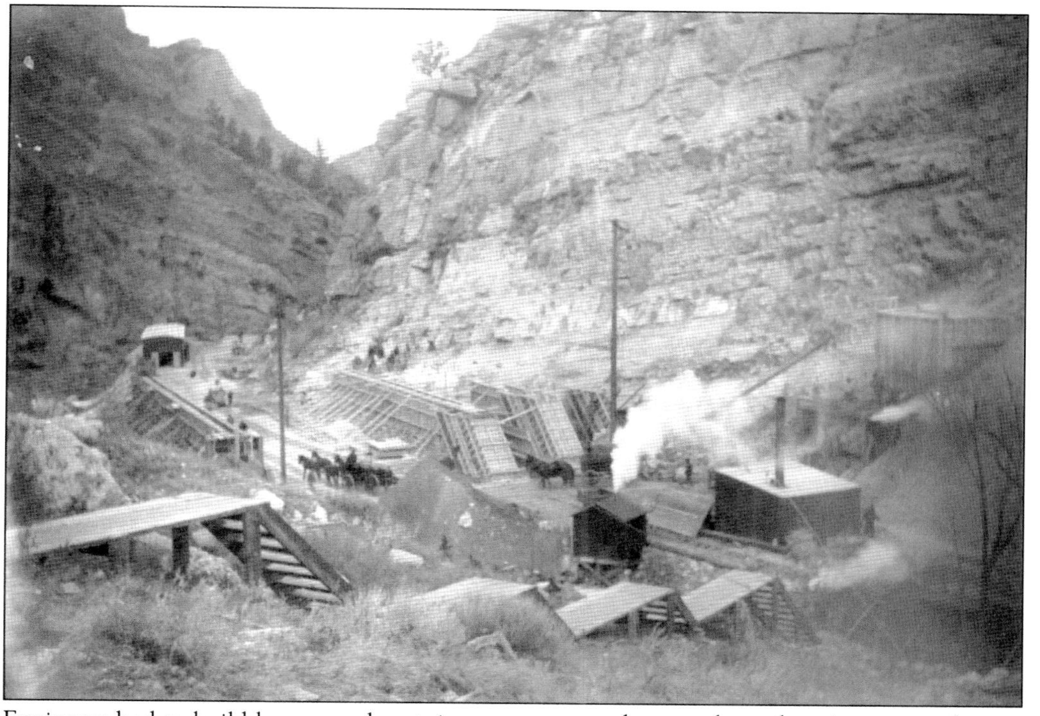

Engineers had to build long, wooden staircases to get workers, tools, and equipment to the site deep within the canyon. Once completed, the dam would store 15,1C0 acre-feet of water.

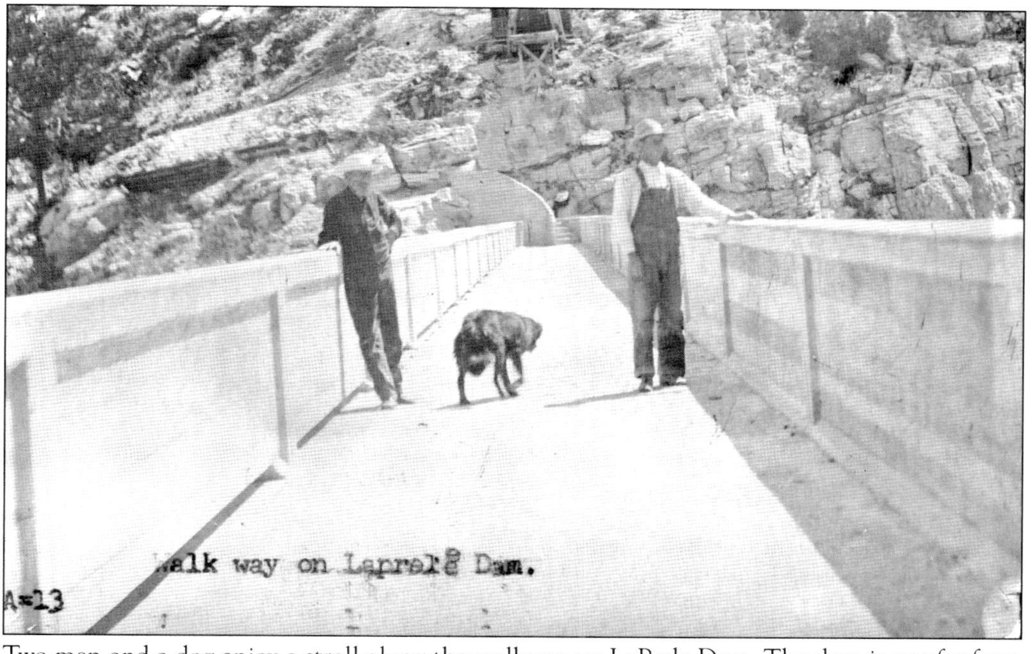

Two men and a dog enjoy a stroll along the walkway on LaPrele Dam. The dam is not far from Ayres Natural Bridge, and it is thought that these two are members of the Ayres family.

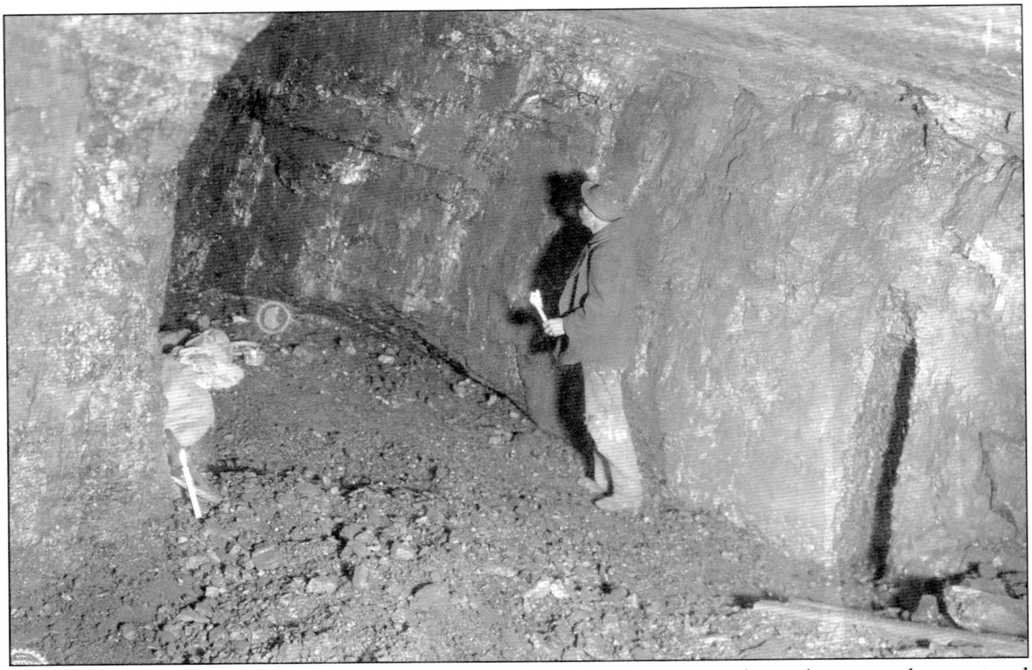

Coal mining was also an industry in and around the Douglas area, where the ground contained millions of tons of coal. Homesteaders and ranchers used the coal primarily for heating and cooking. The fuel was delivered to homes and ranches weekly or sometimes monthly, and cost approximately $2.25 per ton. Industrious prospectors could also find ore, lead, copper, and gold in the ground. In many cases the quality was excellent, but the quantity insufficient to continue operations.

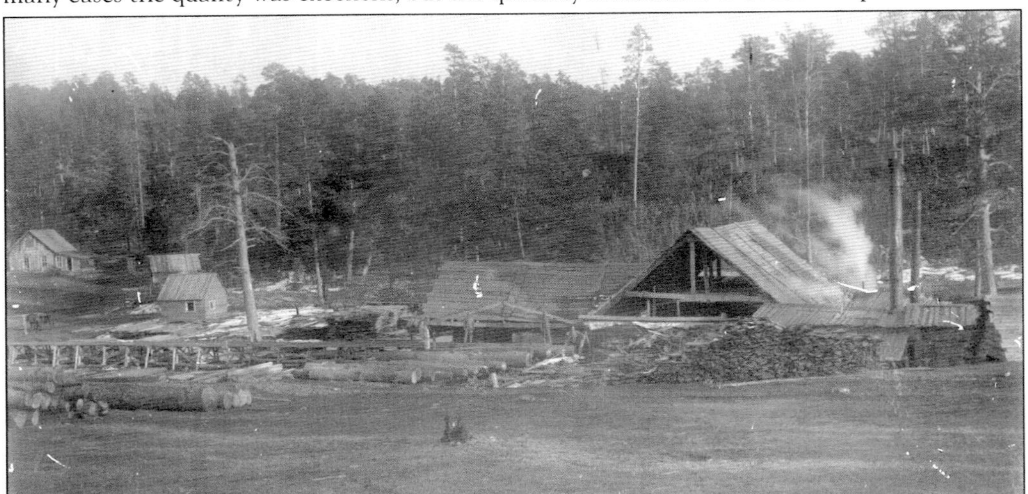

Many sawmills operated in the Cold Springs and Esterbrook areas near Douglas. While a good job, working in the sawmills was very dangerous and labor-intensive, requiring lots of muscle. Product from the surrounding forest was used for all types of construction projects, from houses to businesses to furniture. Logs were also shipped out of the area. The Marshall Saw Mill, above, operated in the Cold Springs area. Other successful operations were run by the Stinson and Russell families.

Five

Some Swell Events

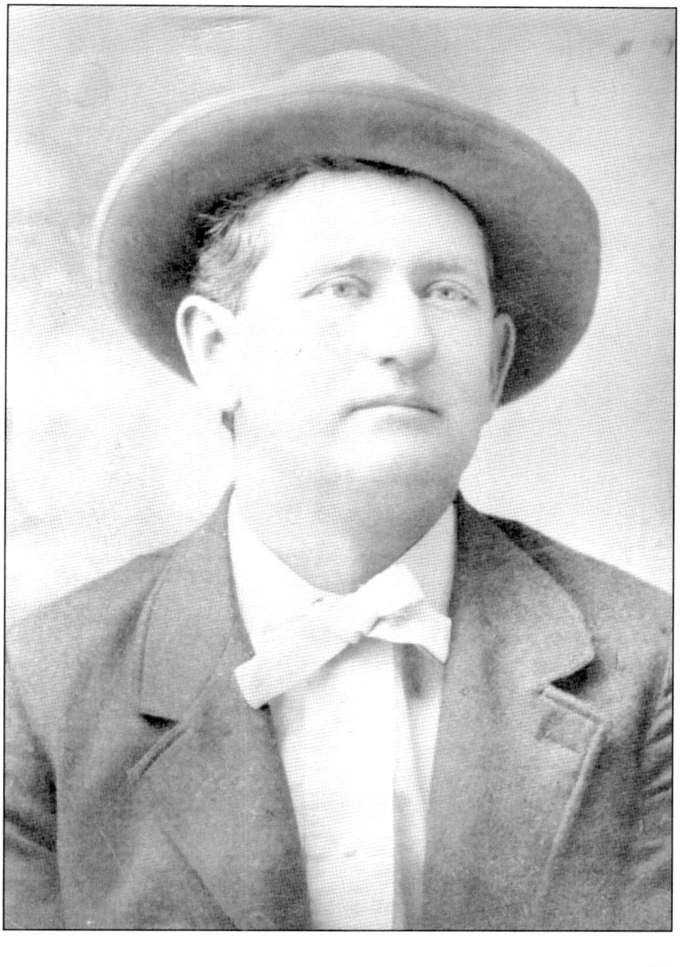

Douglas Budget editor, historian, writer, and sagebrush philosopher Bill Barlow was well respected from the moment he set up the first *Budget* office in a tent at Fort Fetterman in June 1886. While perturbed as to how the town was named, he later called Douglas the "best town in the world" and enjoyed reporting on its "swell events." Bill Barlow's real name was Merris C. Barrow; he and his wife, Minnie, worked together on the newspaper. Barrow served as the first town clerk, and later became mayor in 1890. He died in Douglas on October 9, 1910, and is interred at the local cemetery. His funeral was reportedly one of the biggest the town had ever seen.

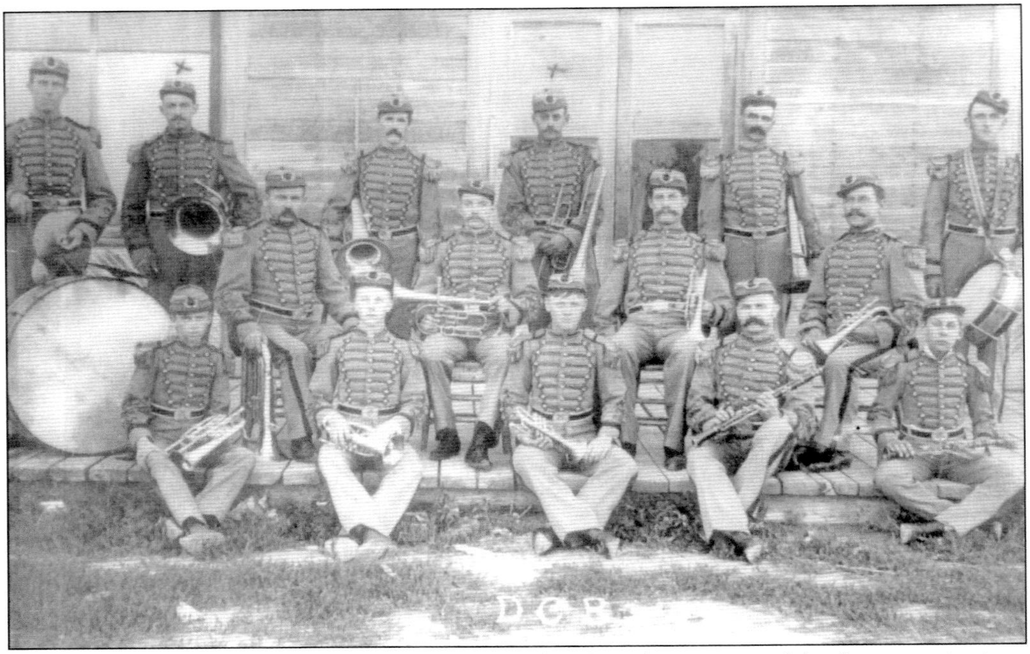

The Douglas Cornet Band organized in January of 1887, making it one of the first organizations in town. According to early newspaper reports, some of the band members had never played an instrument, while others brought years of training with them. The band would use any excuse to play for an audience, including performances at political meetings. Two charter members of the band, John J. Steffen and Harry Ruhl, played with the band for at least 25 years. The *Douglas Budget* reported that "Mister Ruhl has missed but one dance out of the 21 that the boys have given, and that was the year he was in Indiana." Ruhl was a blacksmith and cabinetmaker. Steffen owned the drugstore.

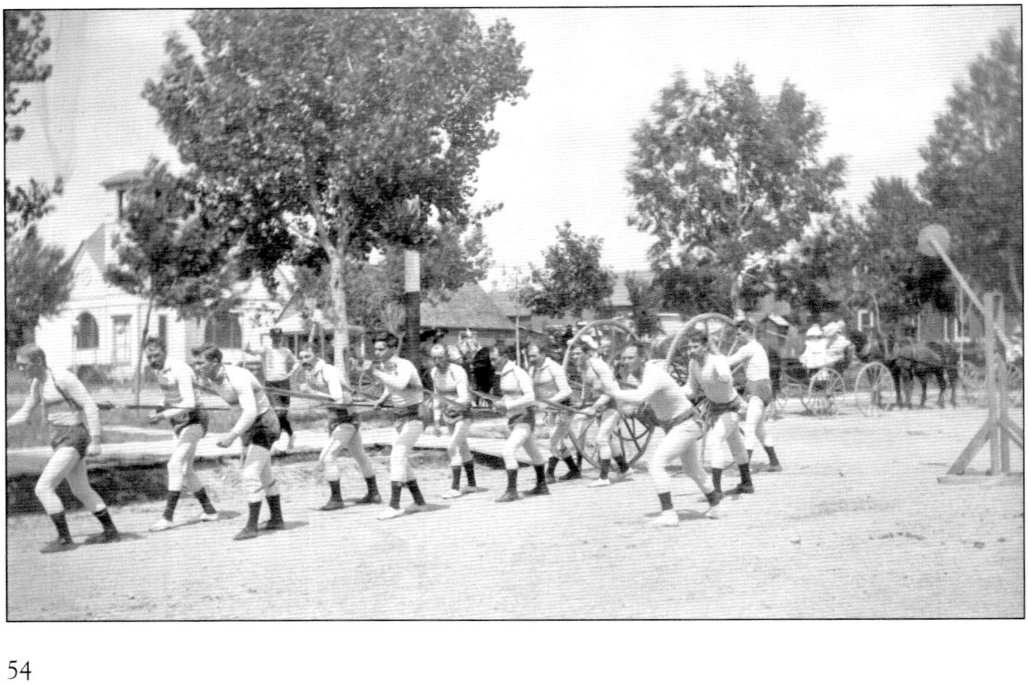

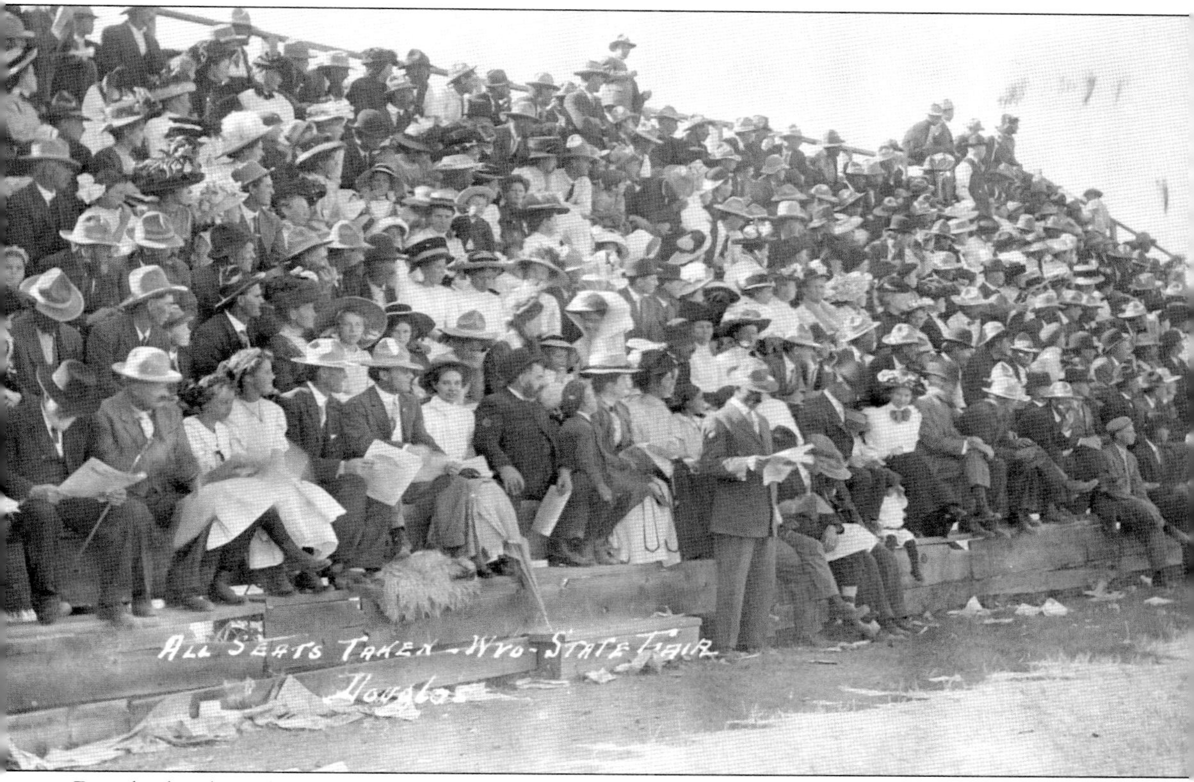

Douglas has been home to the Wyoming State Fair since 1905. The event is an opportunity for the young and old from across the state to showcase their best, whether by showing livestock, demonstrating homemaking skills, or taking part in the rodeo. The Wyoming State Fair celebrates history and culture, and involves education, competition, and entertainment for everyone. People of all ages filled the grandstand to enjoy a fine rodeo.

Opposite Page: The Douglas Hose Company held many events in town to benefit their cause. In March 1902, they staged a benefit ball, proceeds of which would allow them to purchase a ladder and other "badly needed apparatus." On July 4, 1902, the hose company participated in a fire-wagon-pulling contest with other, out-of-town hose companies to see which company was the fastest. The Douglas Hose Company held the speed record for a number of years.

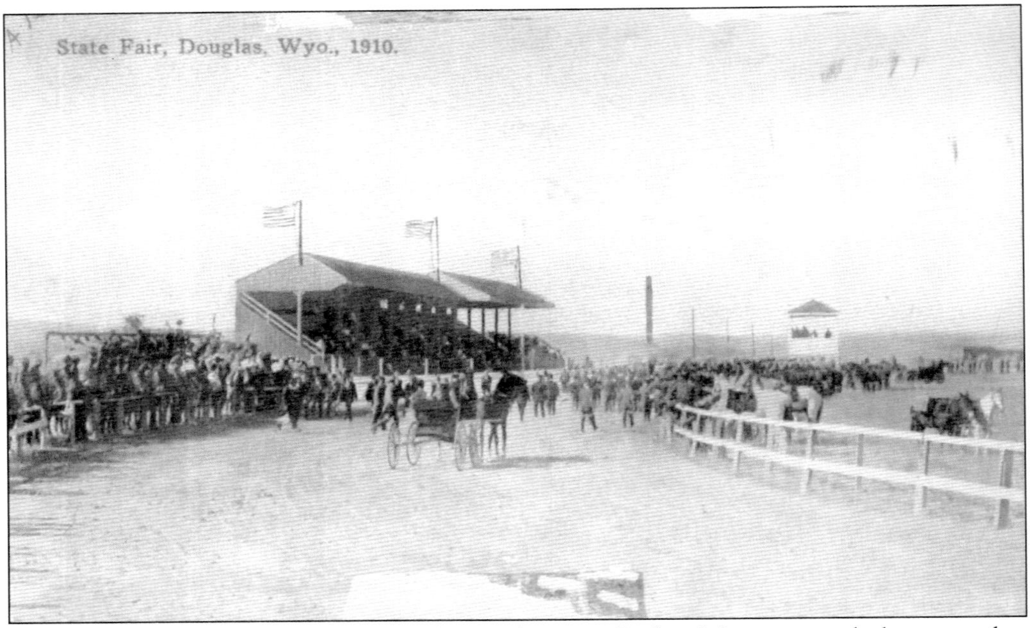

Land for the fairgrounds was donated by the Northwestern Railroad Company with the caveat that "a permanent home is near the Platte River at Douglas, and that at least 25 consecutive events are held, and that it be called the Wyoming State Fair." Events have been held every year since, with the exception of 1935 and 1936 due to the Great Depression, 1937 because of an outbreak of infantile paralysis, and 1942–1945 because of World War II. Many improvements to the grounds have been made over the years.

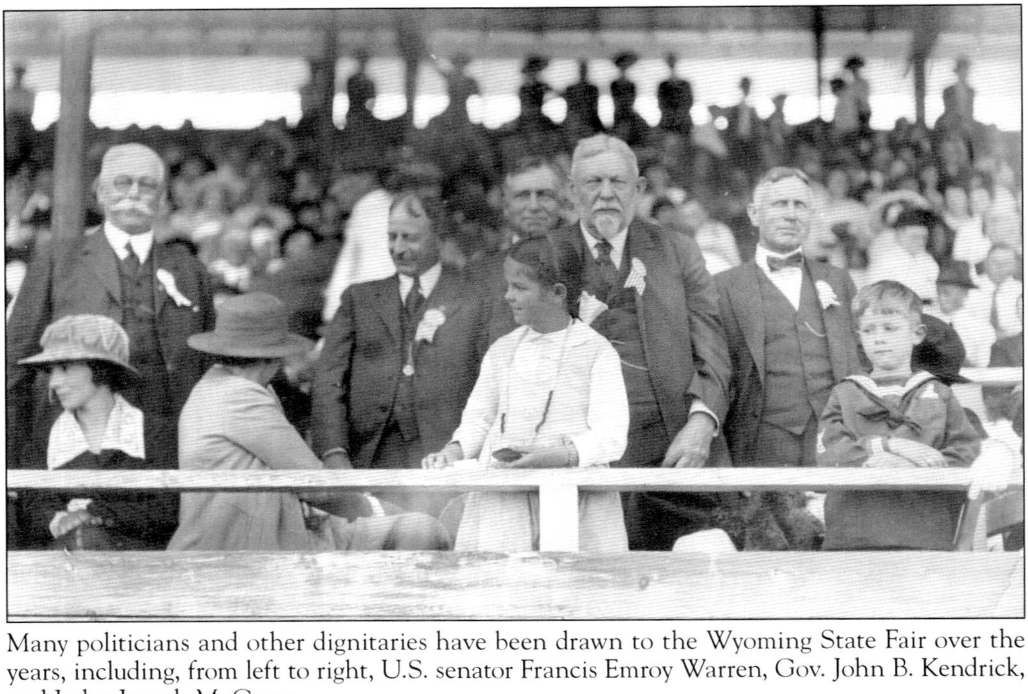

Many politicians and other dignitaries have been drawn to the Wyoming State Fair over the years, including, from left to right, U.S. senator Francis Emroy Warren, Gov. John B. Kendrick, and Judge Joseph M. Carey.

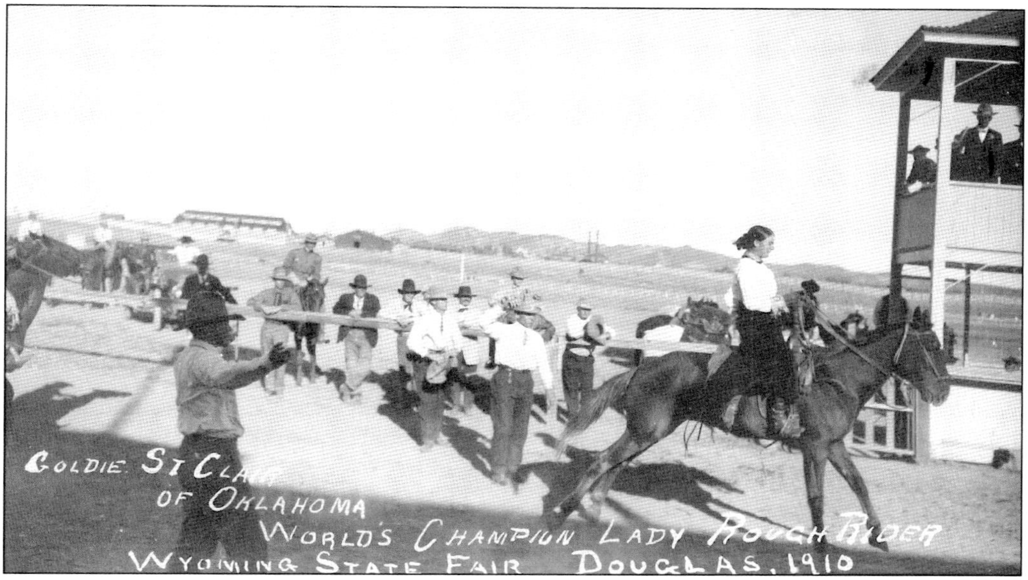

In 1910, women participated in the rodeo right alongside the cowboys. Goldie St. Clair of Oklahoma was the World's Champion Lady Bronc Rider, and no doubt gave a spectacular show.

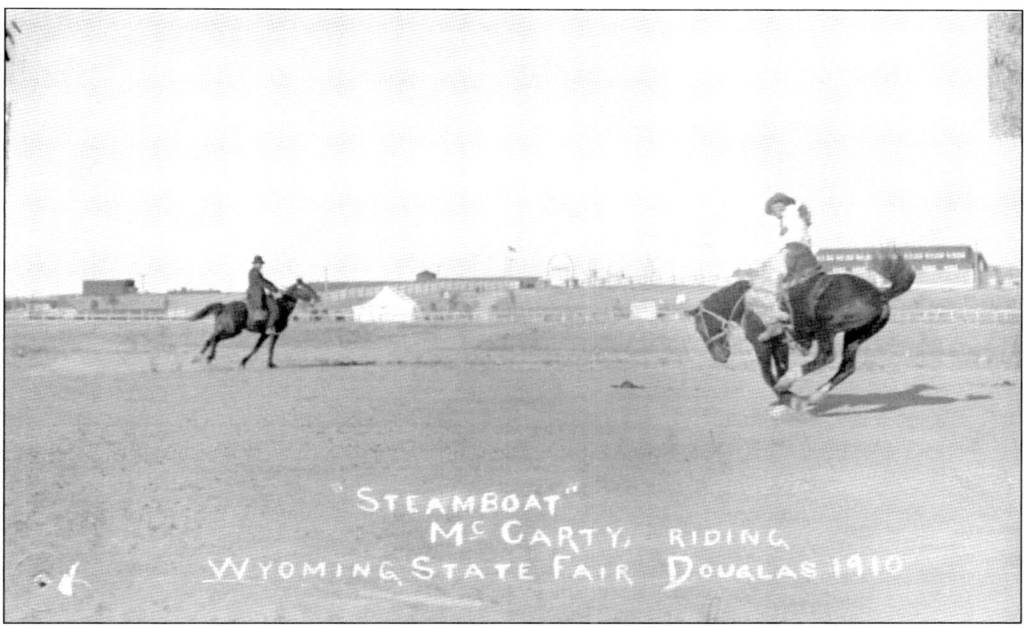

The cowboy known as "Steamboat" McCarty takes his turn at saddle bronc riding, an event as popular then as it is today. Notice the "pick up" man on the left, ready to rescue the cowboy when his time is up. The arena was huge, unlike those of today, which are fenced-in with bleachers and an area for the announcer.

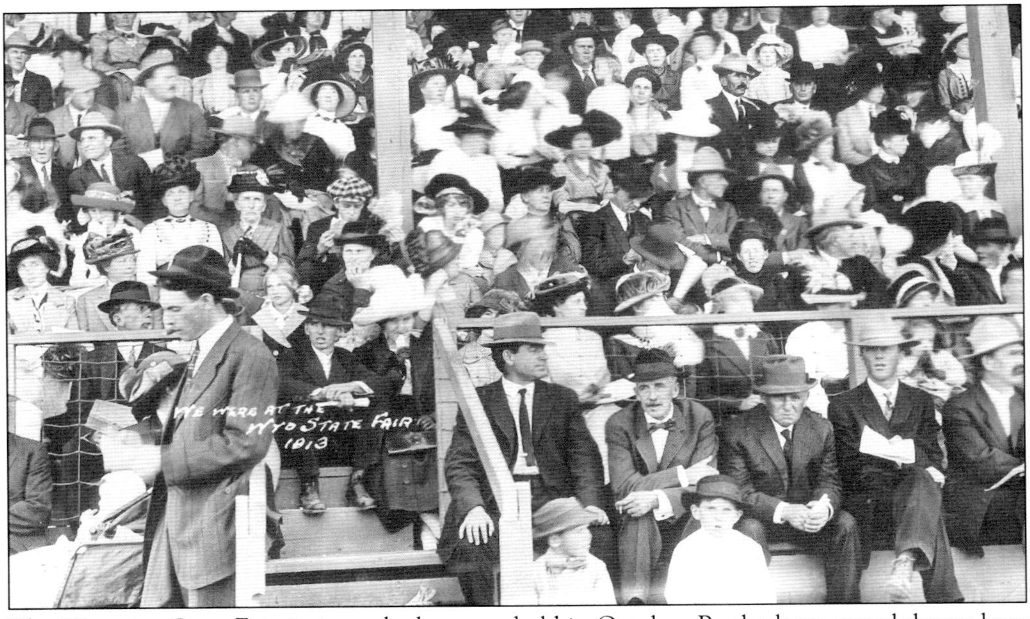

The Wyoming State Fair, in its early days, was held in October. By the large crowd shown here at the 1913 fair, it is evident that nothing, including school, farm chores, or work kept the people away.

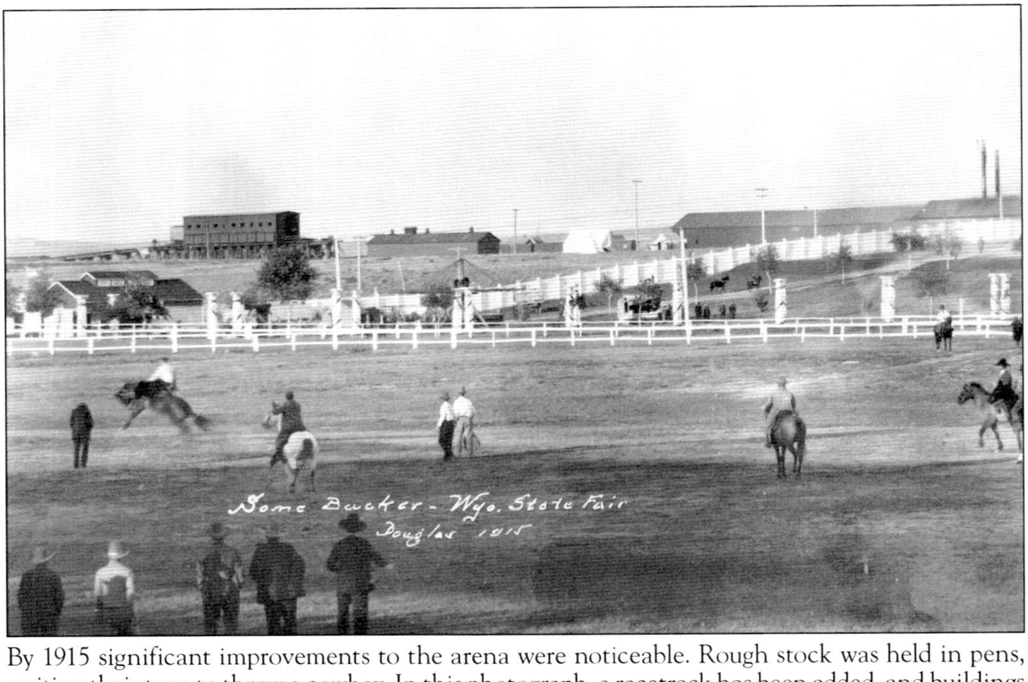

By 1915 significant improvements to the arena were noticeable. Rough stock was held in pens, waiting their turn to throw a cowboy. In this photograph, a racetrack has been added, and buildings and trees are starting to take shape.

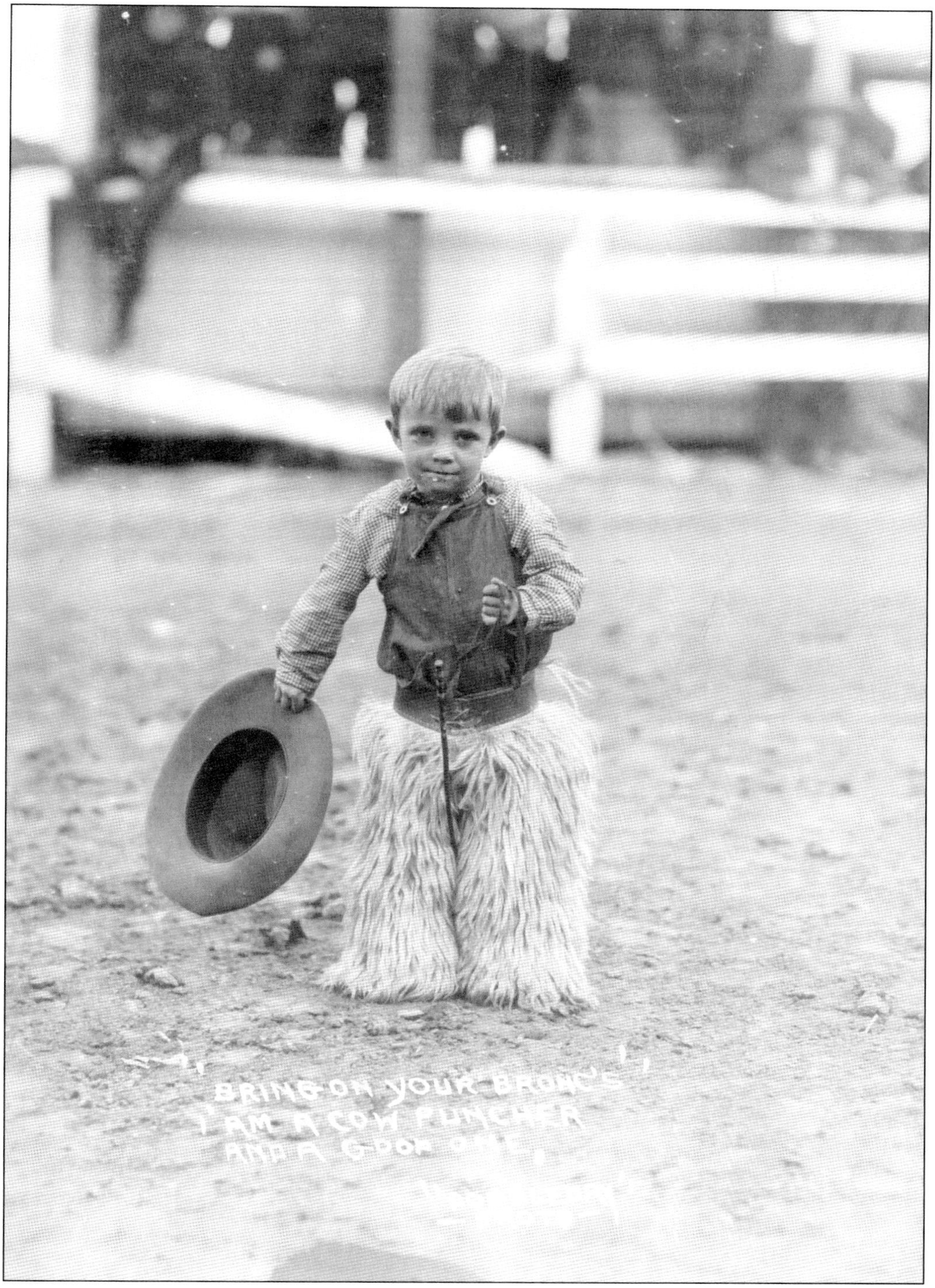

In 1915, this unidentified buckaroo is all decked out for the rodeo with his woolly chaps, cowboy hat, and vest. Underneath his picture is written, "Bring on your broncs; I'm a cowpuncher and a good one!"

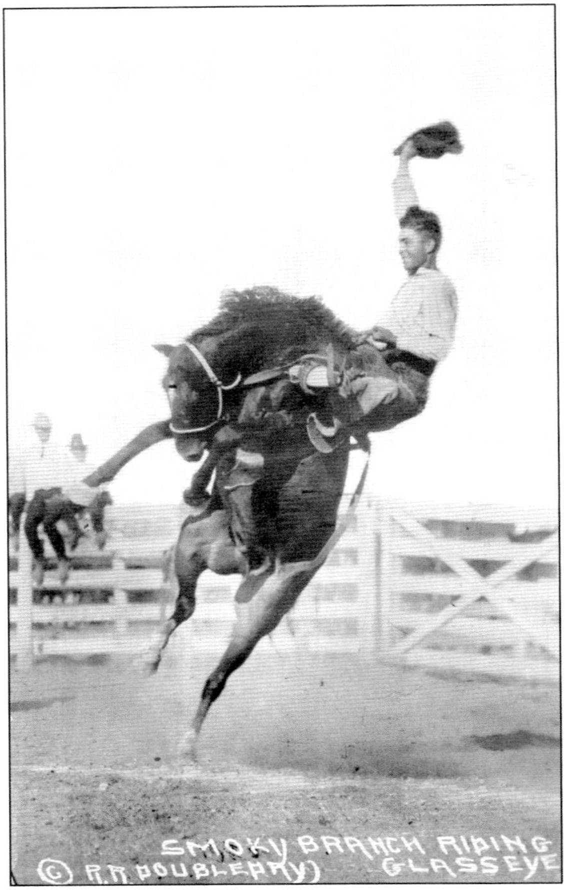

Smoky Branch, shown here atop a horse named Glass Eye, looks like he is having the time of his life.

By the way these fellows are dressed, one can only assume they had some level of authority. They may be explaining a score to a contestant. Their hats are of the 10-gallon variety, each crown shaped somewhat differently than the other.

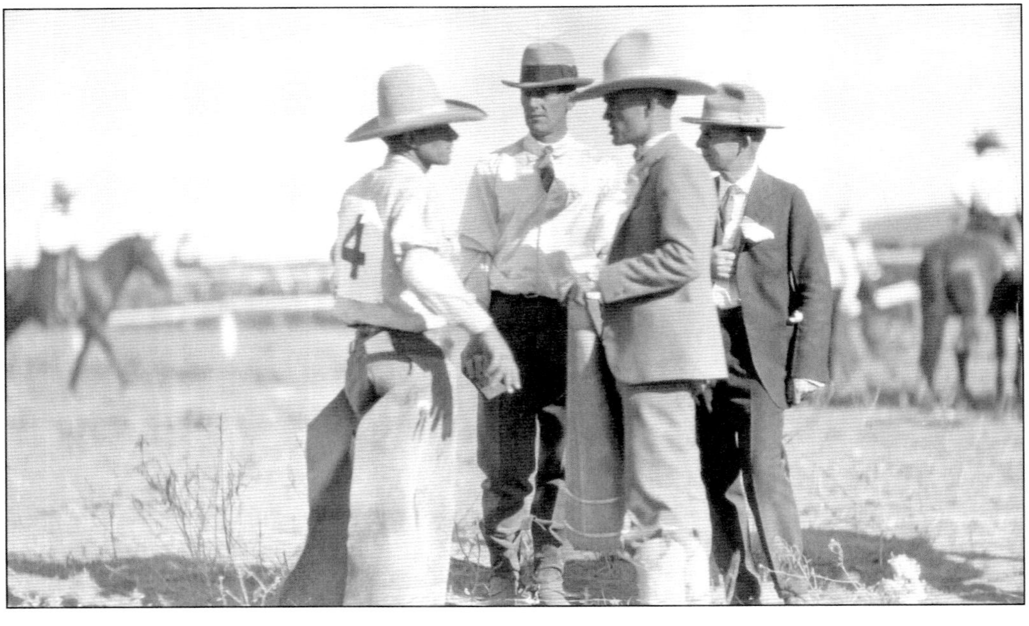

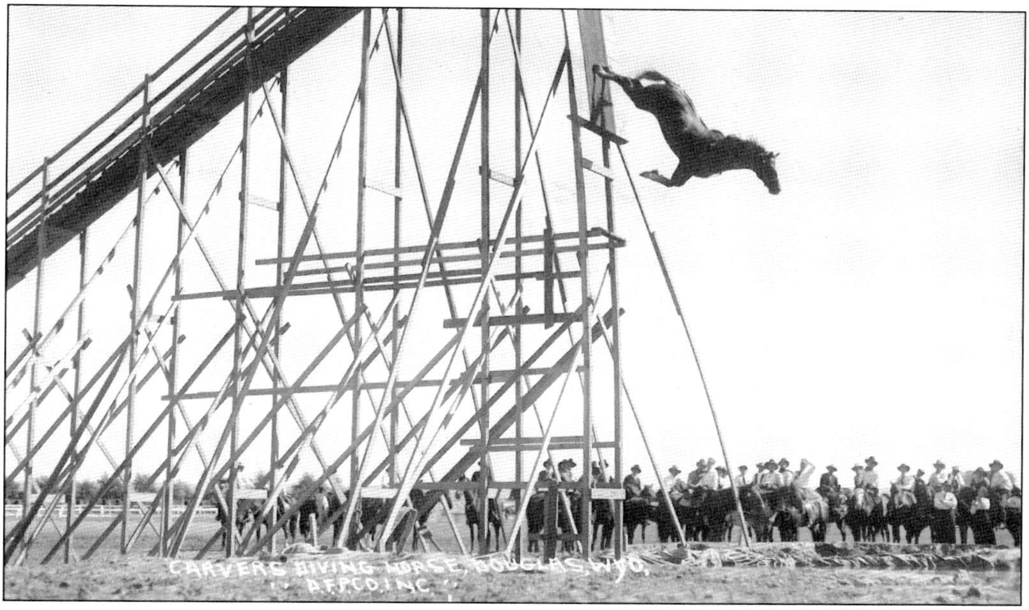

A diving horse was a huge attraction, not only at the Wyoming State Fair in the early 1900s, but around the country. The act was developed by William "Doc" Carver, a performer with Buffalo Bill's Wild West Show. The story goes that Carver got the idea of a diving horse when his own horse either fell or jumped into the water while he was crossing a bridge. Understandably, the act riled early animal rights activists, leading to the decline of its popularity after World War II.

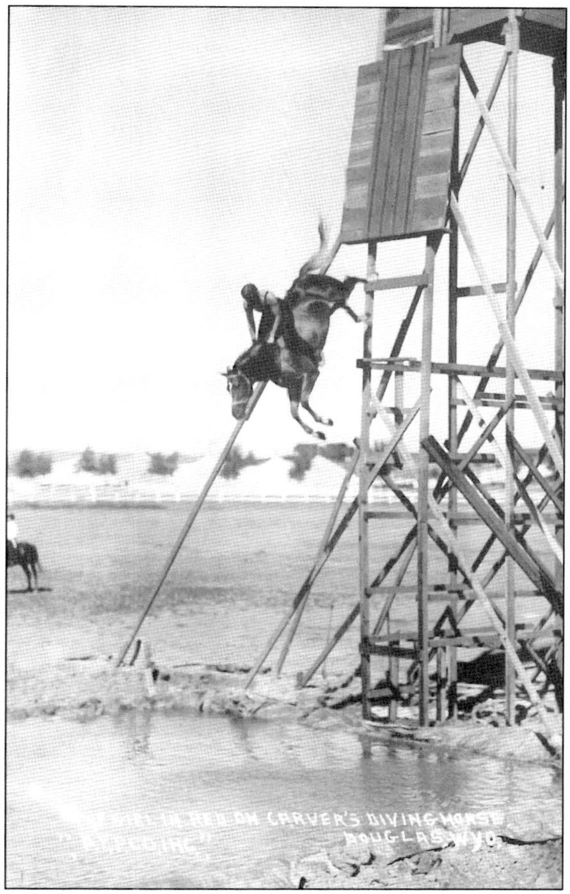

Doc Carver's Diving Horse undoubtedly drew loads of spectators, most of them drawn by curiosity. How could a horse be trained to do this in the first place? Why would anyone actually mount a diving horse before it jumped from a 60-foot-high platform into what must—from the rider's view—look like a puddle?

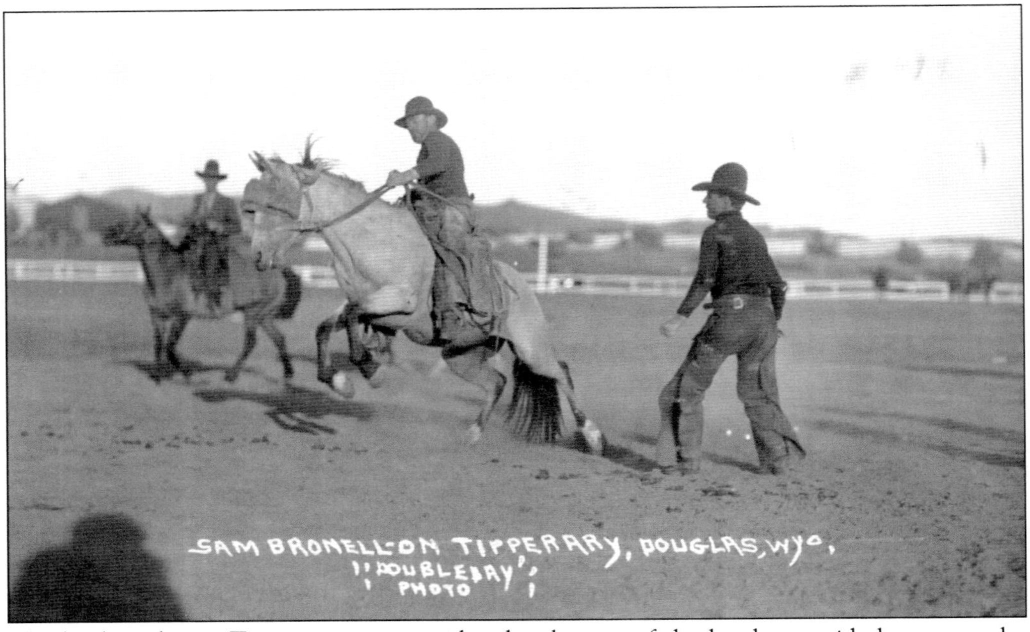

The bucking bronc Tipperary was considered to be one of the hardest-to-ride horses on the circuit. Sam Brownell is the brave cowboy riding the horse here. Brownell also rode Tipperary at Cheyenne Frontier Days in 1918. Of that ride, he said, "It was the hardest-fought battle between a champion man and a horse ever fought to a finish in any arena."

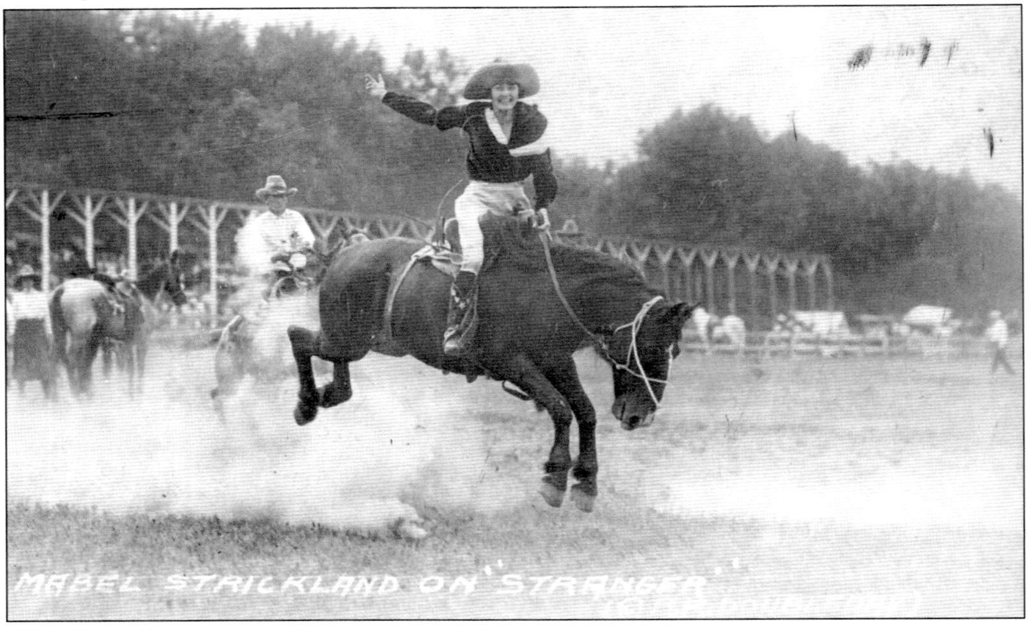

Famous cowgirl Mabel Strickland was well-known on the rodeo circuit, participating in bronc and steer riding, roping, trick riding, and Roman riding. Inducted into the National Cowgirl Hall of Fame in 1992, Mabel starred in several movies and also founded the Association of Film Equestriennes. Most often, cowboys and cowgirls cut their teeth at local rodeos before competing in bigger events like Cheyenne Frontier Days.

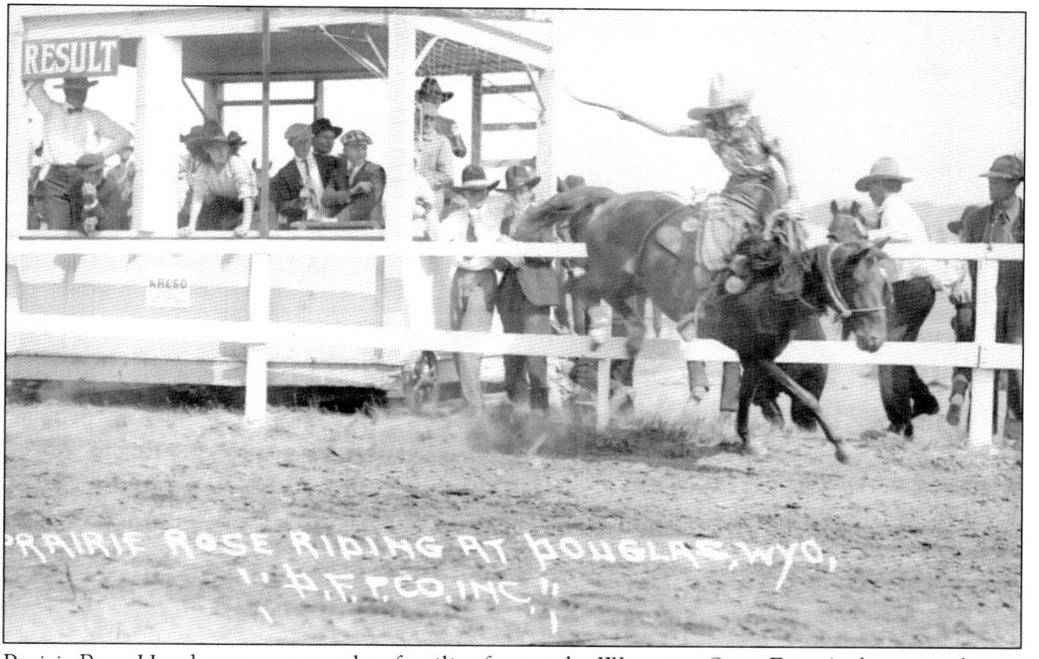

Prairie Rose Henderson was another familiar face at the Wyoming State Fair. A champion bronc rider, the young woman attracted lots of attention with her natural good looks and style.

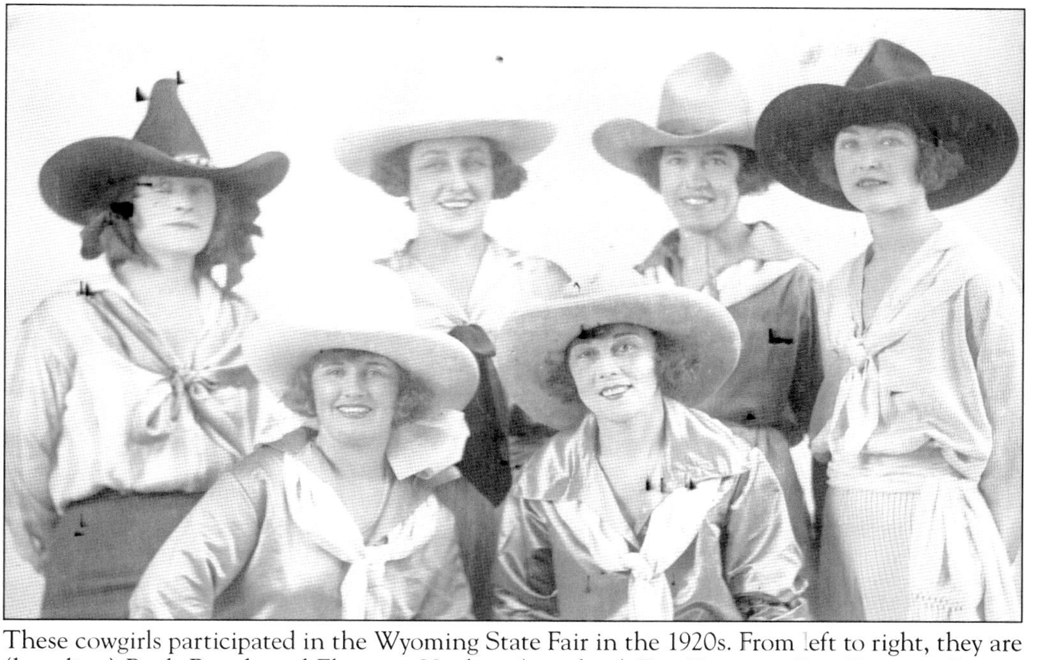

These cowgirls participated in the Wyoming State Fair in the 1920s. From left to right, they are (kneeling) Ruth Roach and Florence Hughes; (standing) Fox Hastings, Bea Kiernan, Prairie Rose, and Mabel Strickland.

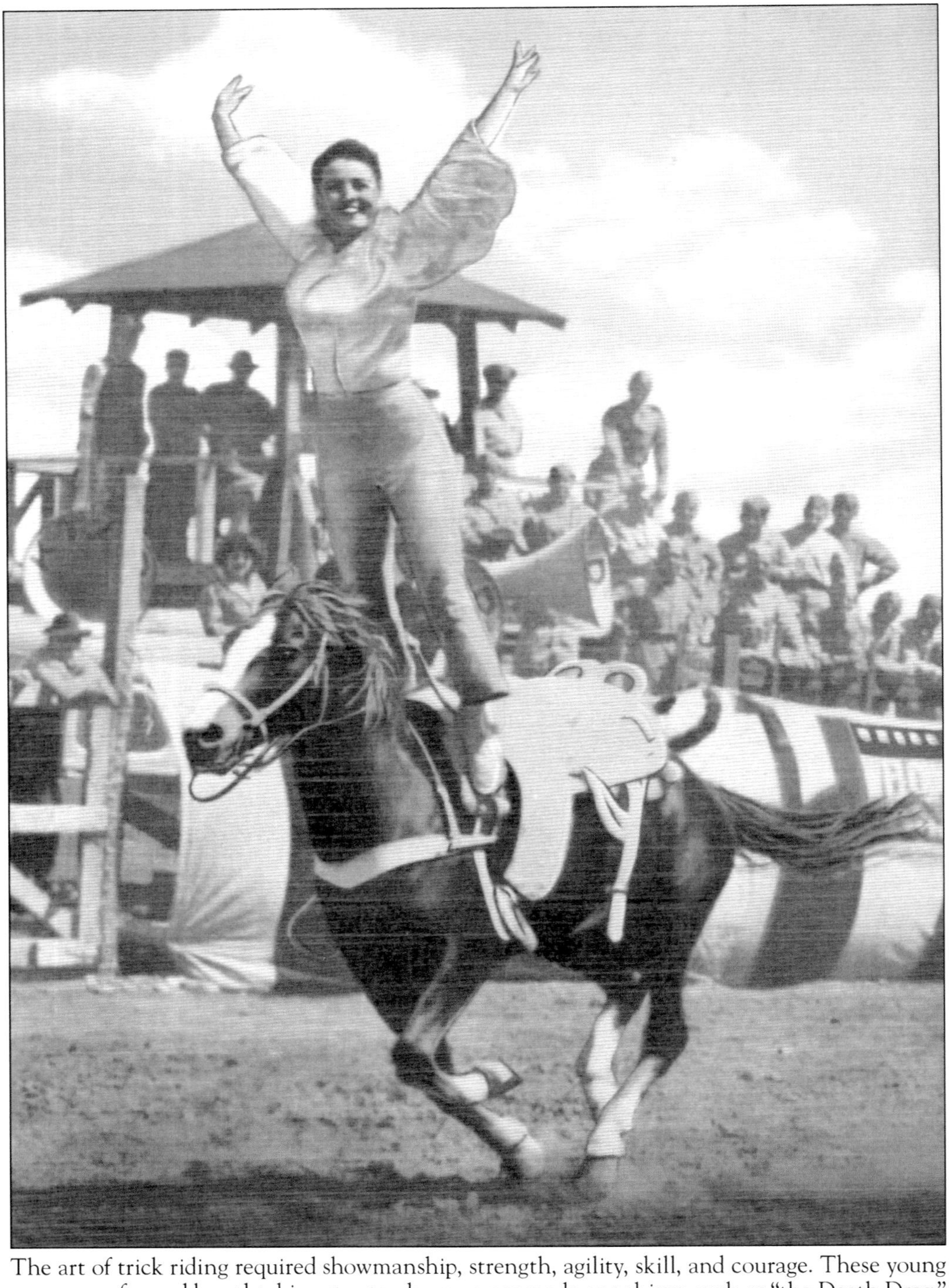

The art of trick riding required showmanship, strength, agility, skill, and courage. These young women performed breathtaking stunts whose names made one shiver, such as "the Death Drag," also known as "the Suicide Drag." This brave rider is "Roman riding," a trick performed standing atop two horses, with one foot on each. Various forms of trick riding have been performed in the movies, and trick riders have often acted as stunt doubles for Western stars.

Chief Yellow Calf was the much-respected, final chief of the Arapaho people. Native Americans were a huge part of any rodeo celebration, and the Wyoming State Fair was no exception. They participated by demonstrating traditional Native American singing, drumming, and dancing.

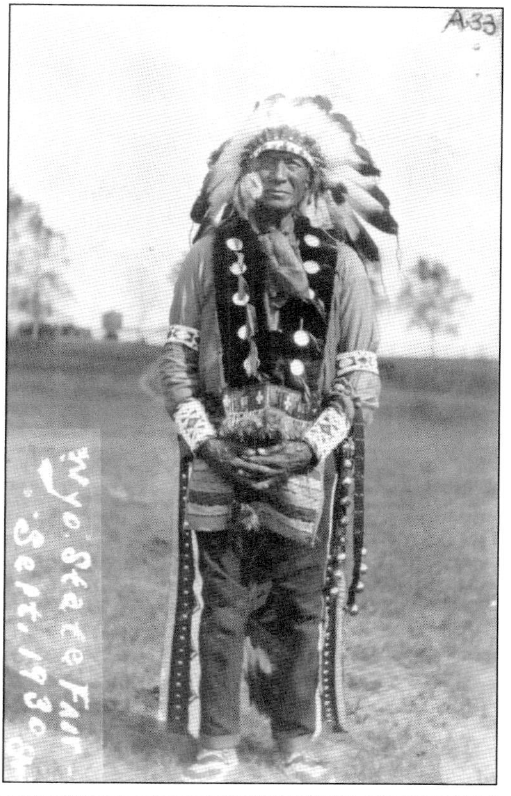

On January 8, 1926, the Wyoming Pioneer Association was formed to "effect a permanent organization for pioneers who had resided in Wyoming 25 years or more." Today it boasts a membership of over 700 people nationwide. The gathering below was held in 1928, and similar gatherings have taken place every year since.

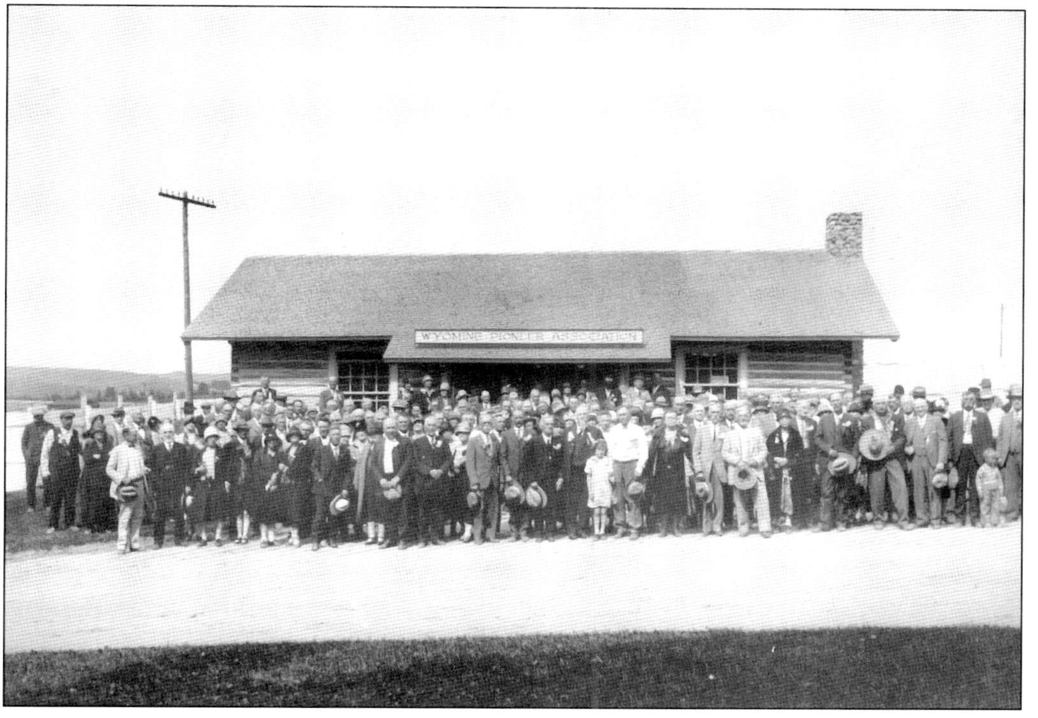

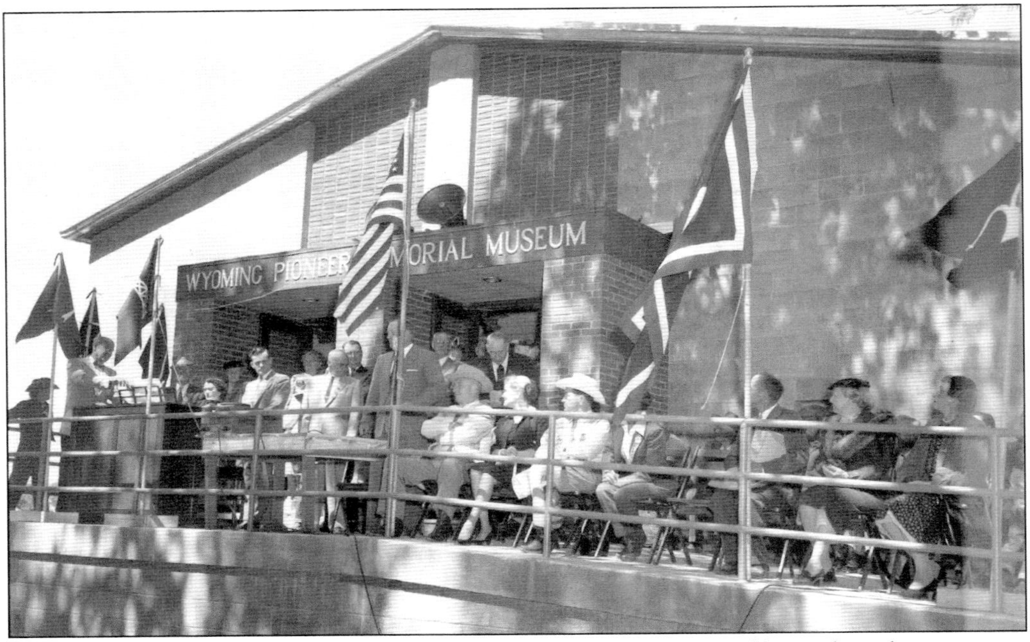

The Wyoming Pioneer Memorial Museum was established in 1925, and housed in a log structure. In 1956, the Wyoming Pioneer Association was instrumental in building a brand new museum. While the association's original mission was to honor Wyoming pioneers, it also serves as an advisory board to the museum.

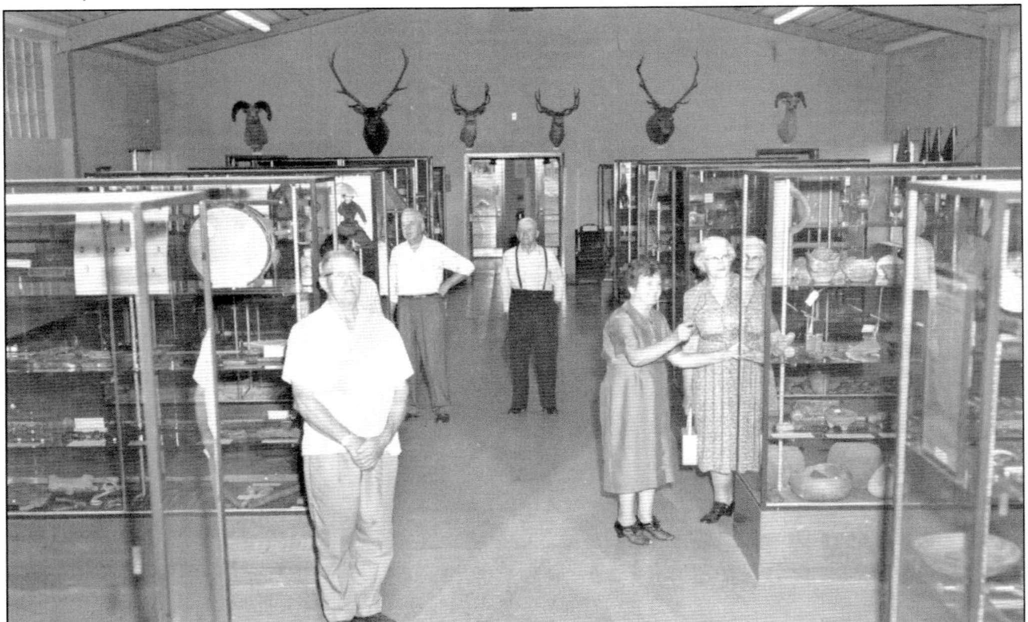

Visitors to the Wyoming Pioneer Memorial Museum enjoy a variety of historical and cultural materials related to westward expansion, to Wyoming pioneers in particular, and to the West in general. Today the museum is administered by the Wyoming Department of State Parks and Cultural Resources.

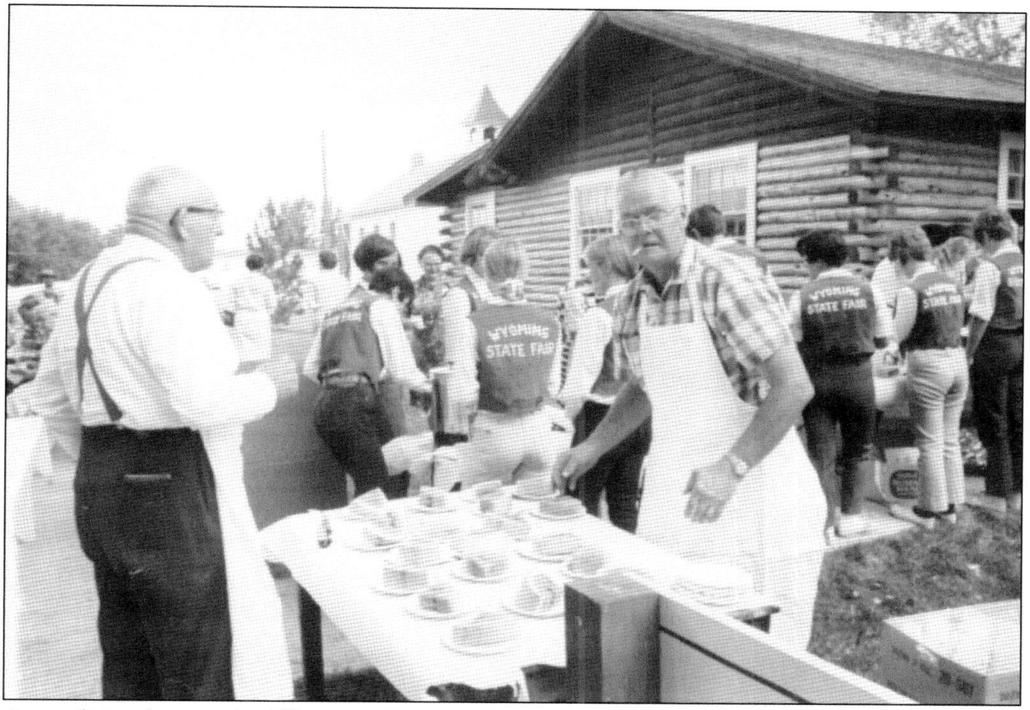

As tradition has it, the Wyoming Pioneer Association hosts an outdoor picnic for all of its members and guests each year following their annual meeting. The picnic is a much-anticipated event, offering an opportunity for old-timers to get together and talk about days gone by. It is also a time that the pioneers introduce old traditions to younger members of the family, taking any opportunity to encourage pride in Wyoming's heritage. In this photograph, Douglas businessman Otto "Beef" Bolln serves up some watermelon. Bolln came from a family of Douglas pioneers, and owned Bolln's Grocery Store.

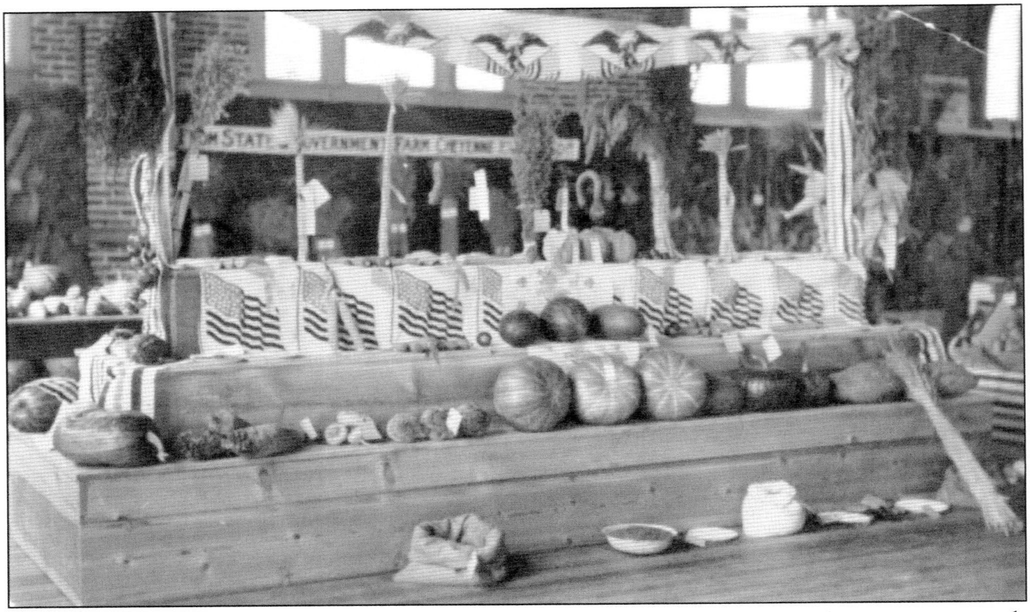

Exhibits are a highlight of the Wyoming State Fair and represent efforts that begin prior to each county fair. Exhibitors can enter in a wide variety of divisions, including floriculture, agriculture, culinary, needlework, and visual arts. Exhibiting at the Wyoming State Fair is an honor for homemakers, youth, and businesses, and usually represents a year's worth of effort. This is an exhibit prepared by the Wyoming State Government Farm.

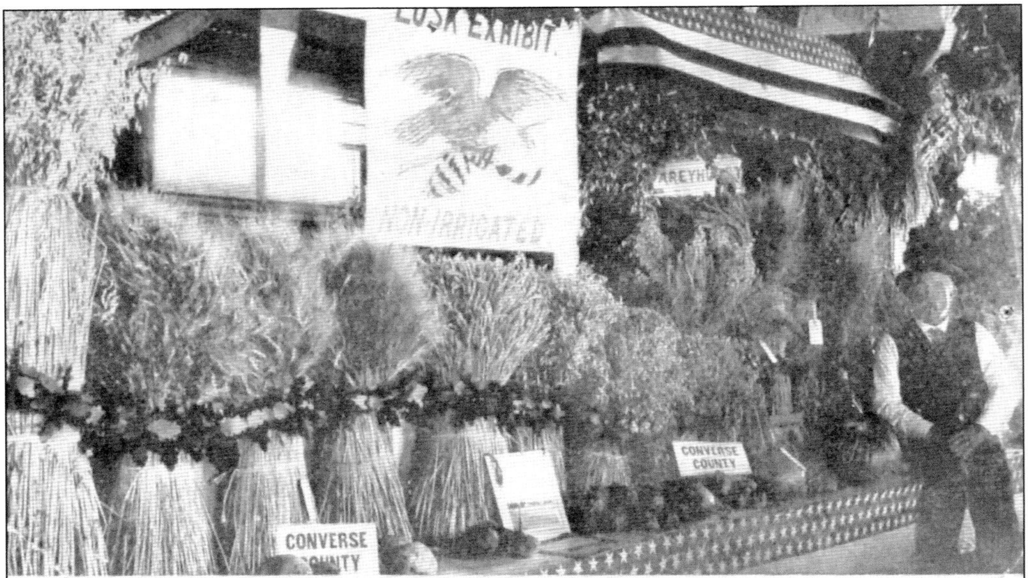

The year 1909 was a good one to grow non-irrigated crops in Niobrara County, east of Douglas. This exhibit at the Wyoming State Fair featured grains of all types. In the foreground of this photograph are vegetables grown in Converse County.

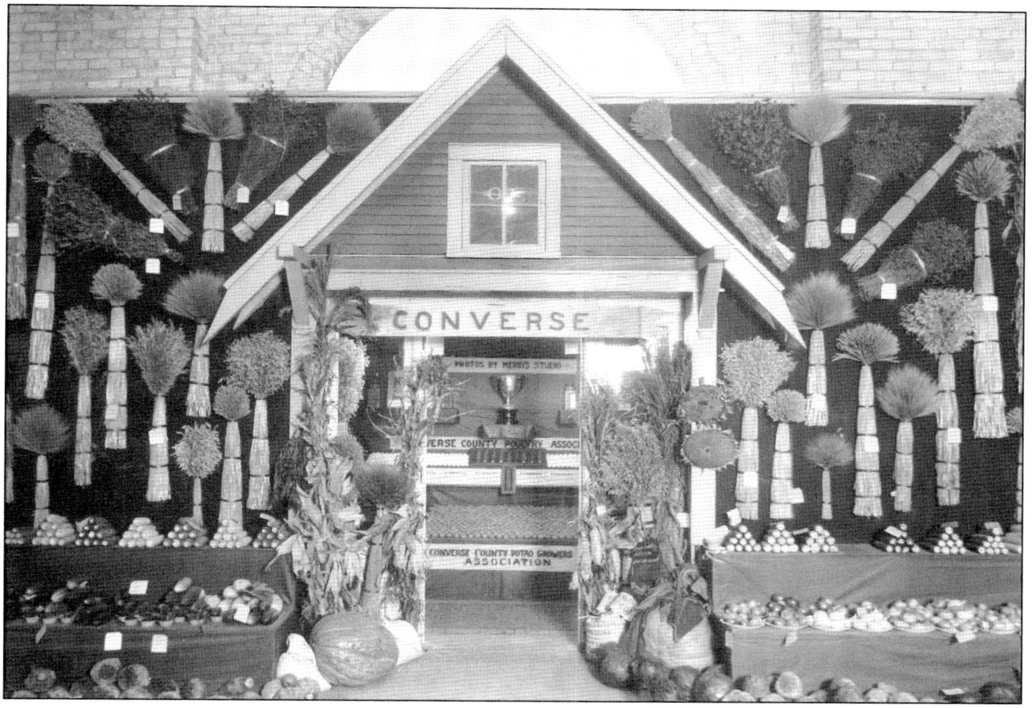

Converse County growers were well-represented in this exceptional 1925 exhibit. Just look at the array of corn, beets, watermelons, cabbage, cucumbers, and even sunflowers. In the background are eggs displayed by the Converse County Poultry Association, and potatoes raised by the Converse County Potato Growers Association.

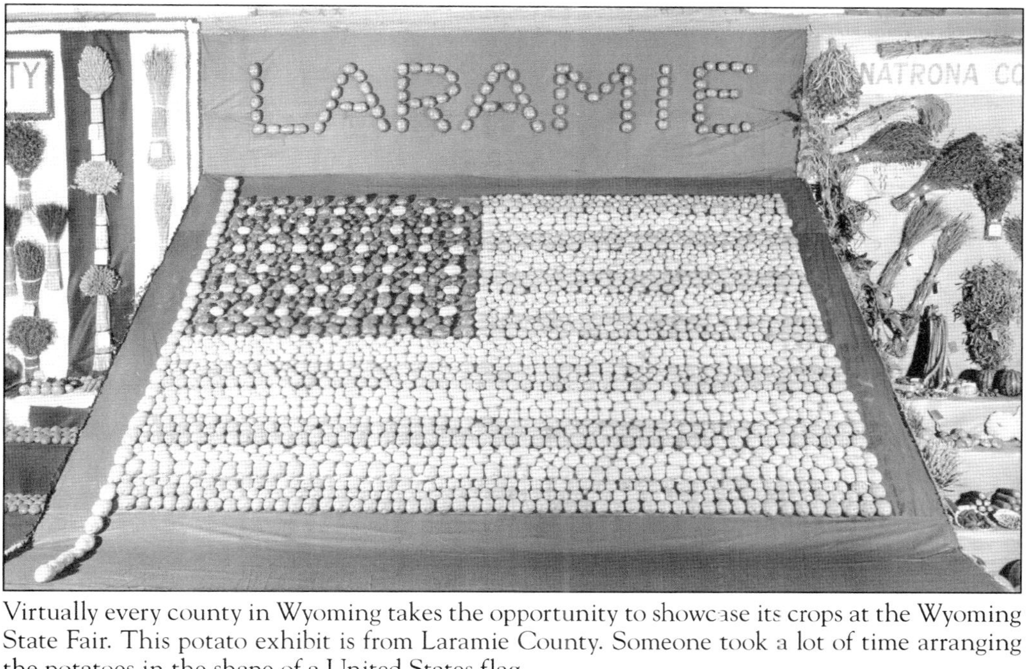

Virtually every county in Wyoming takes the opportunity to showcase its crops at the Wyoming State Fair. This potato exhibit is from Laramie County. Someone took a lot of time arranging the potatoes in the shape of a United States flag.

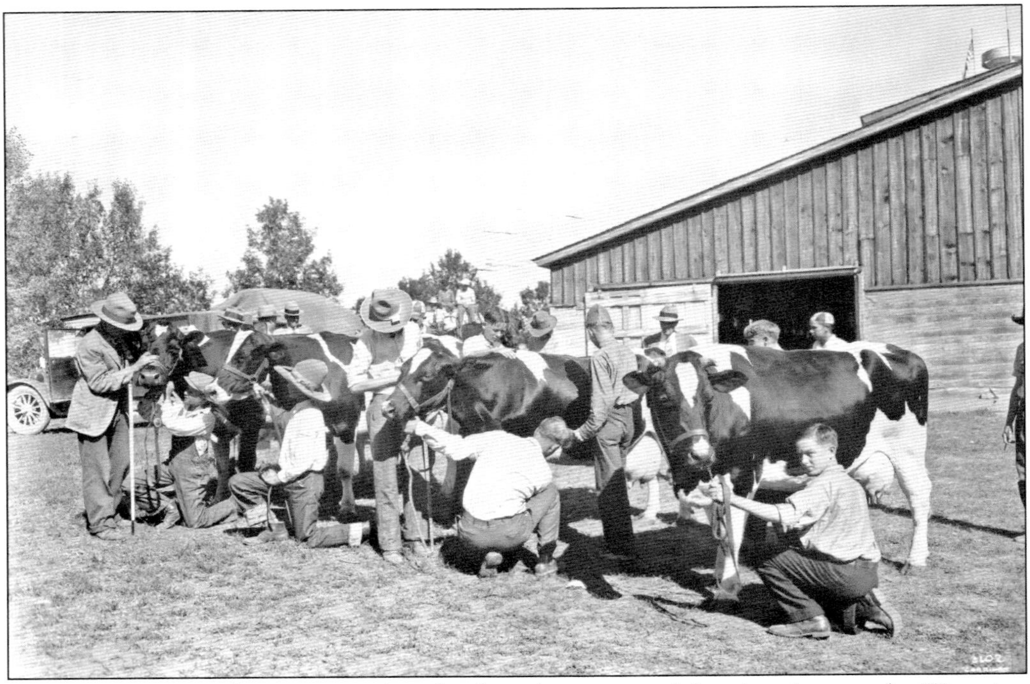

Young livestock producers raise calves for the sole purpose of showing them at the Wyoming State Fair. Judges look for a healthy weight, shiny coat, and good teeth and gums before awarding much-coveted prize ribbons to the deserving animals and their owners. Most of the children and teenagers who show livestock at the state fair are members of a local 4-H club, a nationwide organization dedicated to helping youth become "contributing, productive, self-directed members of society." Ideally, a young person's experiences with the club serve to expand upon the lessons he or she is learning at home and on the farm or ranch.

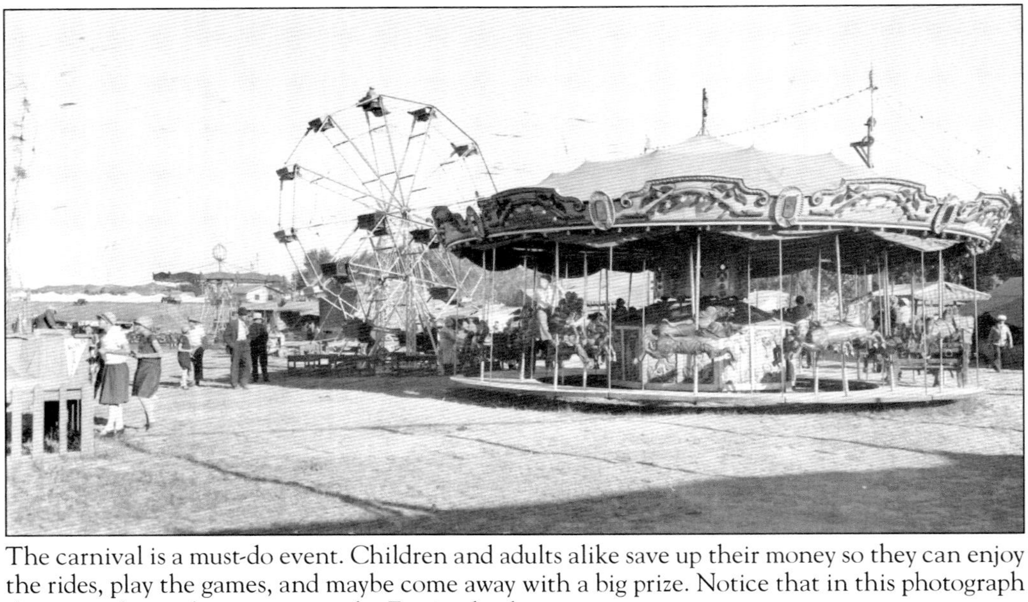

The carnival is a must-do event. Children and adults alike save up their money so they can enjoy the rides, play the games, and maybe come away with a big prize. Notice that in this photograph there is only one brave man on the Ferris wheel.

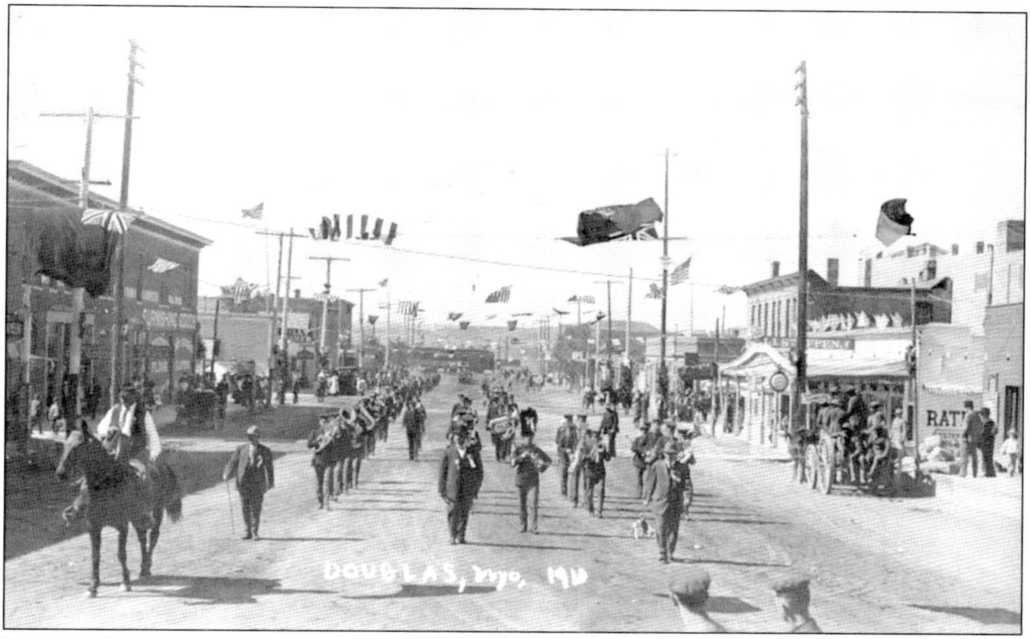

Everyone loves a parade, a staple of the Wyoming State Fair since the beginning. Parades give the town a chance to dress up with flags and bunting, and hold special sales. In this 1910 photograph, the Douglas band marches down an unpaved street.

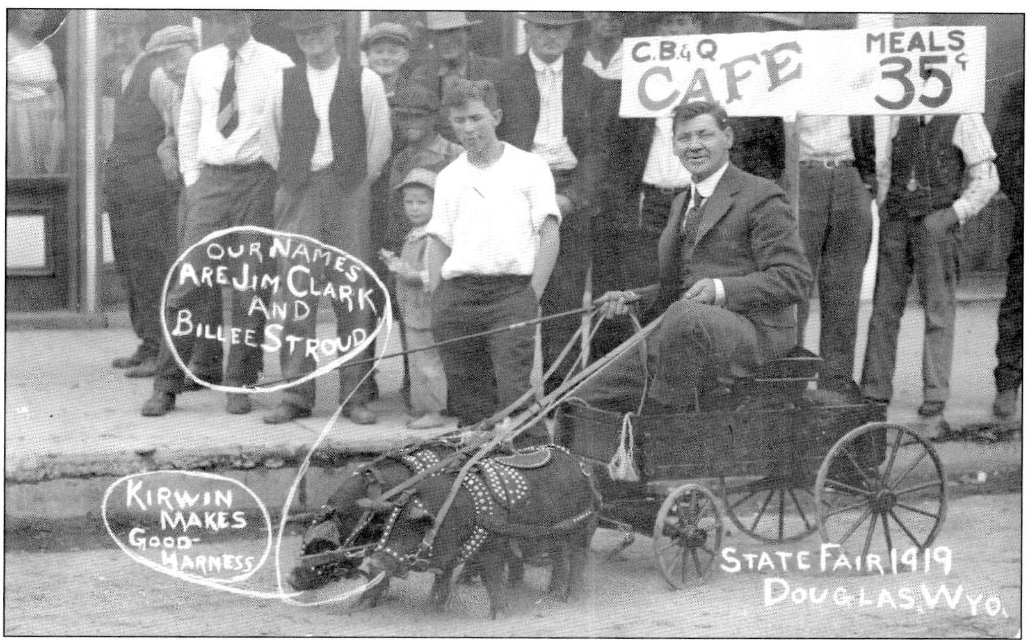

These pigs (who say their names are Jim Clark and Billee Stroud) surely were a crowd pleaser. The man holding the reins trained the two pigs to pull the wagon. A parade gives participants an opportunity to display their talents, no matter how unusual. Notice that in 1919, when this photograph was taken, lunch at the CB and Q Cafe was 35¢.

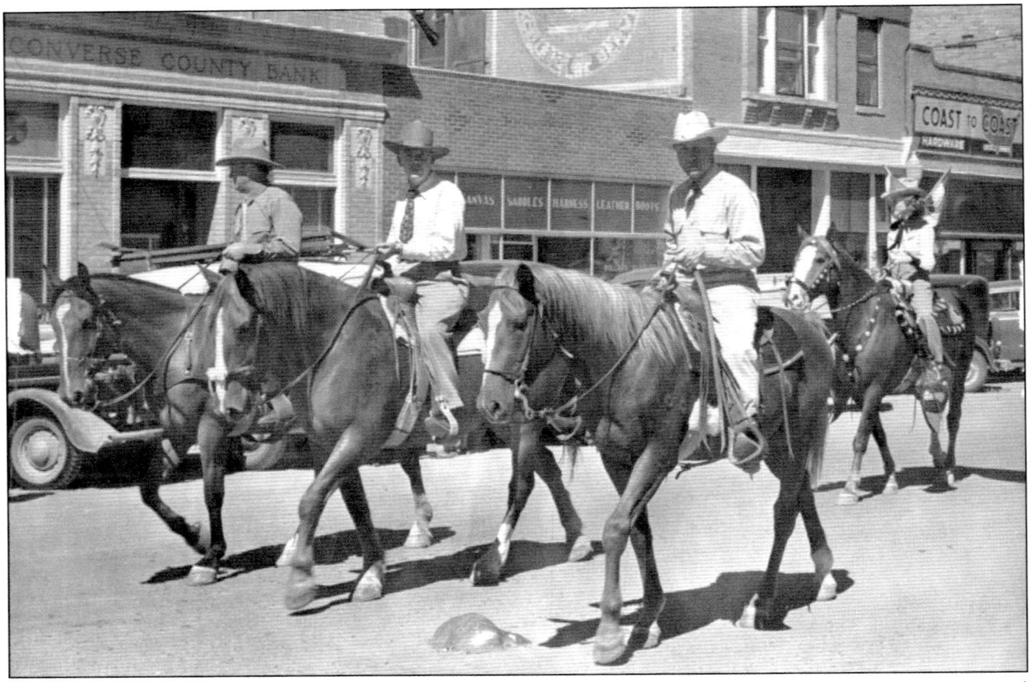

Distinguished citizens and politicians are commonly asked to lead parades. Douglas mayor Leonard Shaw, Red Fenwick, newspaper columnist for the *Denver Post* (center), and an unidentified man ride their horses down Second Street.

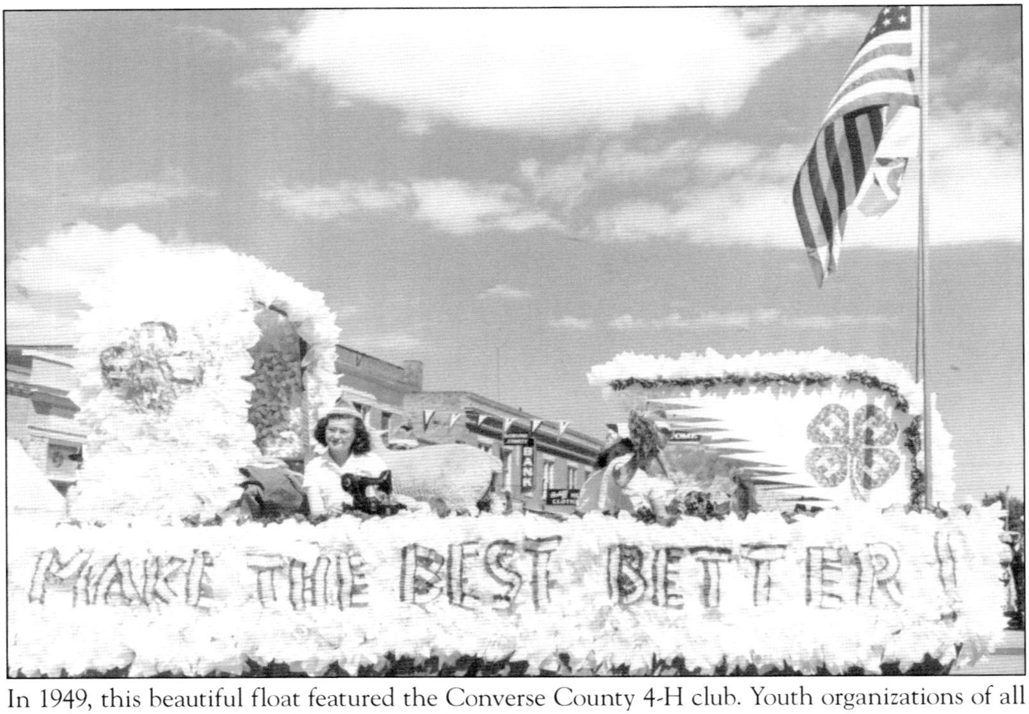

In 1949, this beautiful float featured the Converse County 4-H club. Youth organizations of all types were well-represented in the annual parade.

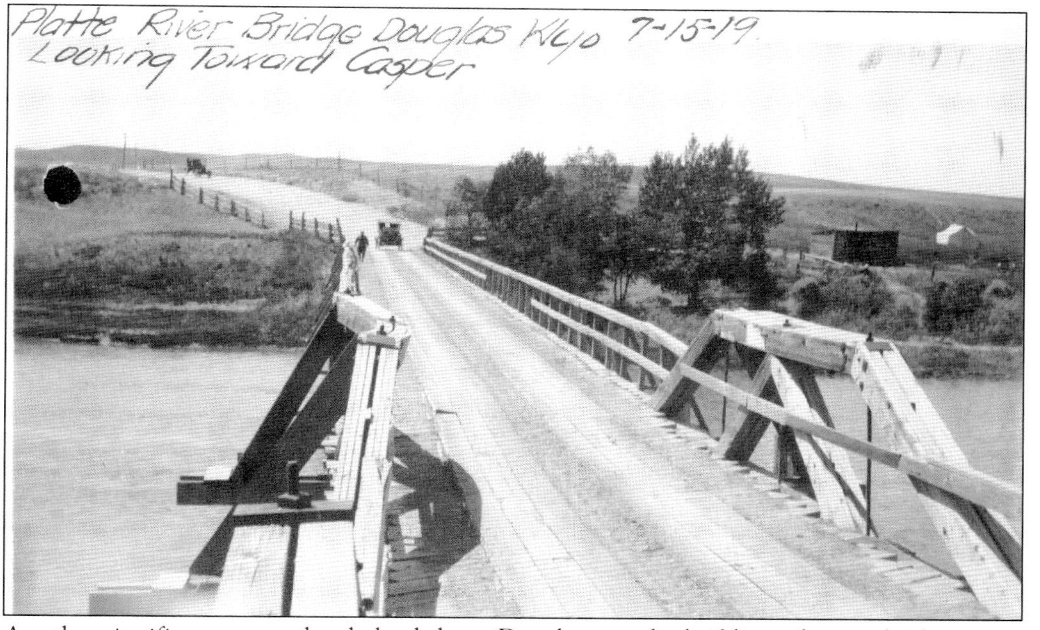

Another significant event that helped shape Douglas was the building of a new bridge across the North Platte River. In 1922, the newspaper announced the construction of a new federally funded bridge along the Yellowstone Highway over the North Platte River on the west side of Douglas, "replacing the old wooden structure, which has been repaired until there is scarcely a place left solid enough to hold a nail."

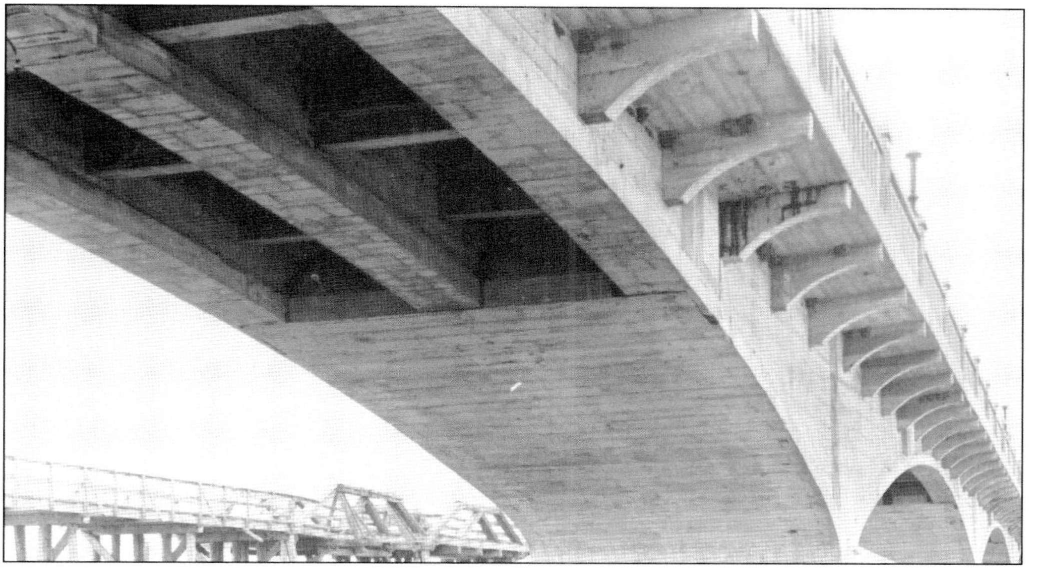

Completed in May 1923 under the supervision of Wyoming State Highway Department engineer John E. Walter, the five-span cantilevered, 416-foot-long concrete structure was roundly proclaimed, "one of the finest bridges in the state." The new bridge cost $58,549.33. The original wooden bridge had not yet been removed when this photograph was taken. By the 1950s the 1923 bridge was declared too narrow for the increased amount of traffic, and in 1953 the bridge was widened to 30 feet.

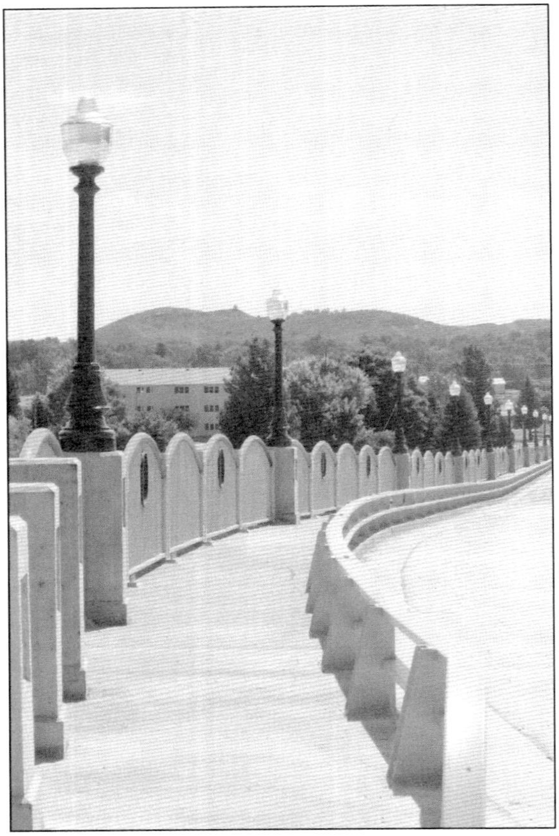

In the early part of the 21st century, the bridge across the North Platte River was found to be outdated once again, and plans for a new bridge were developed. On Thursday, July 30, 2009, a ribbon-cutting ceremony celebrated the completion of the new bridge. Douglas's acting-mayor Marilyn Werner, Wyoming Department of Transportation (WYDOT) commission chair Susie Dziardziel, and WYDOT director John Cox participated in the celebration. The new bridge features this inviting and safe pedestrian walkway. (Courtesy WYDOT.)

Construction on the new bridge began in 2008, causing traffic to be re-routed for a little less than a year. The new five-lane bridge is 430 feet long, not including the approaches. The bridge itself cost $7.5 million. (Courtesy WYDOT.)

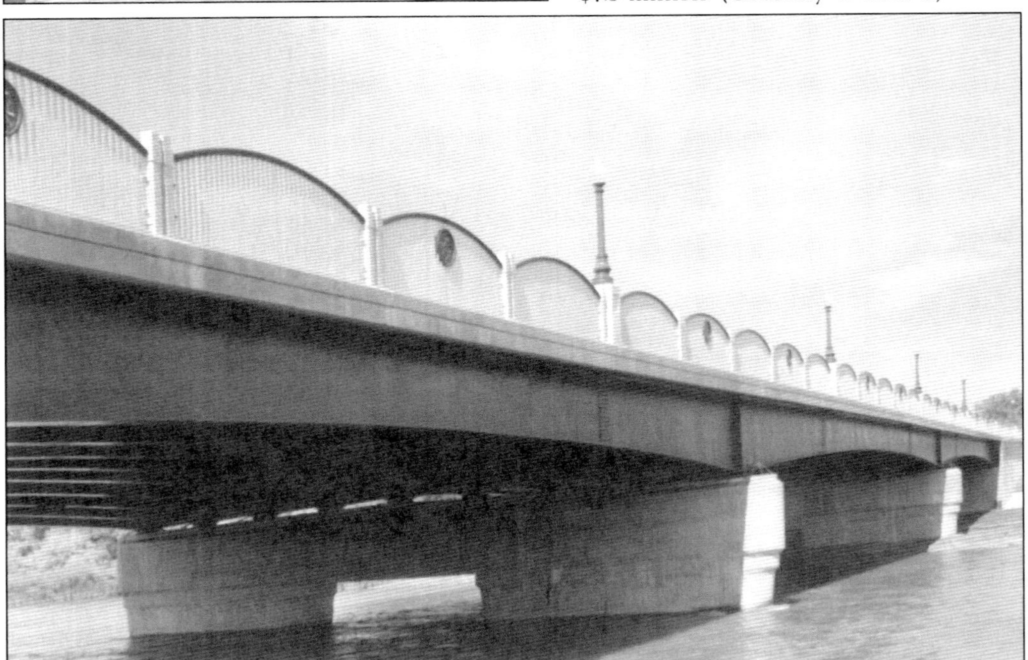

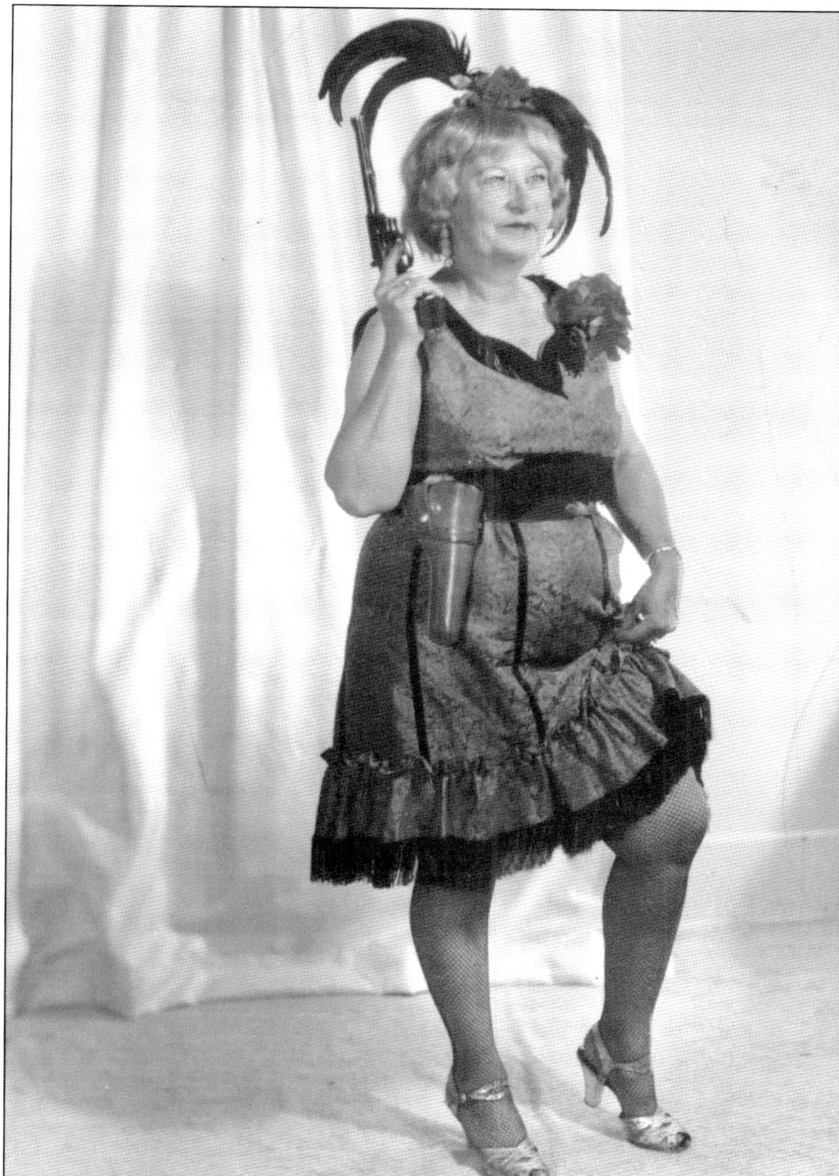

Alice Messick, alias "Flamin' Mame," was named chairman of the 1962 Douglas Diamond Jubilee Days celebration. Planning for the event began in 1961, and publicity played a key role in getting everyone involved. Other officers included vice-chairman Raymond Combs, treasurer Cecil Coe, and secretary Pearl Eathorn. The Douglas Diamond Jubilee Board of Directors included chamber president Jack Ward, then-mayor Dr. William Hinrichs, superintendent of schools Charles Wenger; Sam Morvee, Fred Schultheis, Bill Cannaday, and Harriett Perrotti. Citizens of all ages were encouraged to wear period costumes, and it seemed like every man in town who could grow a beard, did. Events included such contests as a greased-pole climb and greased-pig contest, parades, free food, Red Fenwick Day, mock hangings, fireworks, shaving contests, staged shootings, wagon rides, melodramas, cancan dancers, Pioneer King and Queen contests, a penny scramble, and more. Douglas's celebration was a prelude to the state's 75th anniversary in 1965.

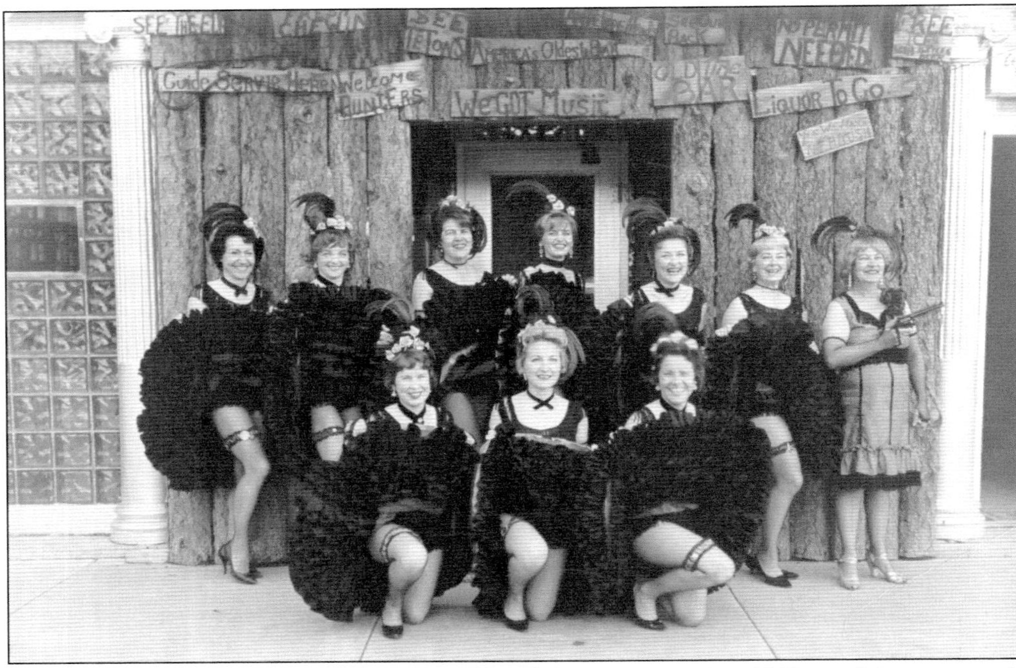

The Diamond Jubilee Can-Can Dancers of Douglas was organized in 1962 to celebrate not only the Douglas celebration, but to get ready for Wyoming's 75th anniversary in 1965. For the three years leading up to the celebration they performed throughout Wyoming and the area in an effort to boost enthusiasm for the big event. The troupe performed at conventions, fairs, and parades across Wyoming, Nebraska, and Colorado. According to the *Douglas Budget*, "The local lovelies received exceptional reception and applause everywhere they went." Seen here from left to right, the dancers are (first row) Vi Fleck, Harriet Perrotti, and Marilyn Werner; (second row) Georgia, Graves, Ginny Nuhn, Jo Roush, LaRae Hanks, Aliene Rohlff, Gwen Adams, and Alice Messick. "Flamin Mame" escorted her girls everywhere they went. She was well-known for "not takin' nothin' from nobody," and, in fact, used her six-gun when necessary. Messick and her husband, Ray, owned the local car dealership. She went on to become chair of Wyoming's 75th anniversary commission, appointed by Gov. Cliff Hansen.

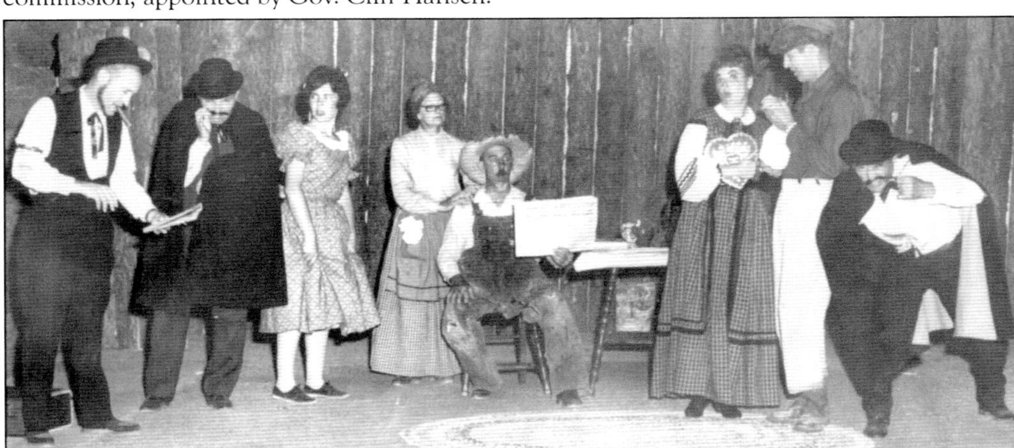

The "Jubilee Mellerdrammer" featured local residents in a variety of roles. Audiences especially loved the villains and weren't shy about booing and hissing when necessary.

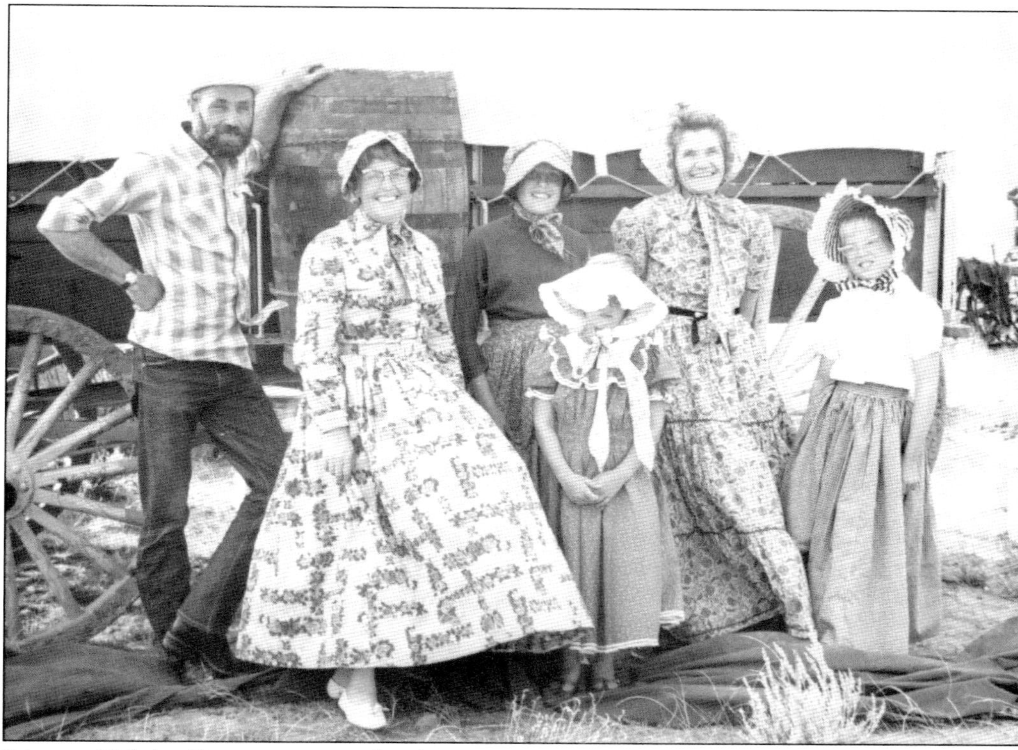

Diamond Jubilee Days gave entire families a reason to participate. These folks are getting into the spirit by modeling their pioneer costumes, made especially for the celebration. While the event was officially held July 4–8, 1962, it took a year's worth of planning. Douglas didn't stop there, continuing their celebration through the state's 75th anniversary in 1965.

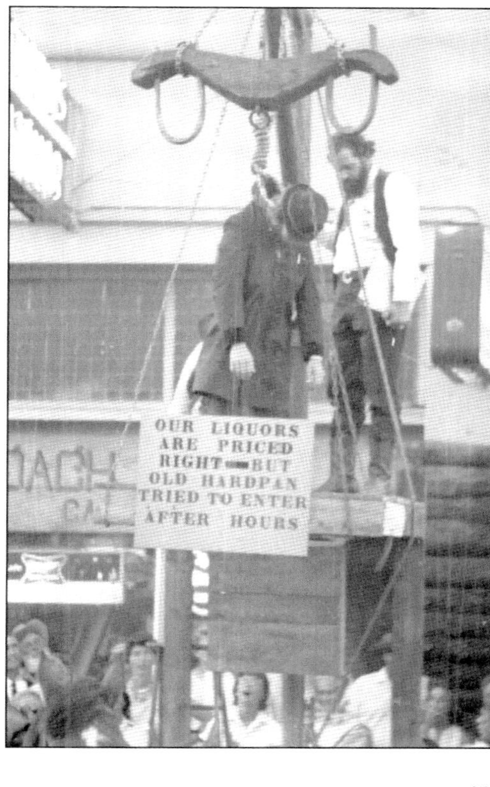

Mock hangings were an everyday event during the celebration, promoted by "the Wild Bunch," a band of individuals with questionable morals. They could find any excuse for a daily hanging, innocent or not, with or without a beard, and often simply for sport. Given the expression of the woman at the bottom of the photograph, she may have thought this execution was real.

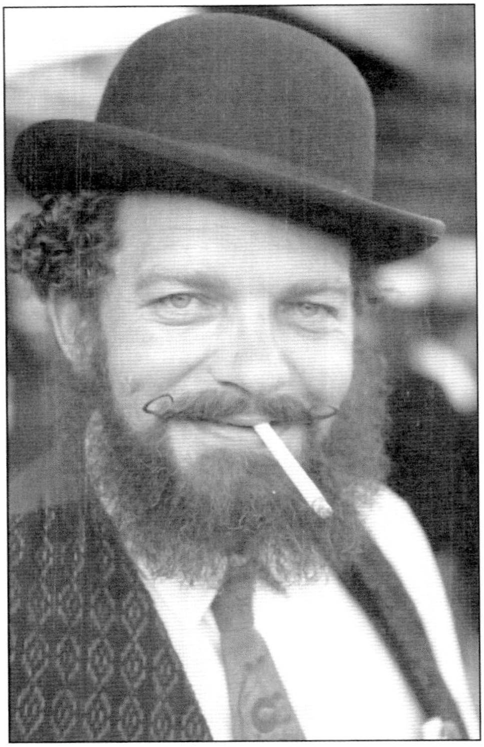

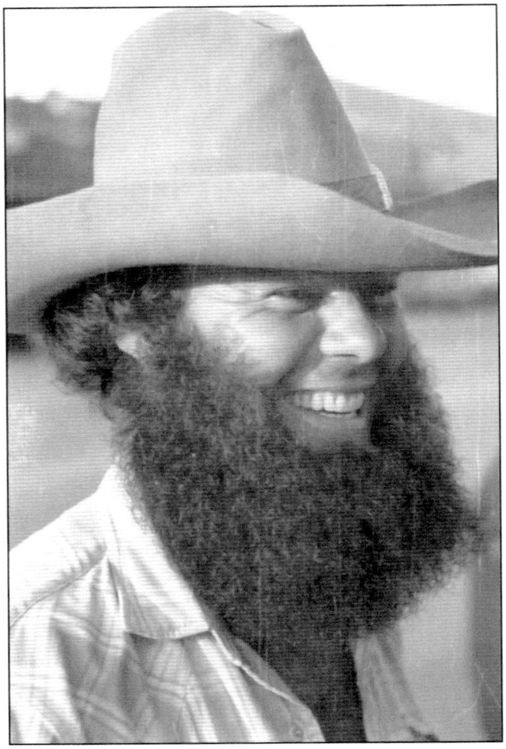

Beards were required attire; a clean-shaven violator might suffer a serious fine, and could even get hanged. Curly Epperly (above left) won the award for "Scraggliest Beard," and Clarence Ramseier (above right) won "The Best Overall Beard."

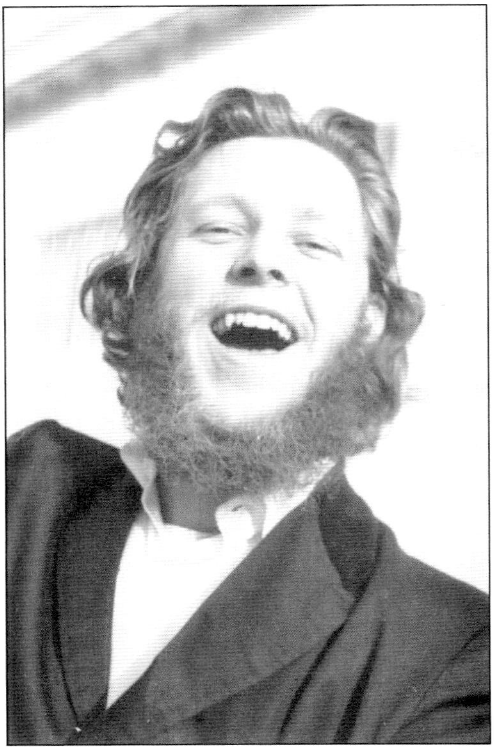

Peter Mike Curtin was named winner of the "Best Baby Beard." The three winners went on to participate in the state beard contest in 1965.

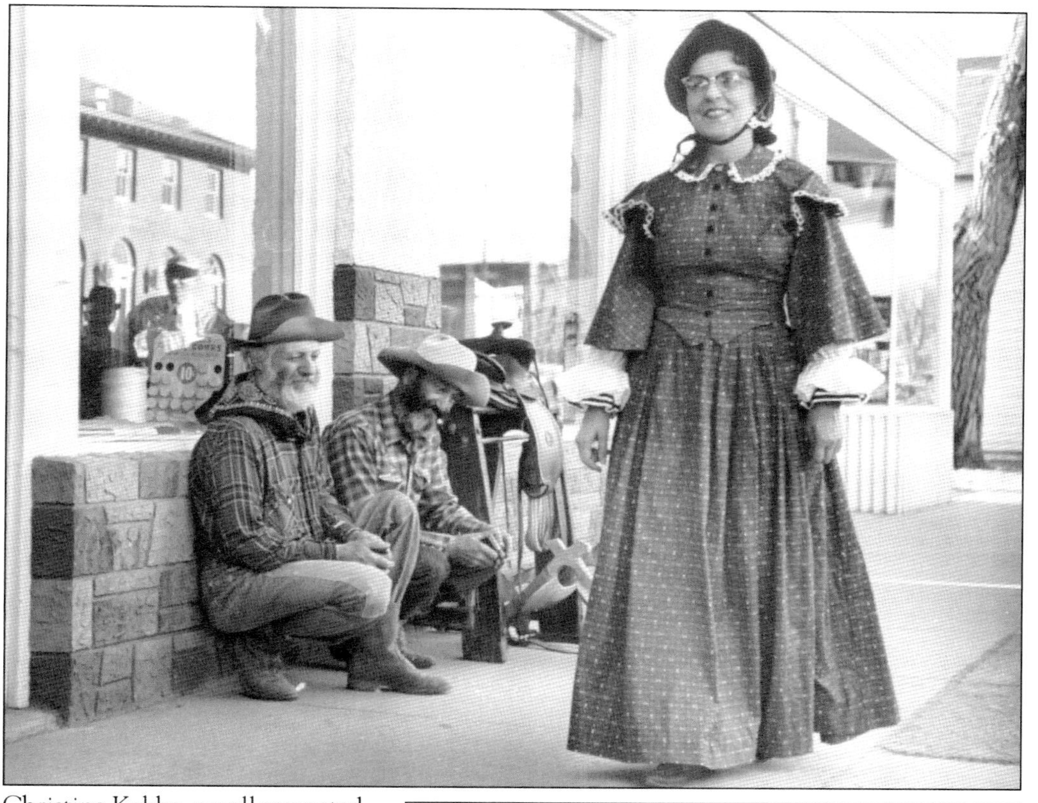

Christine Kobbe, a well-respected junior high math teacher, strolls down the sidewalk in her authentic period costume. Appreciating her presence are Ferris Bruner and Rody Brow.

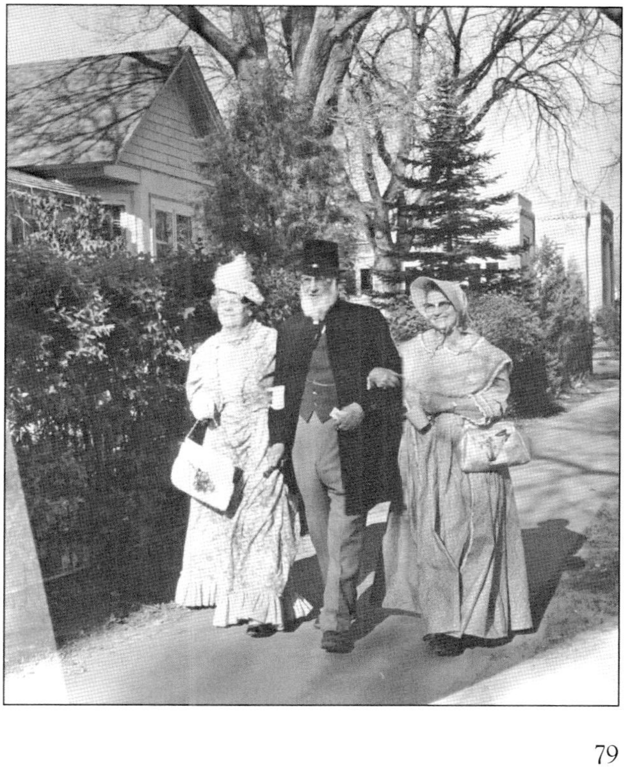

Emma Adair, Fred Graves, and Ada Hildebrand are a striking threesome in their jubilee garb. The spirit of the celebration is fondly remembered today. It took many people, money, time, and effort, but the results were well worth it. One would be hard-pressed to remember any other time in Douglas's history where everyone participated in a civic event.

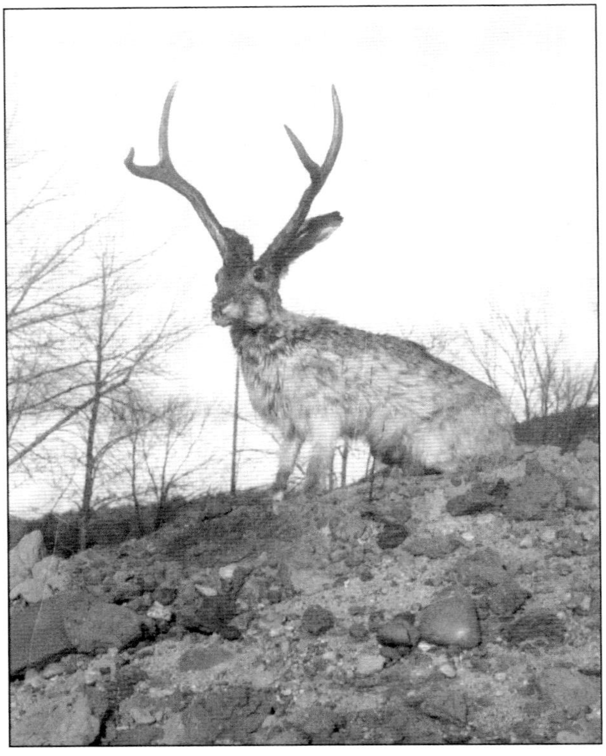

According to lore, the first Jackalope to appear in Douglas was made by taxidermist Doug Herrick in 1939. The Jackalope, a cross between a jackrabbit and an antelope, both prolific throughout the Douglas area, has been written about in magazines and newspapers throughout the world. It has been the subject of poems and songs, and can only be hunted on June 31 from sunrise to sunset. The 1939 version was sold and put on display in the LaBonte Hotel where it stayed until it was stolen in 1979. A $500 reward was offered for its safe return, which did not happen. In 1960 the term "Jackalope" became a registered trademark for the Douglas Chamber of Commerce, and in 1970, the town of Douglas was given a registered trademark as "Home of the Jackalope." Town vehicles and equipment carry the symbol of the Jackalope as part of the logo.

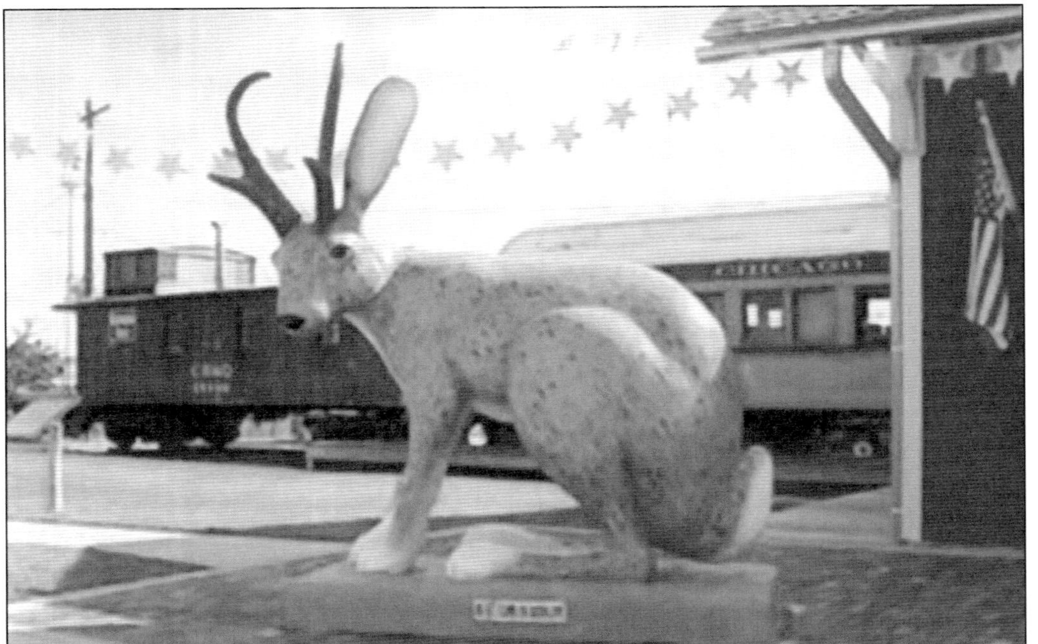

The historic and elusive Jackalope is honored with this statue in downtown Douglas at Jackalope Square. Every year, the town celebrates Jackalope Days with a variety of events for all ages. (Courtesy Douglas Chamber of Commerce.)

Six

UNEXPECTED COMPANY

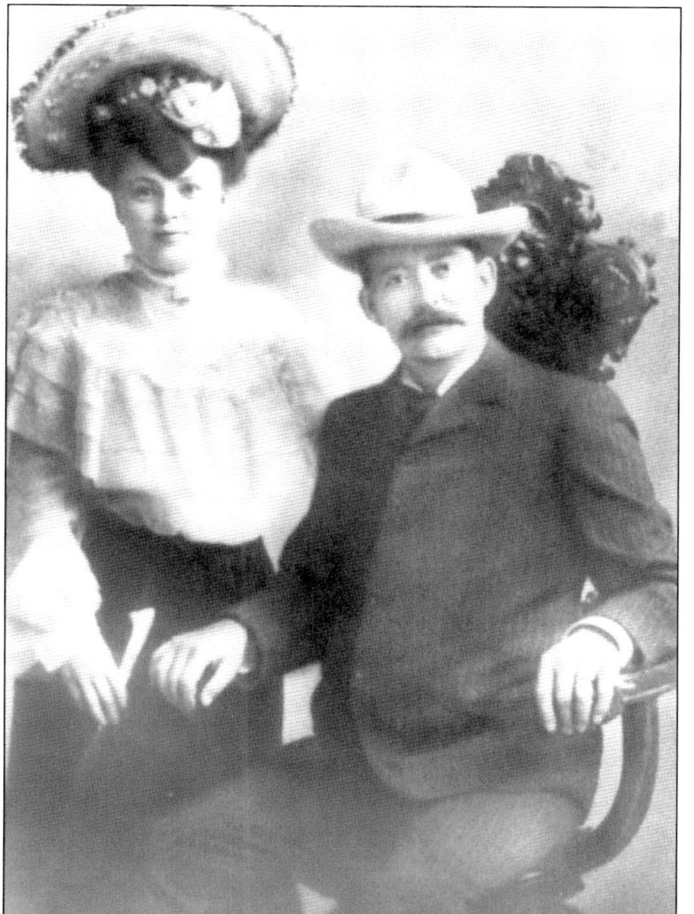

In the early 1900s, young Maggie AuFrance came to Douglas with a "professional paramour." After he disappeared, Maggie entered the field of prostitution herself, recruiting young women to be escorts and serving as their madam. For several years, Maggie and her "girls" were well known, business boomed, and she grew wealthy. In 1913, Maggie married the 55-year-old Benjamin Wheelock, a well-respected Civil War veteran and sometime Native American-language interpreter for the U.S. Government. In 1940, the Wheelocks died within seven weeks of one another and are buried side by side in the Douglas Cemetery.

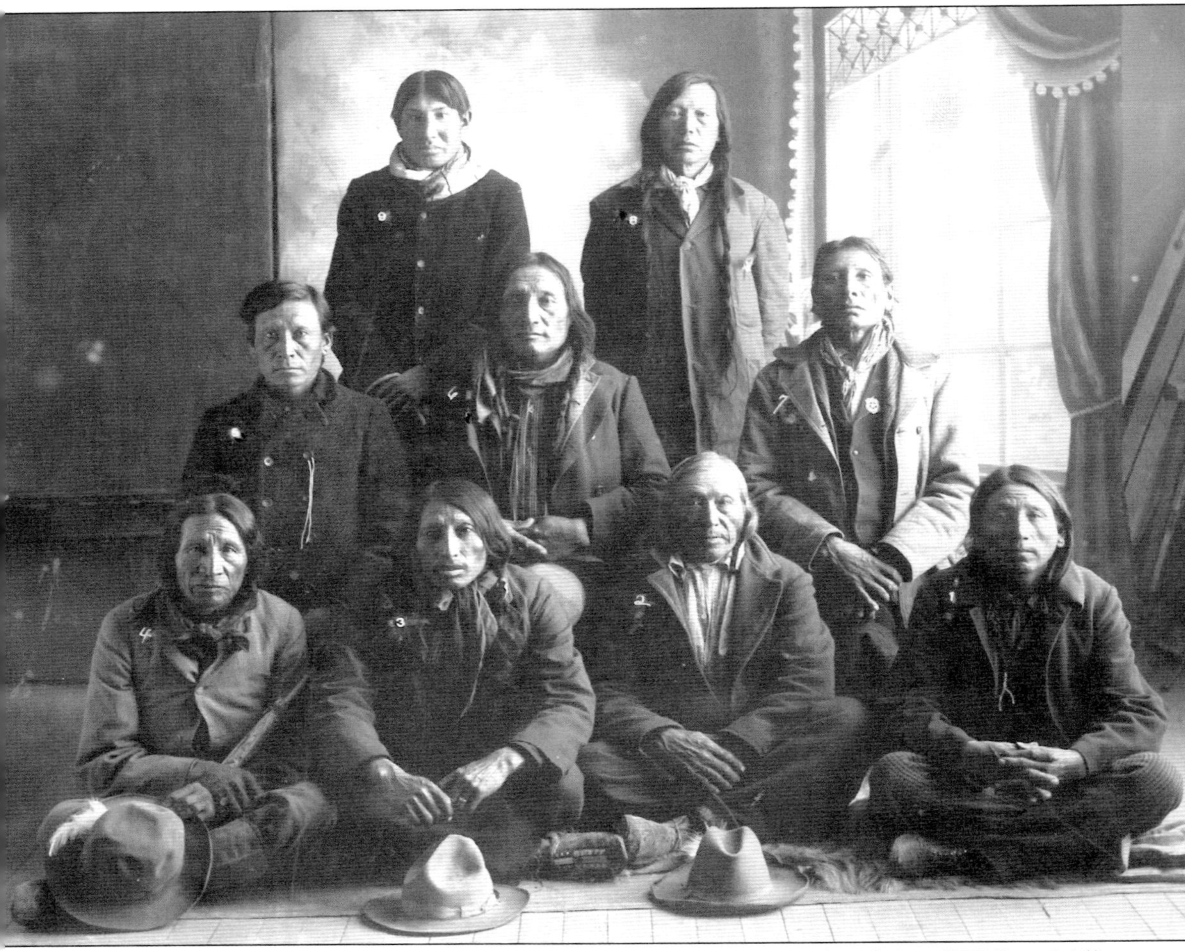

This group of Sioux Indians was held in the Douglas jail for the murder of Sheriff William Miller and Deputy Sheriff Louie Falkenberg in one of the region's last Native American battles. The Battle of Lightning Creek took place 45 miles northeast of Douglas. In October 1903, Falkenberg had joined a posse pursuing nine Sioux suspected of a string of property crimes in 1903. In the ensuing skirmish, Falkenberg was killed, along with four Native American warriors. Iron Shield, Chief H. E. Crow, Red Pin, High Bull, Broken Nose, High Dog, James White Elk, Charge Wolf, and Jessie Little War Bonnet were eventually captured and taken to Douglas to stand trial. They were later released for lack of evidence.

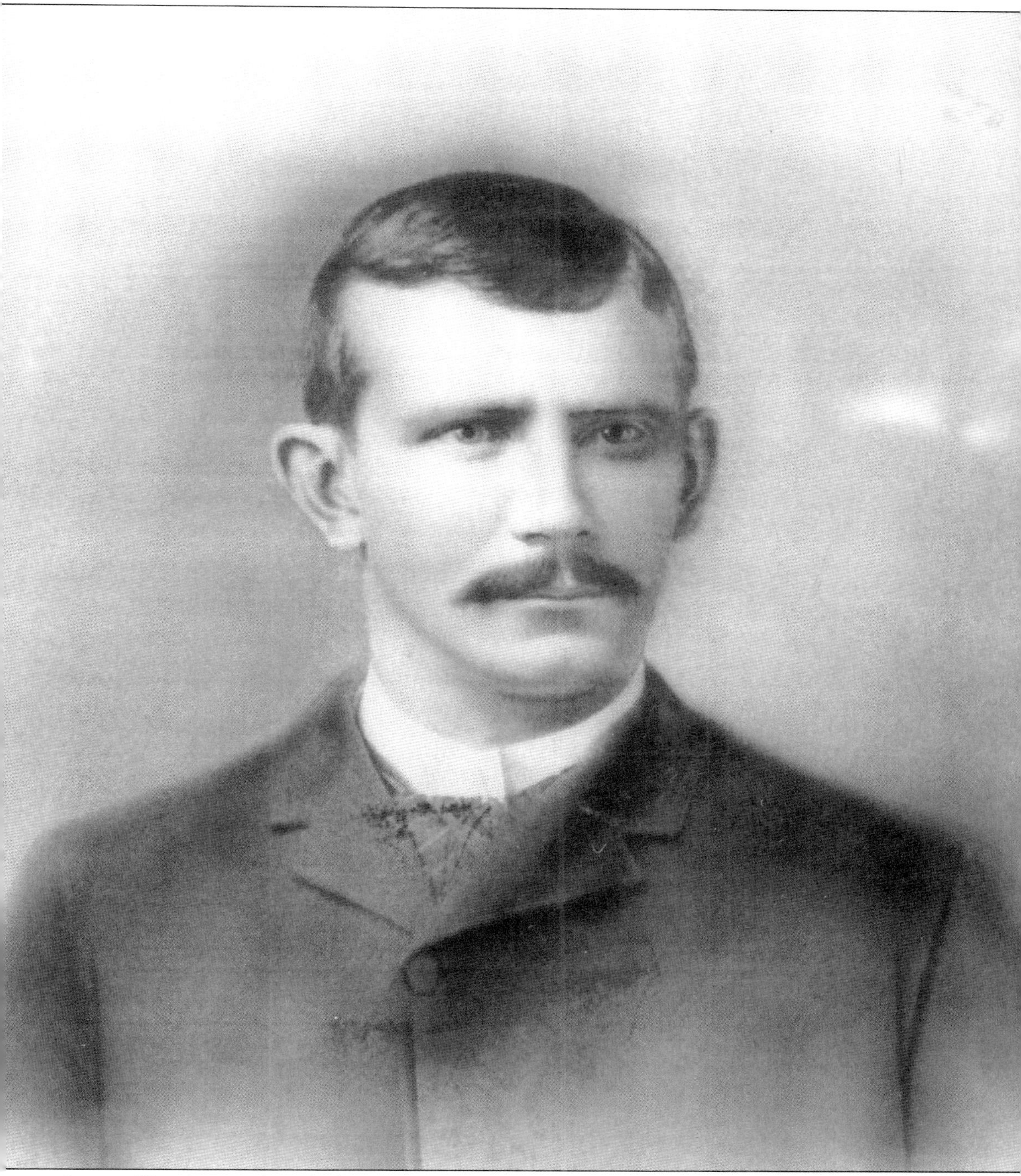

George W. Pike was described as a gallant and unusually successful horse thief. He arrived in the town of Antelope in 1885. He thrived as a gambler and petty con man, and presumed to be a "rancher" which, in his case, meant a horse thief. Pike is buried in the Douglas Cemetery. The epitaph on his tombstone calling him "the wildest one of the wayward West," was composed shortly after his death in 1908 by an anonymous writer for the *Denver Post*.

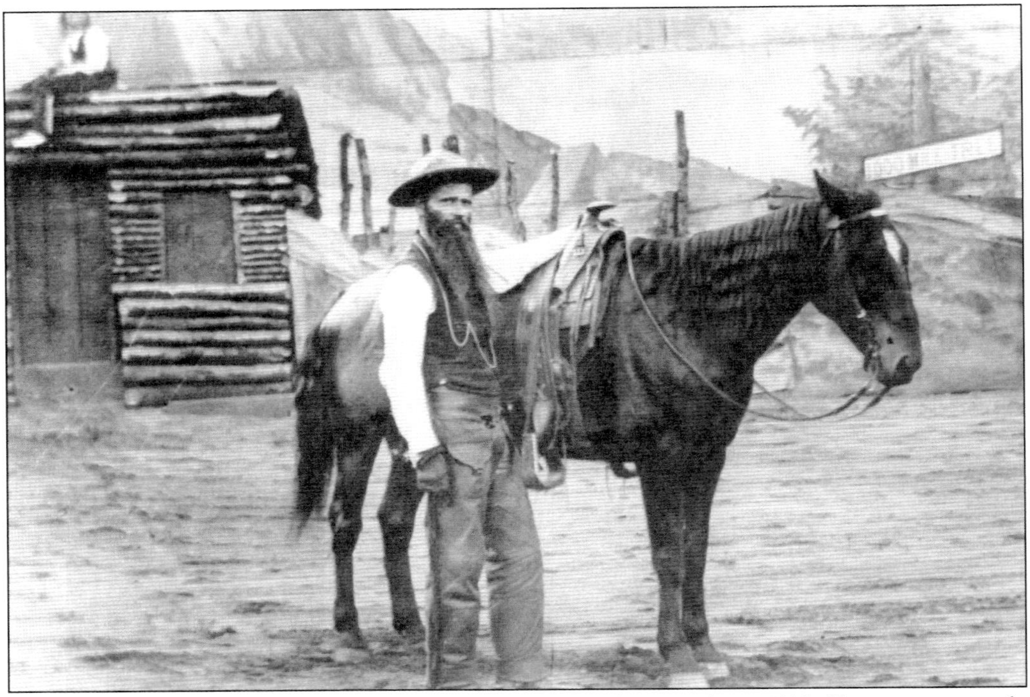

Doc Middleton arrived in Douglas at the ripe old age of 62, in about 1913. He was apparently planning to retire here from a life of crime. A regular in Buffalo Bill's Wild West Show, and a participant in Cheyenne's big rodeo, he became best known for participating in the Chadron to Chicago horse race in 1893. A favorite to win, Doc's horse troubles forced him out of the race, and he only received a $75 consolation prize. Implicated in several murders, thefts, and cattle rustlings, Doc served time for only a single murder conviction—until he arrived in Douglas. After opening a saloon near Orin, Doc was convicted of selling alcohol illegally, and confined to the county jail. He became very ill while serving his sentence, and later died in the Douglas "Pest House."

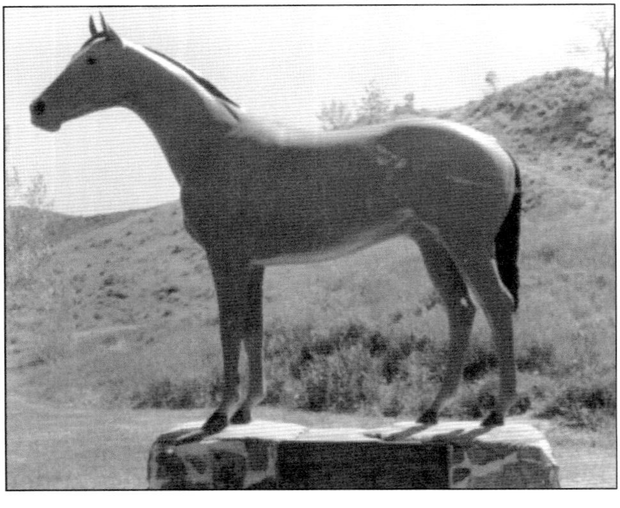

Sir Barton was a prize-winning horse belonging to Dr. Joseph R. Hylton of Douglas. Sometime during the early 1900s, Dr. Hylton acquired Sir Barton, perhaps best known as the first Triple Crown winner in history (though at that time the "Triple Crown" distinction had not yet been made). After winning many races, the champion thoroughbred lived out his life on the Hylton ranch and was buried there. His remains were later moved to Washington Park to rest beneath this memorial. This original statue was recently replaced by a sturdier version.

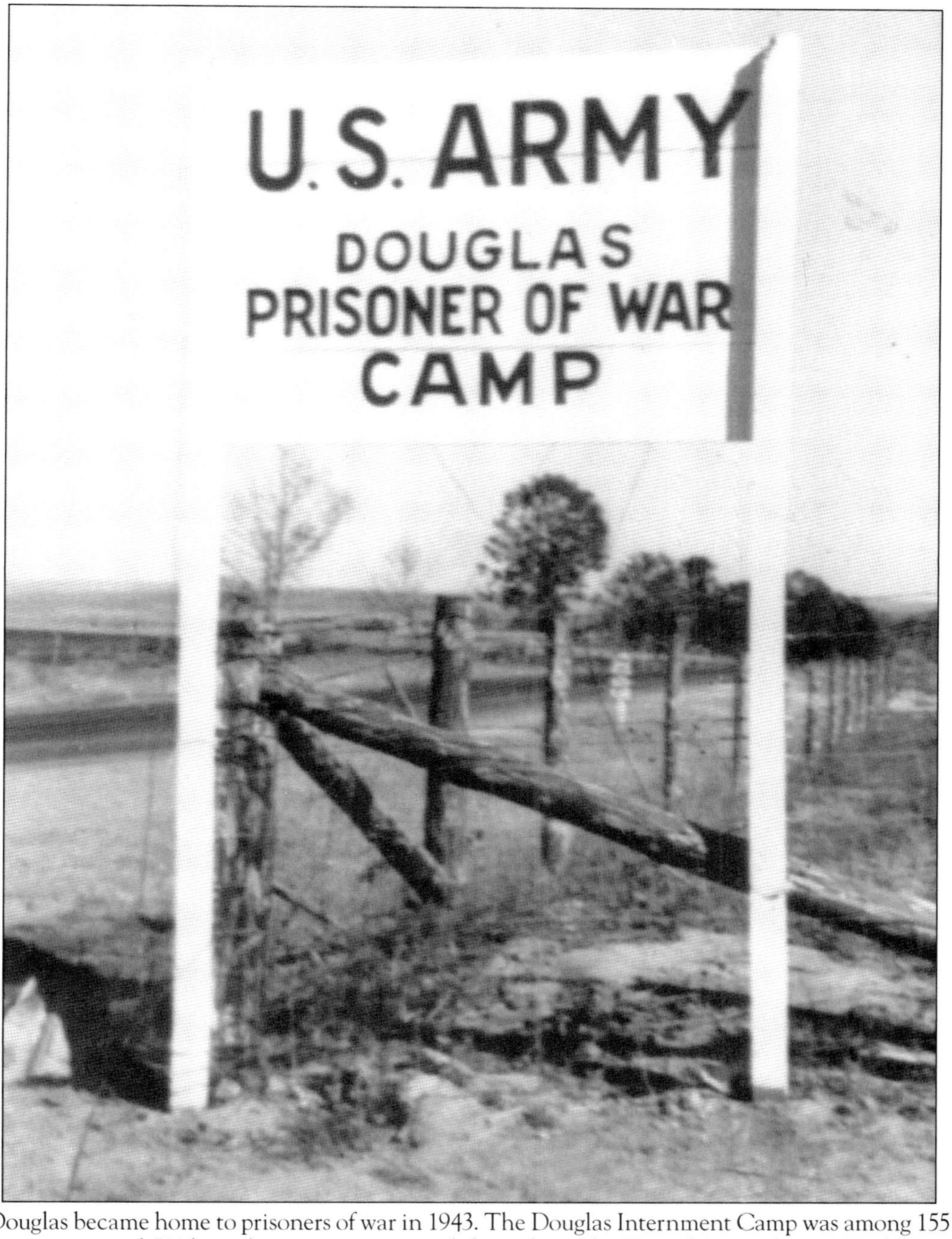

Douglas became home to prisoners of war in 1943. The Douglas Internment Camp was among 155 base camps and 511 branch camps constructed throughout the United States during World War II to house enemy captives from Europe, mostly Italian and German soldiers. According to the May 1943 Completion Report prepared by the Office of the Area Engineer, U.S. Engineer Office in Douglas, the camp was built in 95 days, largely by an engineering company out of Denver, and a contracting company out of Omaha. The report noted that work was often delayed due to the shortage of laborers. As a result the contractor received an extension of just 20 days, making the contract completion date May 22, 1943.

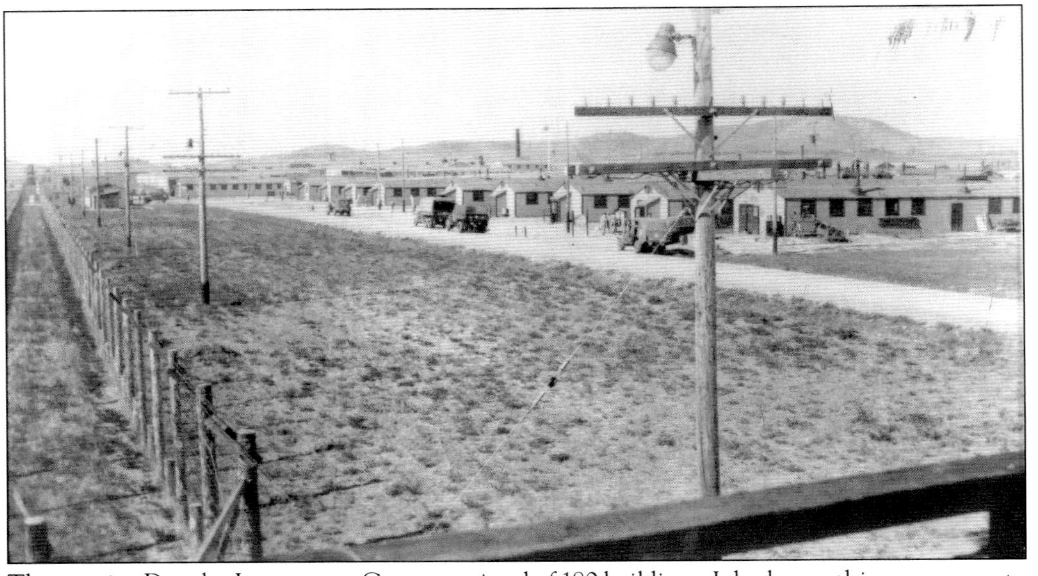

The massive Douglas Internment Camp consisted of 180 buildings. It had everything necessary to meet the needs of the prisoners. Many of the prisoners worked on local ranches during the day.

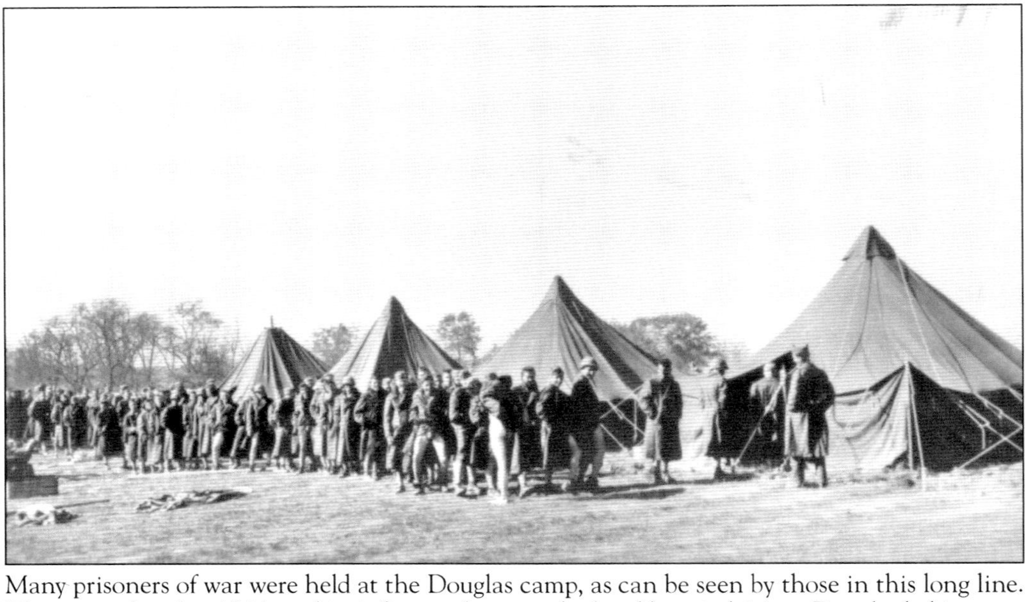

Many prisoners of war were held at the Douglas camp, as can be seen by those in this long line. The camp closed in 1946, and its infirmary became the local hospital. Many Douglas babies were born there between 1946 and the early 1950s, when the new hospital was built.

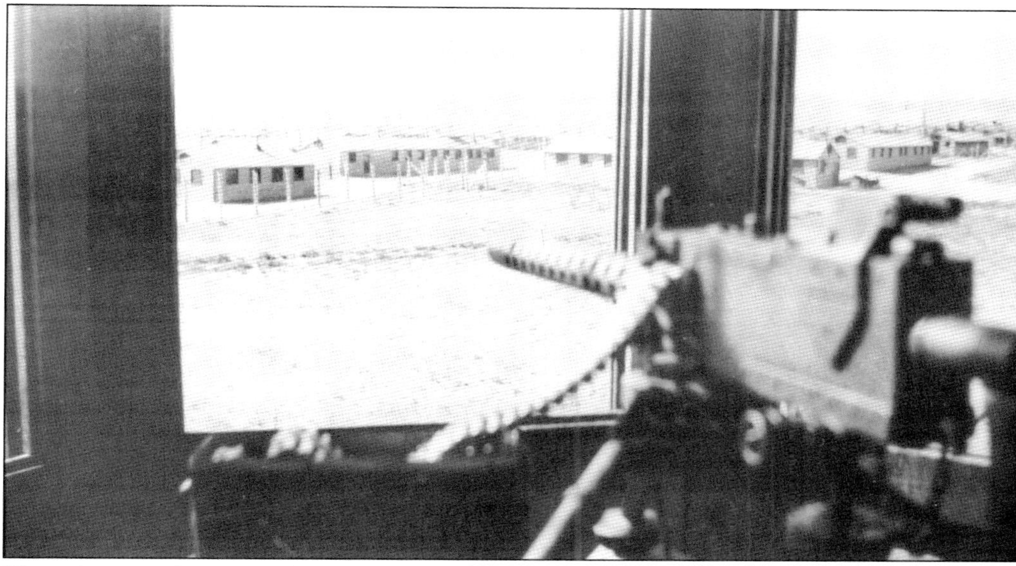

The prisoners of war were shown respect and a certain amount of freedom, but this machine gun in the guard tower testifies that the men were not free by any means.

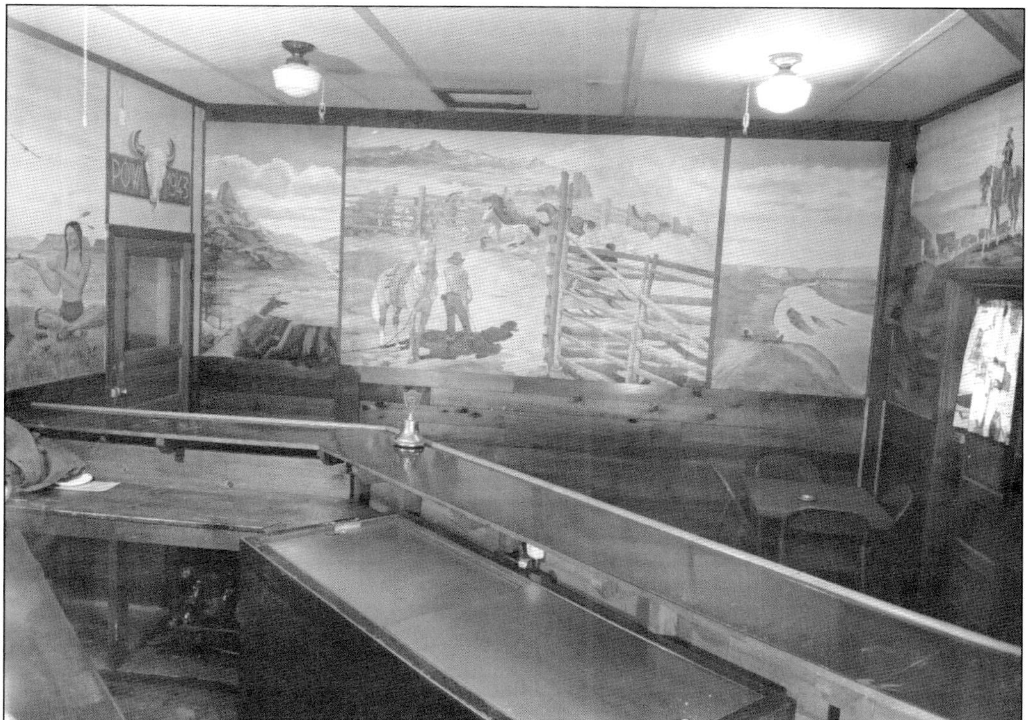

The Officer's Club is still standing. After the camp closed, it was purchased by the Independent Order of Odd Fellows. Inside are 16 murals painted by three Italian prisoners of war during their incarceration. The Odd Fellows, Town of Douglas, and the Douglas Historic Preservation Commission have maintained the building, taking great pains to protect the murals depicting the American West. The building is listed on the National Register of Historic Places.

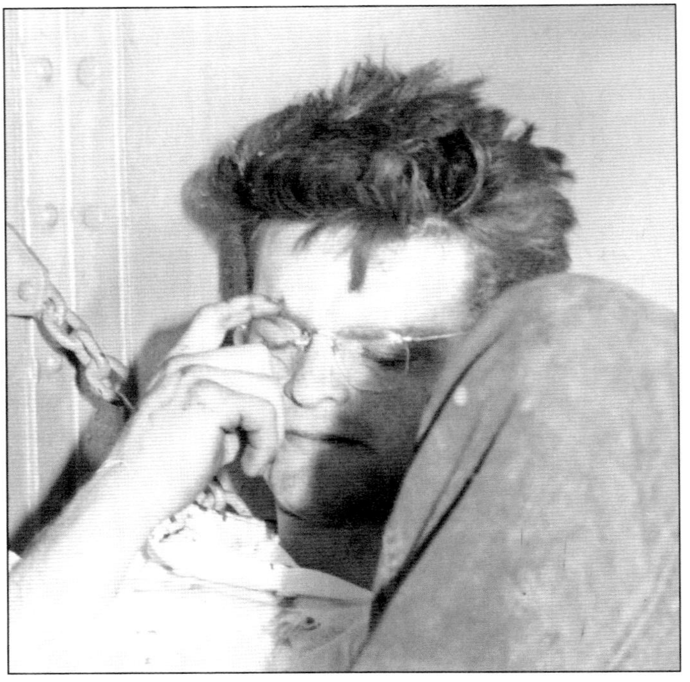

In 1958, Douglas became the center of attention when mass murderer Charles Raymond Starkweather was captured. Starkweather, age 20, along with his 14-year-old girlfriend, Caril Ann Fugate, was accused of killing 11 people in Nebraska and Wyoming. After a high-speed chase through Douglas and an exchange of gunfire, Starkweather stopped the stolen car he was driving (with the body of the car's owner inside) and was immediately arrested. He was convicted of the killings and died in the electric chair at the age of 20. In 1973, the duo was depicted in the movie *Badlands*, starring Martin Sheen and Sissy Spacek.

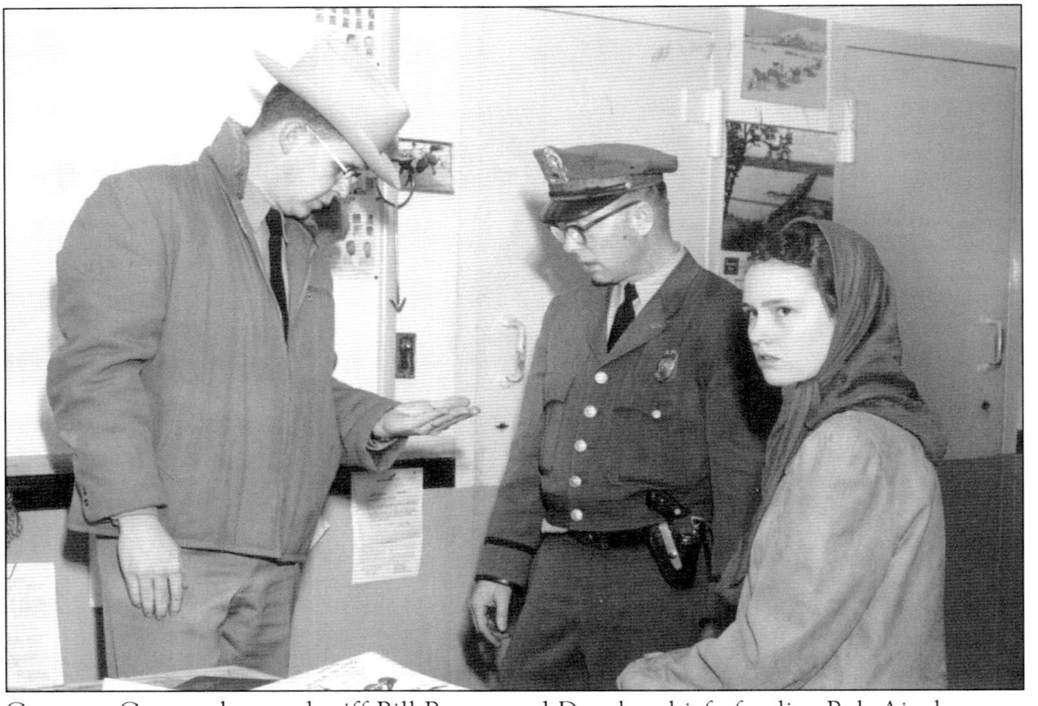

Converse County deputy sheriff Bill Romer and Douglas chief of police Bob Ainsley were instrumental in the capture of Charles Starkweather. Starkweather's accomplice, Caril Ann Fugate, was sentenced to life in prison but was paroled in 1976.

Seven

PEOPLE AND PASTIMES

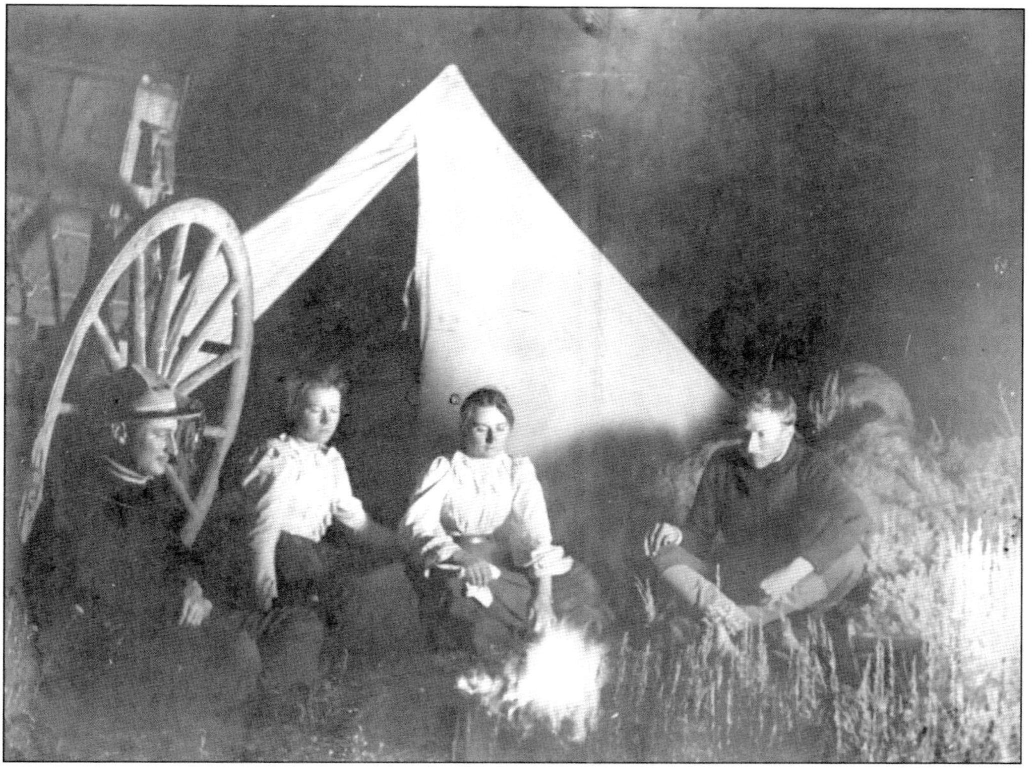

Sitting around a campfire has always been a pleasant way to pass the time. In the summer of 1898 Joe Lowndes, Lena Smith Peyton, Effie Daniel Lowndes, and Hiram Daniels enjoyed camping on Rabbit Creek. There are many wonderful areas to camp and fish in what is now Medicine Bow National Forest southwest of Douglas.

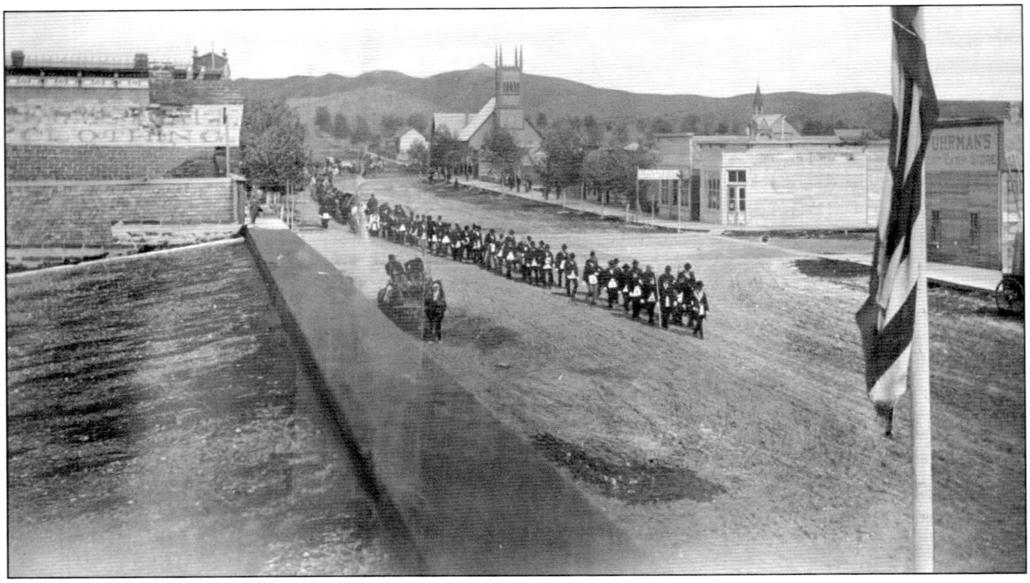

While not a pleasant activity by any means, funerals always brought out a large crowd of mourners. In 1899, Converse County sheriff Josiah "Joe" Hazen was killed in the line of duty while attempting to apprehend a group of train robbers near Kaycee, Wyoming. His funeral was one of the largest the town had ever witnessed, and was attended by Gov. DeForest Richards. Governor Richards had early ties to Douglas, owning a mercantile and helping to found the First National Bank of Douglas. He and Sheriff Hazen were most likely friends.

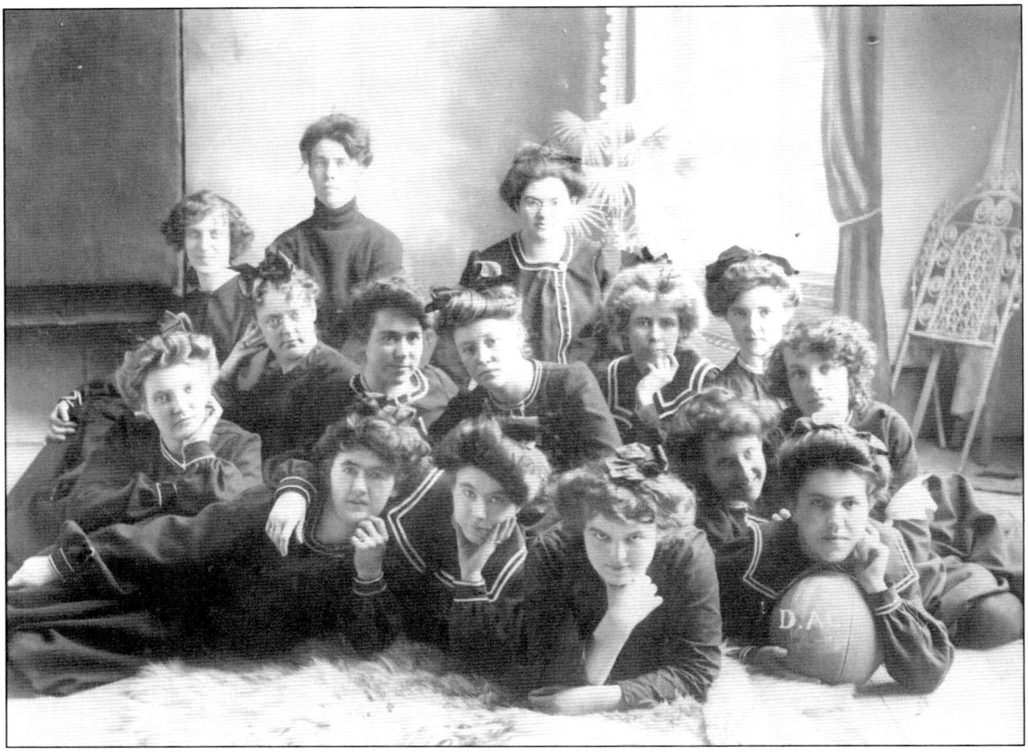

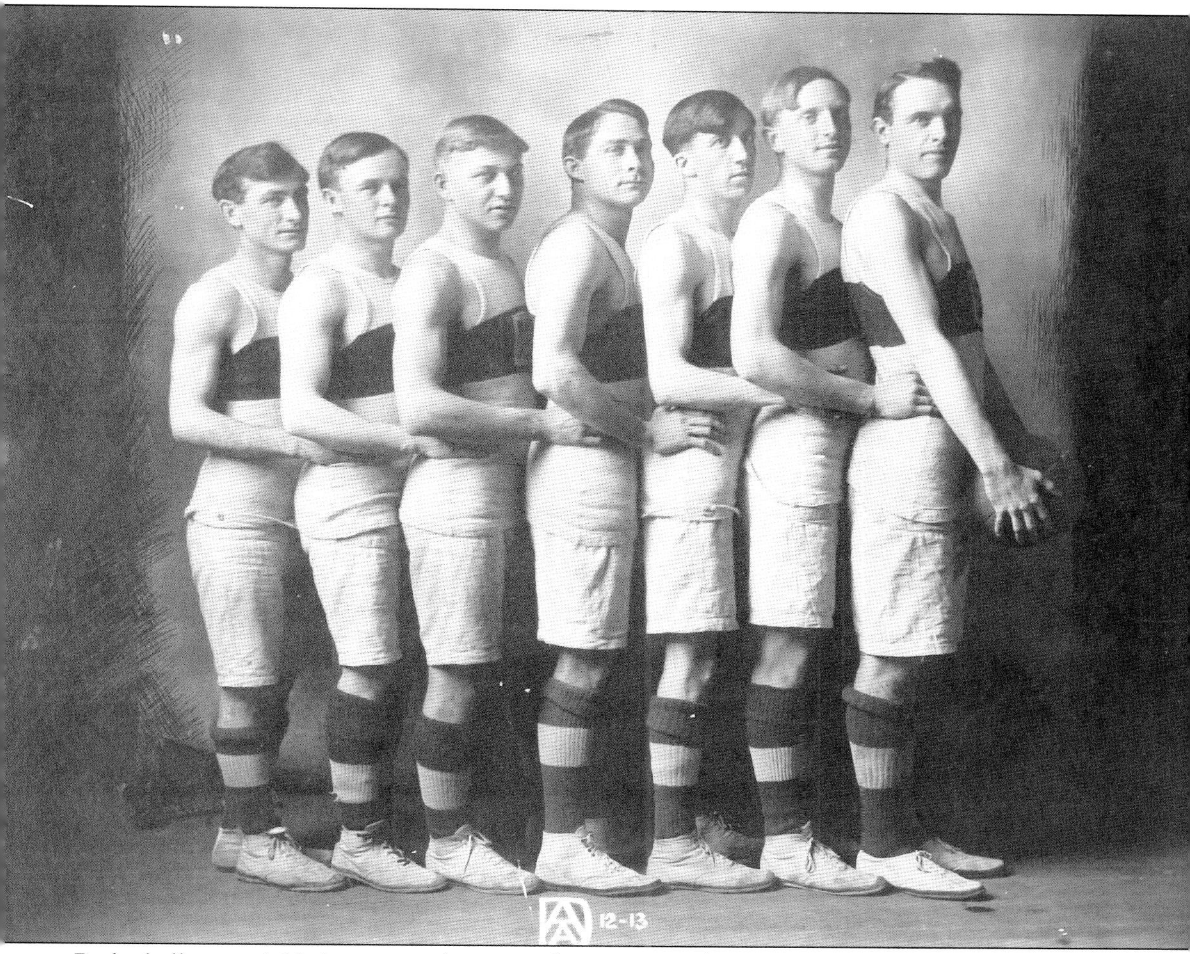

Basketball was quickly becoming the new indoor sport, with teams forming at all levels, at high schools, universities, and through community organizations such as the YMCA. The Douglas High School boys' basketball team is shown here in 1912. They are Ed Peyton, Rhea Tillard, Jess Morsch, E. M. Thompson, Bud Flannagan, Art Daniels, and Jim Price.

Opposite Page: In 1905 the Douglas High School girls' basketball team posed for this photograph. Research failed to reveal their record. The teammates included Florence Shepard, Stella Smith, Elsie Kimme, Claudie Sims, Katherine Quinn, Sadie Messenger, Jessie Wright, Ethel Cook, Sadie Kidwell, Mae Morris, Belle McDermott, Peggy Stocket, Mayme Jarchow, Josie Jarchow, and Louise Olivereau.

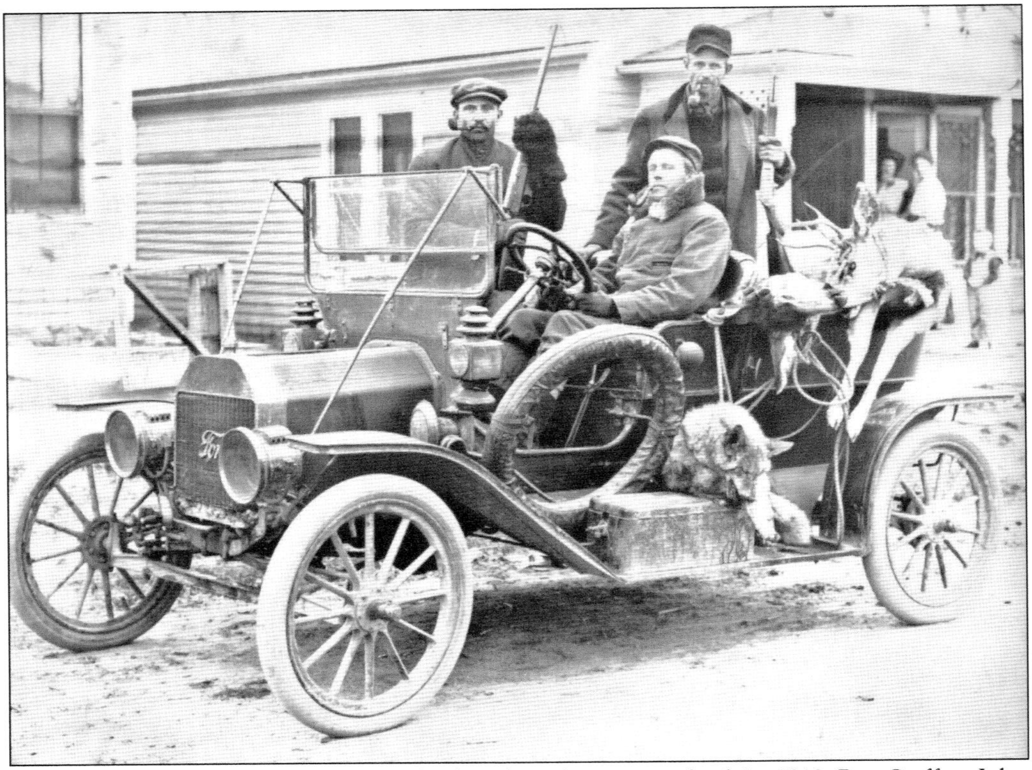

Hunting has always been a pastime, whether done for sport or food. In 1910, Ben Steffen, John Orwin, and A. R. Merritt were proud to show off their bounty that included a wolf and deer.

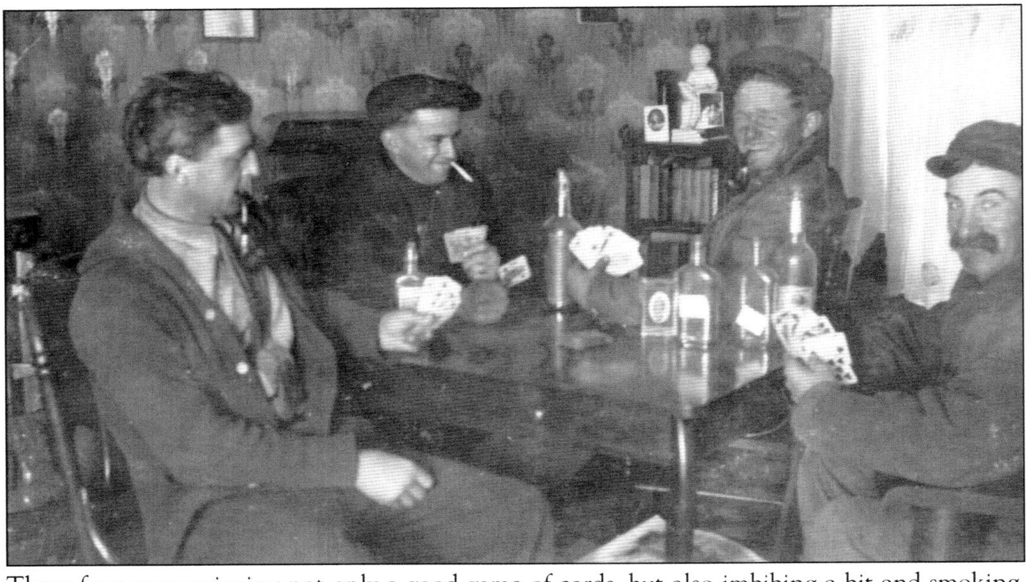

These four were enjoying not only a good game of cards, but also imbibing a bit and smoking, too. Early pioneer and railroad worker Martin Price is on the right.

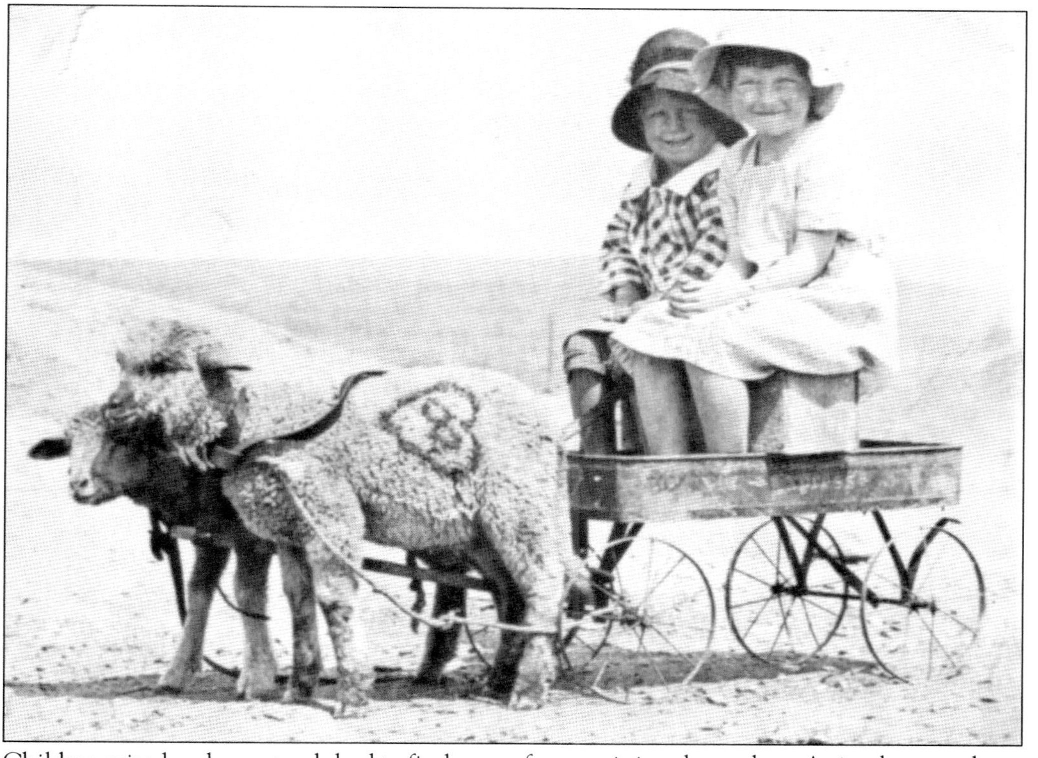

Children raised on homesteads had to find ways of entertaining themselves. Animals were a huge part of their day-to-day lives, making pets out of chickens and, in this case, sheep. Sisters Gladys and Bernice Graves, shown here in 1919, taught willing sheep to lead their wagon. The Lazy Heart 8 brand is still held by the family whose homestead was 7 miles north of Douglas.

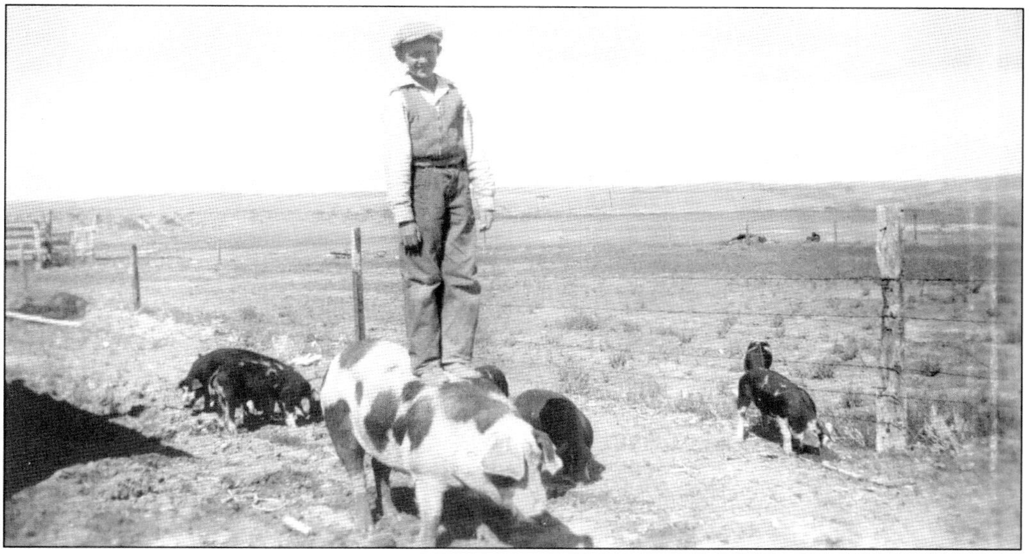

This little boy got a kick out of using his pig as a stepping stool. (It is doubtful the hearty animal even knew he was there.) Homesteaders raised all kinds of livestock including pigs, chickens, sheep, cattle, and in some instances, turkeys.

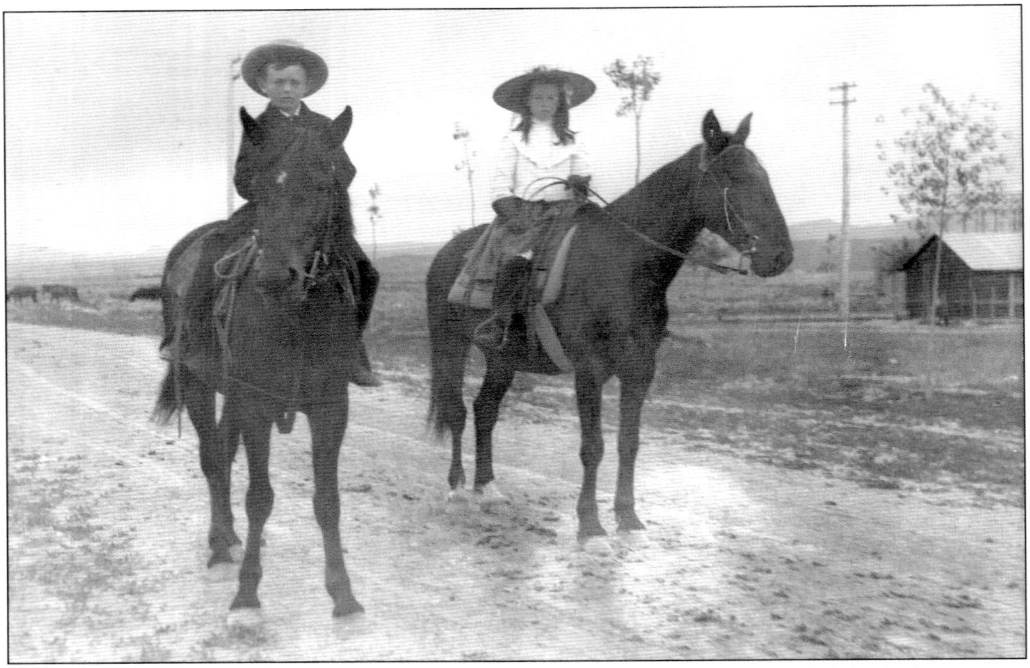

Children learned early how to saddle and ride their favorite pony. Not only did the little pioneers use horses to explore their surroundings, but they also understood the valuable role horses played in everyday life, like getting them to church and school.

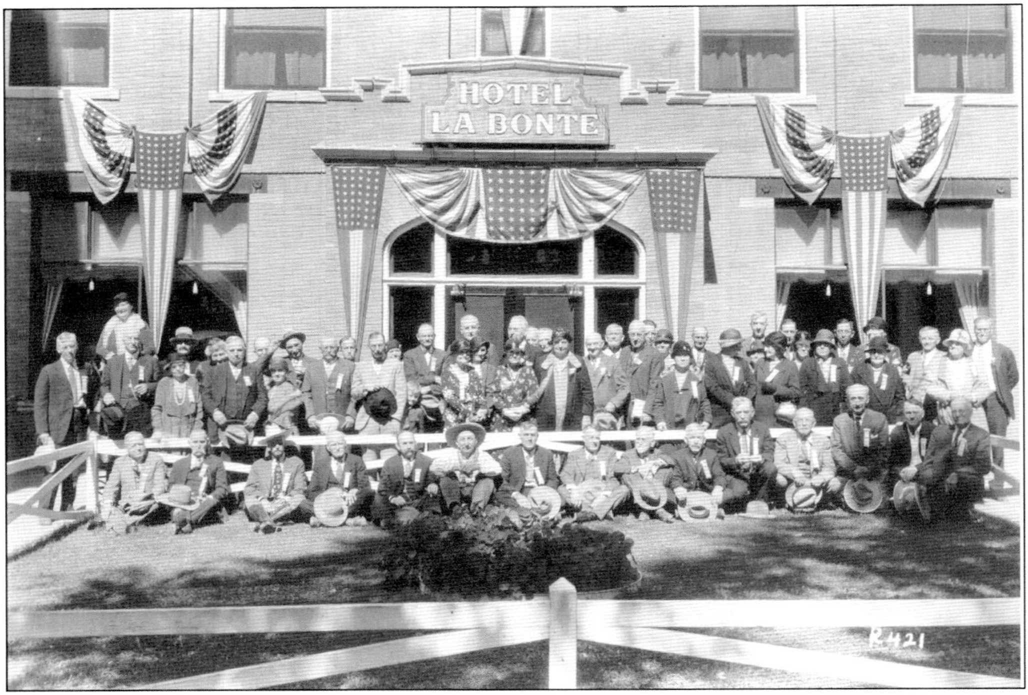

Any celebration was cause for having one's picture taken. In this instance, the LaBonte Hotel was the backdrop for a party recognizing early pioneers.

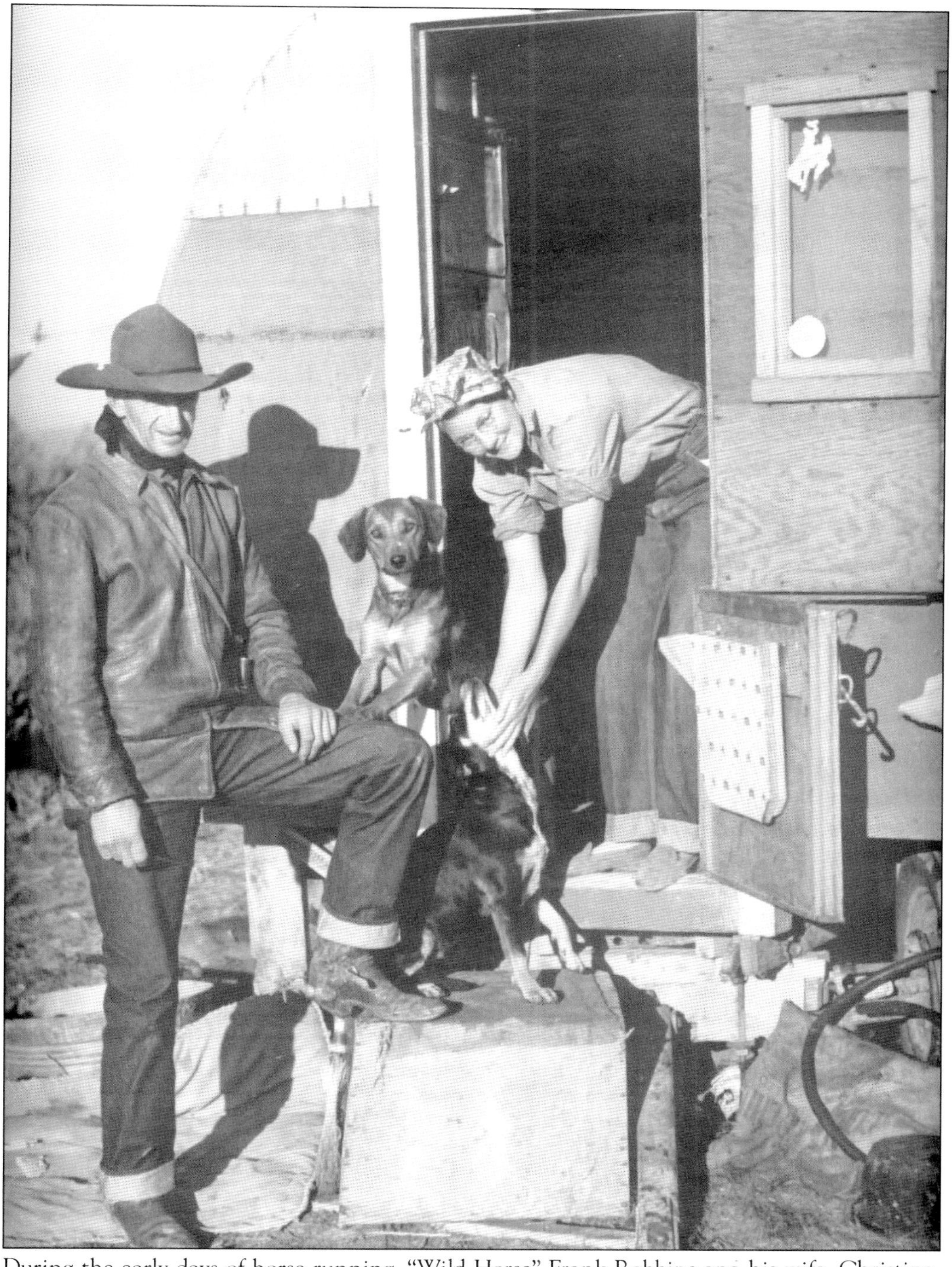

During the early days of horse running, "Wild Horse" Frank Robbins and his wife, Christina, camped in tents or makeshift shelters, usually sleeping on the ground. Later, Frank decided to build a sheep wagon to pull behind his truck. Before his death in 1984, Frank estimated that he caught up to 30,000 wild horses in his day.

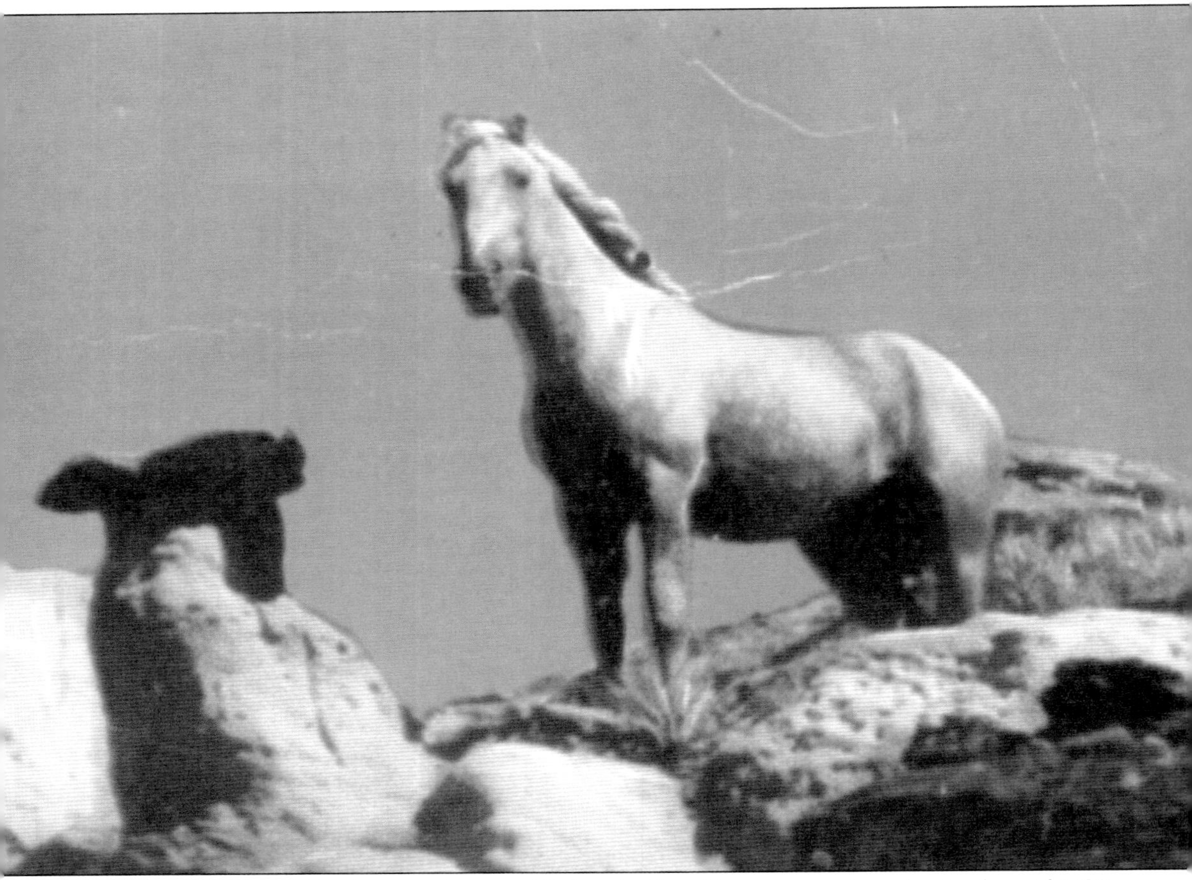

"Wild Horse" Frank Robbins was born in 1894 in the Boxelder area near Douglas. In the mid-1930s and 1940s, he legitimately earned his nickname by rounding up wild horses in the Red Desert. The horses sold for $18 a head, most for rodeo stock. Frank captured a beautiful palomino named Desert Dust, which sired 19 colts on the Robbins ranch, and earned a lot of attention in movies, magazine articles, and billboards.

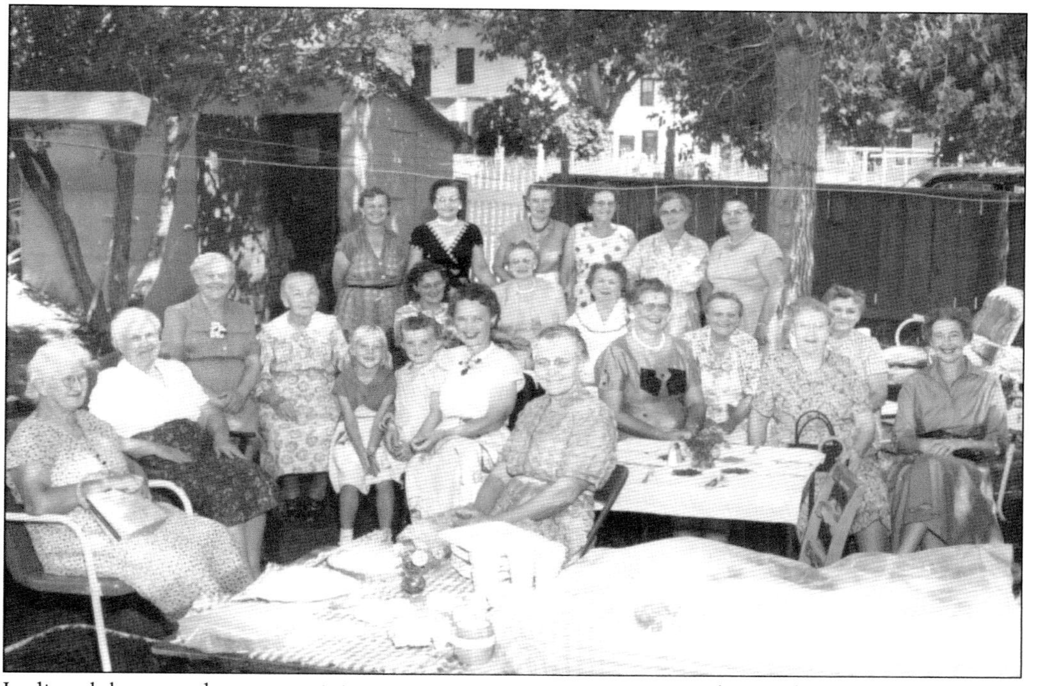

Ladies clubs were the norm, giving women an opportunity to socialize and conduct business for the good of the community. There were several such organizations, including the Townsend Club, Homemakers Club, Methodist Women's Club, Douglas Civic Club, Red Cross Gray Ladies, and the American Legion Auxiliary.

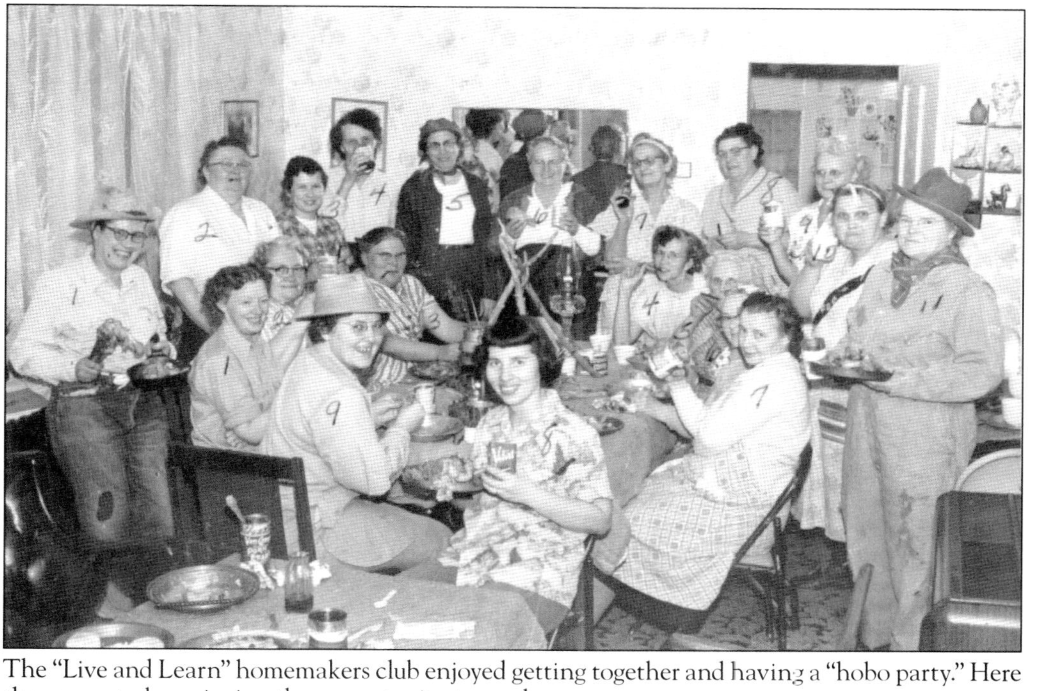

The "Live and Learn" homemakers club enjoyed getting together and having a "hobo party." Here they seem to be enjoying the opportunity to cut loose.

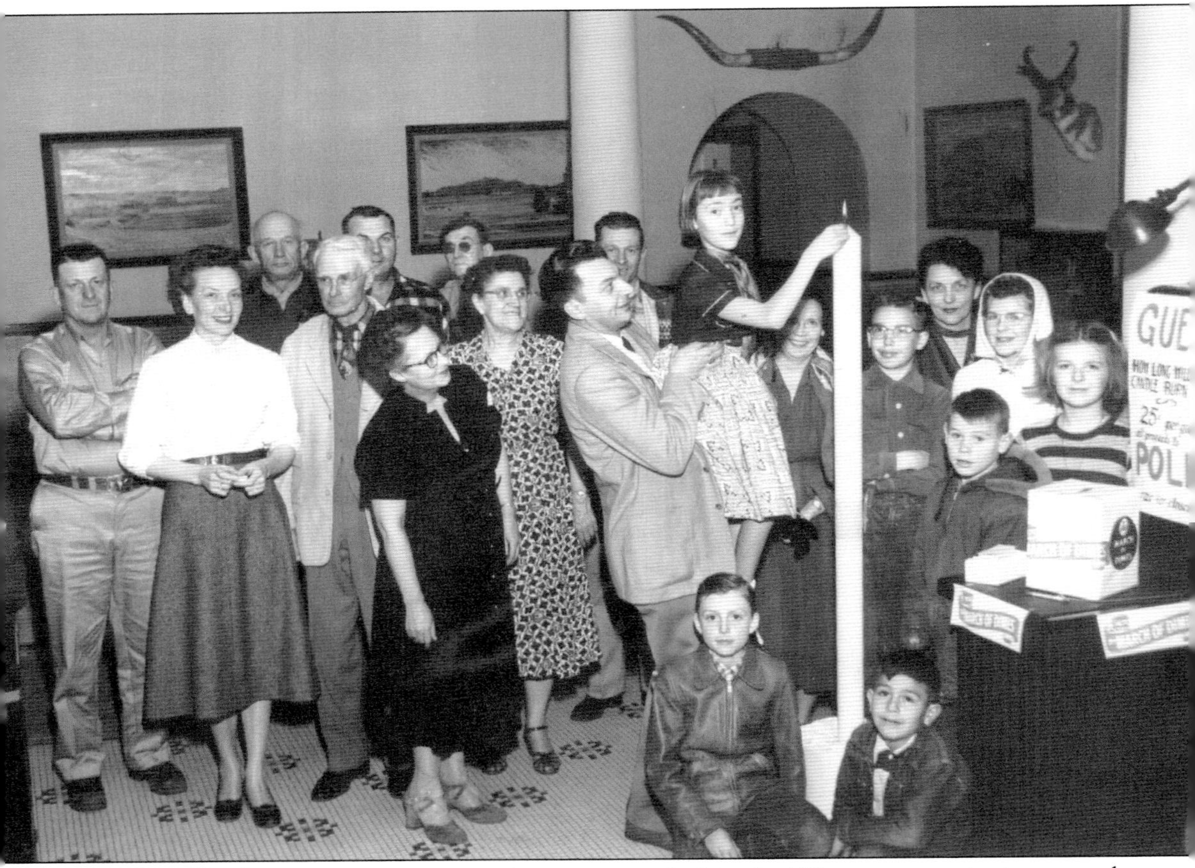

In the 1950s, the community came together to support the March of Dimes, an organization created to help stamp out polio. At this event they are lighting a candle and encouraging people to spend 25¢ to guess how long it will burn. Schoolchildren and adults alike participated in activities like lining up dimes on the sidewalk, or taking a turn at hitting an old car with a sledgehammer. Pres. Franklin D. Roosevelt started the March of Dimes organization in the late 1930s to raise funds for research in an effort to put an end to polio.

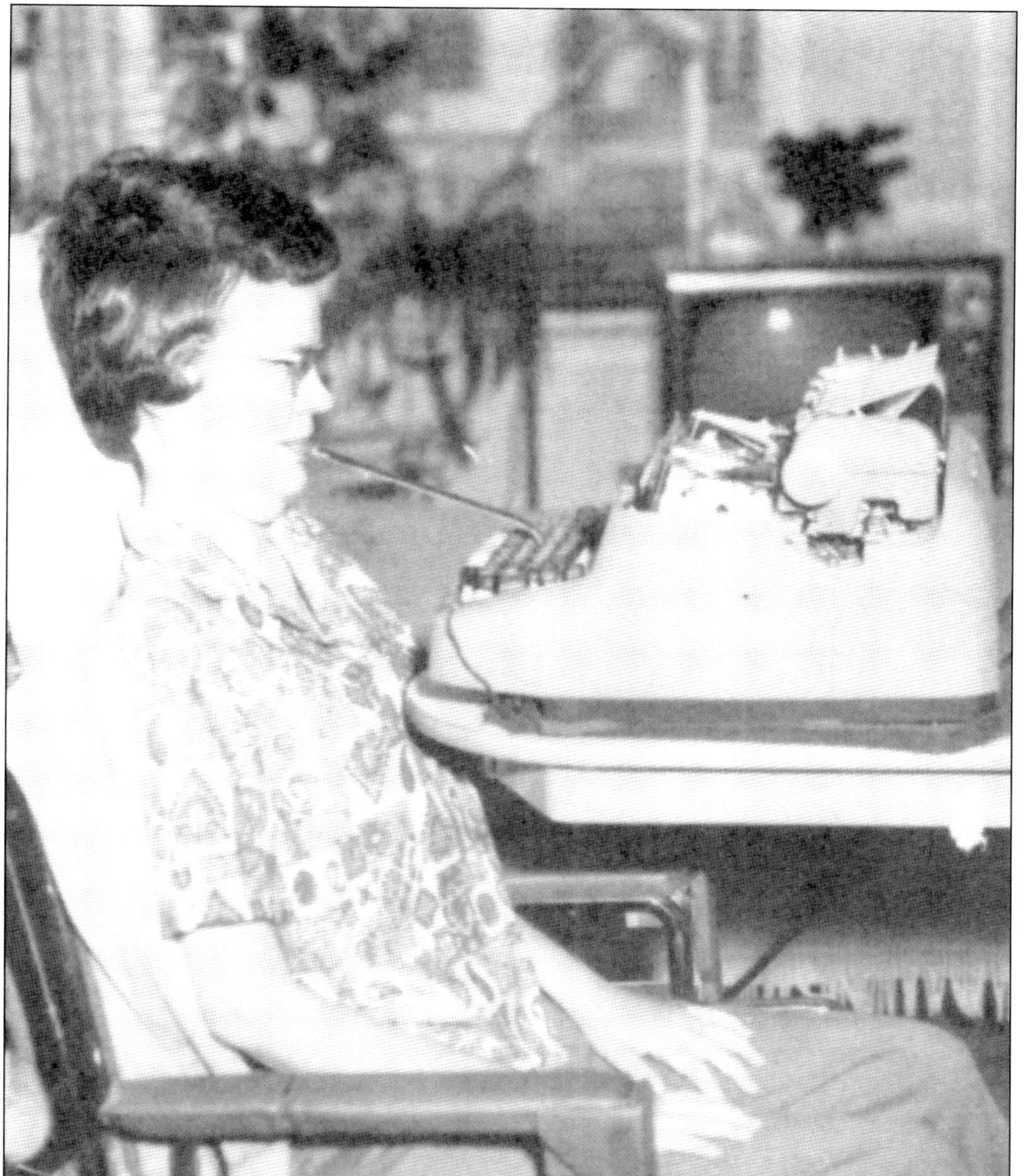

Knowing Peggy Layton Leonard was an invaluable lesson for Douglas citizens. Born in Douglas in 1931 to Scott and Virginia Layton, Peggy became afflicted with polio during her college years. At home she was confined to an iron lung. Peggy enjoyed going out and was a regular at the Mesa Theatre. Away from the restraints of the iron lung, she was restricted to a specially equipped wheelchair and could breathe only with the aid of a respirator. What might be devastating for some didn't stop Peggy. She became an accomplished mouth wand typist and a respected journalist. She discovered a penchant for history, writing a book about Pierre LaBonte. That effort moved her to discover more about early Wyoming and Douglas, in particular. Whenever Peggy had to fly somewhere for medical attention, the entire town would rally around her to show their love. Peggy died in 1983 at the age of 52.

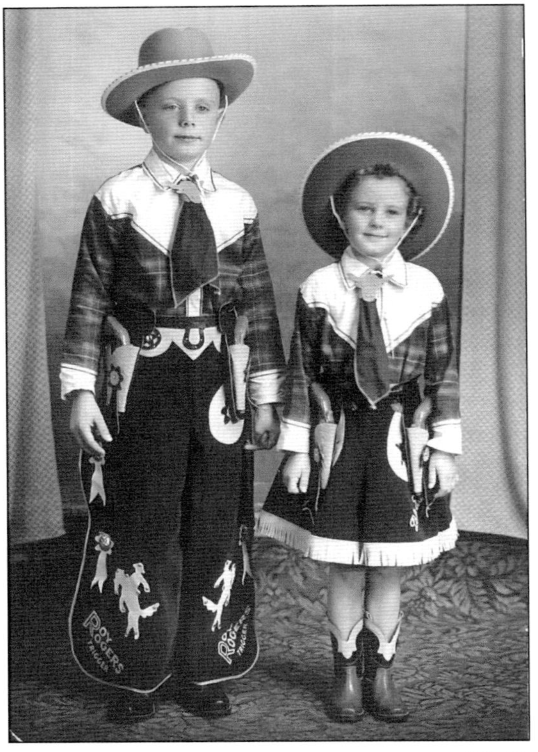

Roy Rogers and Dale Evans were as popular in Douglas, Wyoming as they were throughout the country. Brother and sister Royce and Carol Ann Price were happy as larks when their parents surprised them at Christmas with these authentic outfits, complete with the signatures of the famous cowboy couple on the outfits themselves. Royce and Carol literally wore the costumes out by playing in them almost every day.

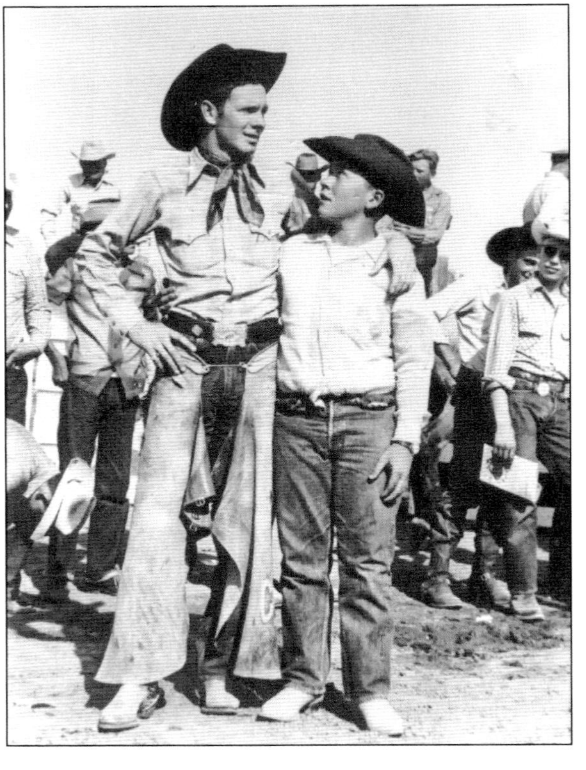

A young Lee Combs (right) looks up to famous cowboy Casey Tibbs. An icon on the rodeo circuit, Tibbs was always easy to approach and readily available to children in particular. Lee, the son of Roy and Muriel Combs, grew up to be an active and beloved citizen in Douglas. An Eagle Scout, Lee understood the value of giving back to his community. He is especially remembered as Santa Claus, a role he played for decades.

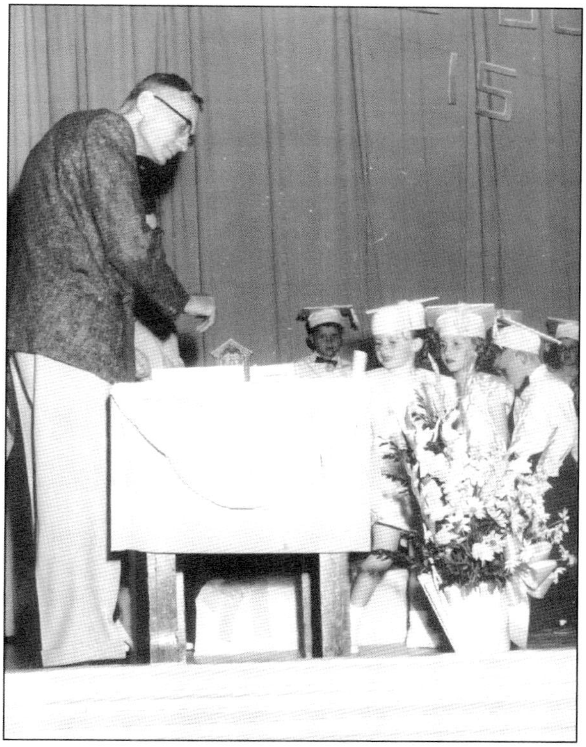

South Grade Elementary School principal Herbert Pearson served the school district for many years. He was a very tall man, with a deep voice and a slight limp. Many children feared him, but he was well respected by parents and students alike. Here he is presenting diplomas to the kindergarten class of 1956.

Local politicians were active in the community and always in every parade. Below, Converse County commissioner Bud Turner leads an uncooperative horse down the parade route, while fellow commissioner John Pexton mans the reins. A rancher born and raised in Douglas, Pexton is a well-respected local historian. Turner ran the local hardware store, Gamble's. Commissioner Gordon Taylor and his young son appear to be enjoying the ride. Following close behind is Converse County clerk Dorothy Taylor.

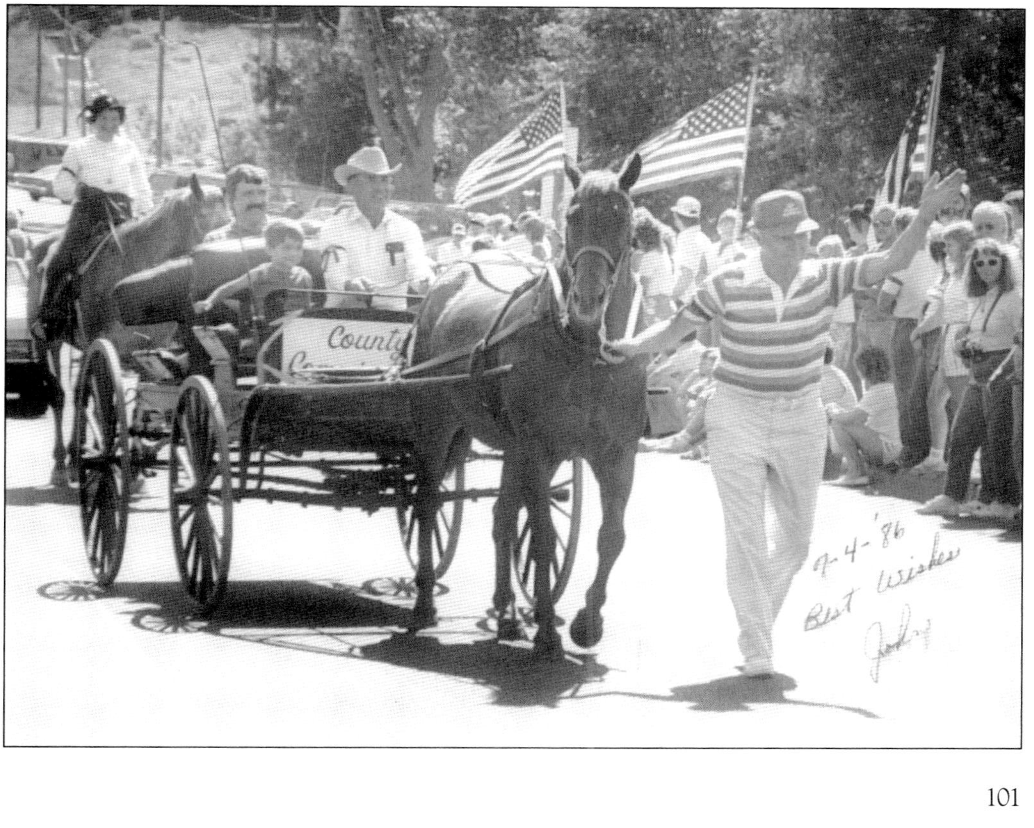

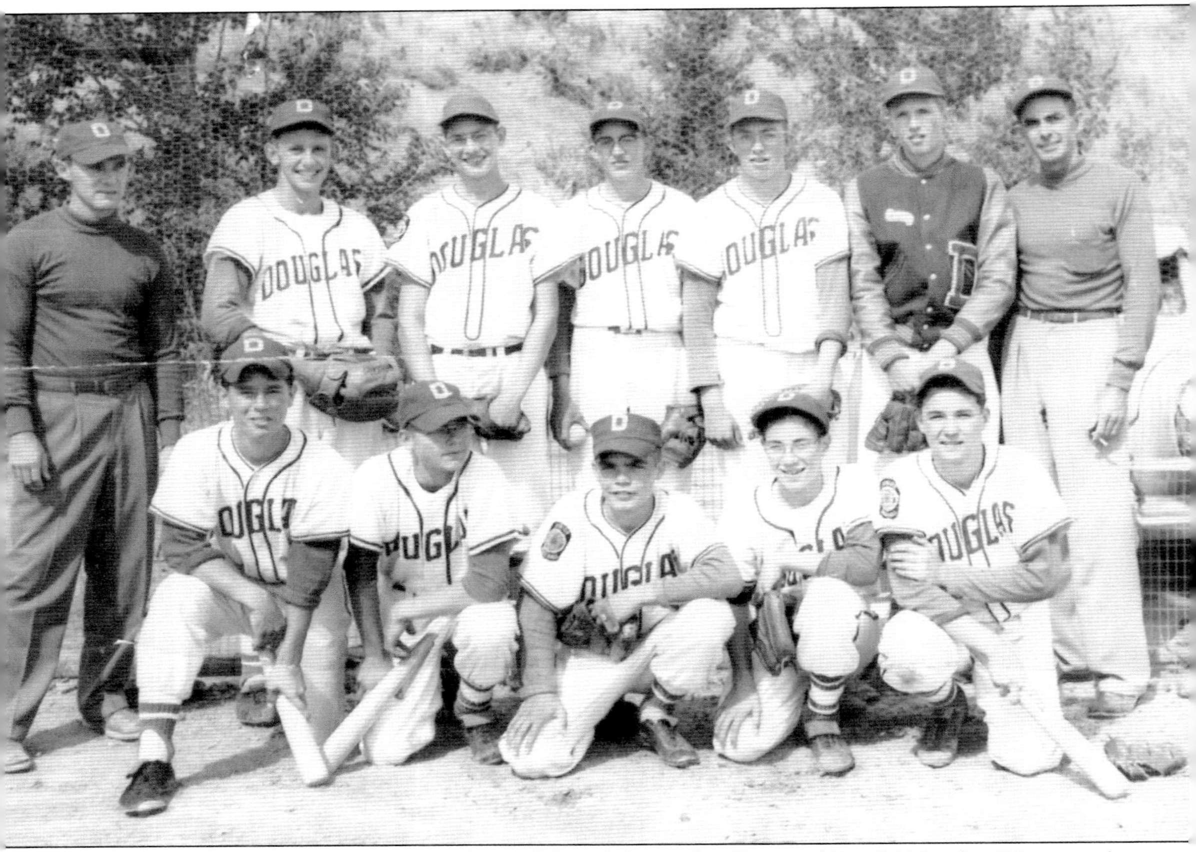

The Douglas baseball team was made up of, from left to right, (first row) Ray Valdez, Jim Thurmond, Joe Poirot, Mike Sullivan and Bill Graves; (second row) Dick Halsted (manager), Dean Dalziel, Bob Hall, Roy Hinton, Barry Nelson, Jim Hanlin, and Keith Nelson (manager). They were third-place winners in the District Junior Legion Tournament held in the early 1950s. Mike Sullivan went on to become Wyoming's 29th governor. Bill Graves was killed in Vietnam in 1967.

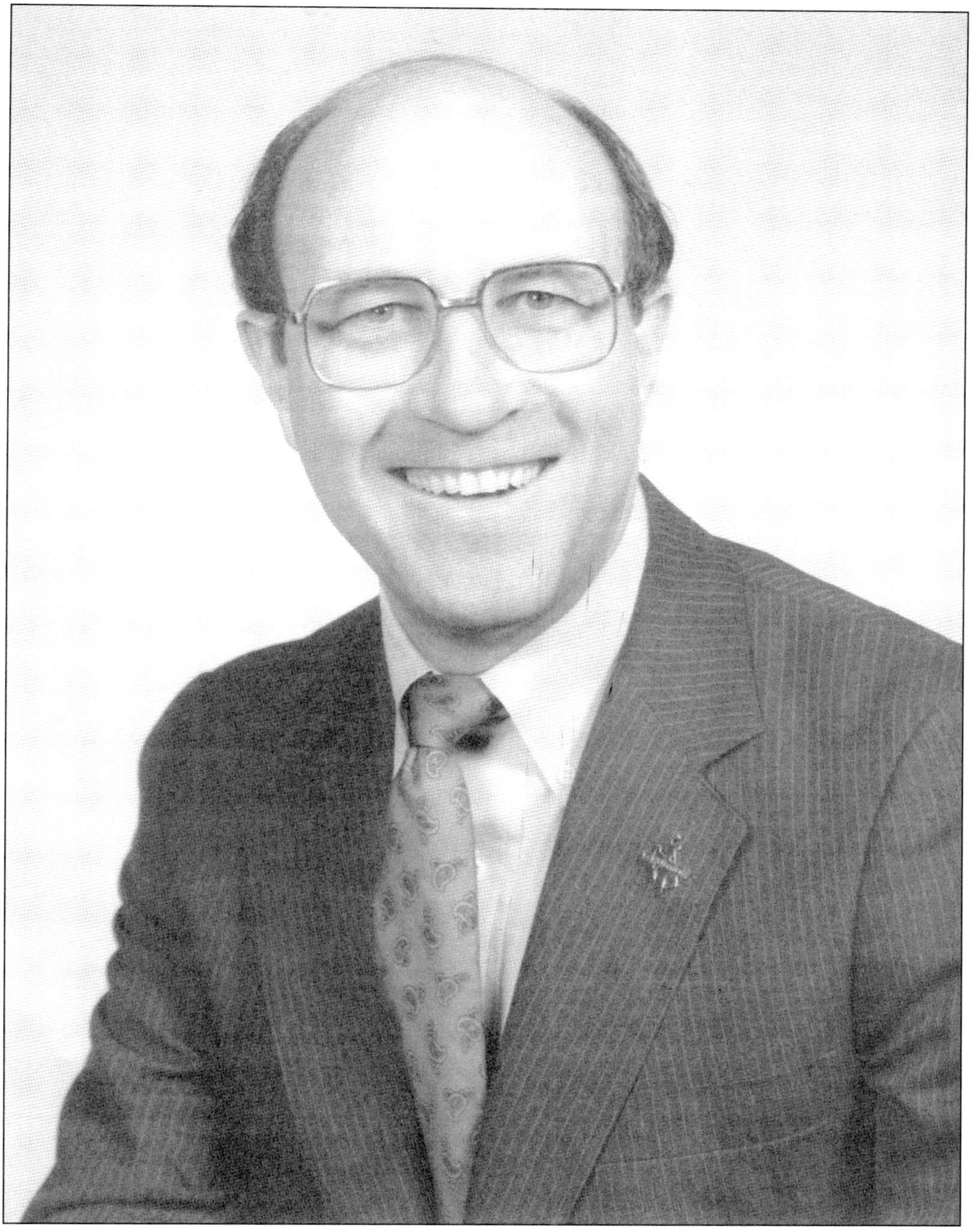

Mike Sullivan graduated from Douglas High School in 1957 as the class salutatorian. He received a bachelor's degree in petroleum engineering and a law degree from the University of Wyoming. Sullivan went on to become one of the state's most popular governors, serving two terms from 1987 to 1995. He often referred to Wyoming as "a small town with unusually long streets." In 1999, Pres. William J. Clinton appointed the former governor as U.S. ambassador to Ireland. Today, Sullivan and his wife, Jane, reside in Casper, Wyoming, where he maintains an active law practice. (Courtesy Wyoming State Archives.)

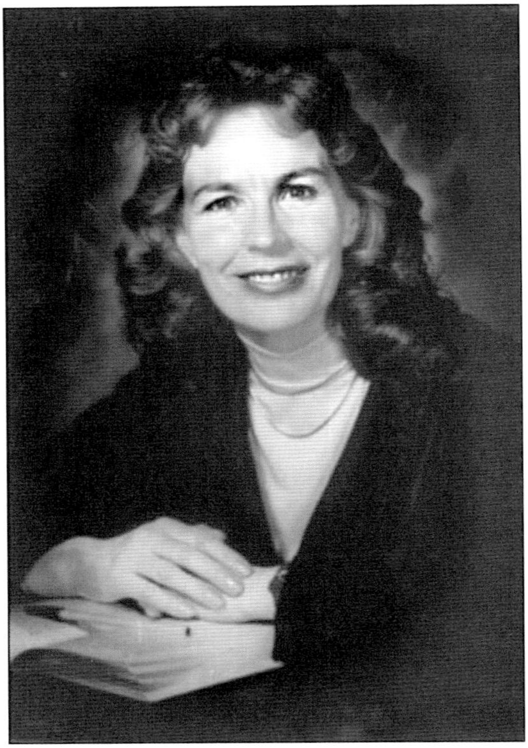

Hazel Cannon Smathers was born and raised in Lost Springs; she graduated from Douglas High School in 1949. After a successful newspaper career, Hazel went on to own and operate a photography studio in Douglas, with her husband, Lee. Hazel was the primary photographer for school pictures, and many students had their pictures taken by her from kindergarten through high school. From 1980 to 1982, Hazel served as the town's first woman mayor. (Courtesy City of Douglas.)

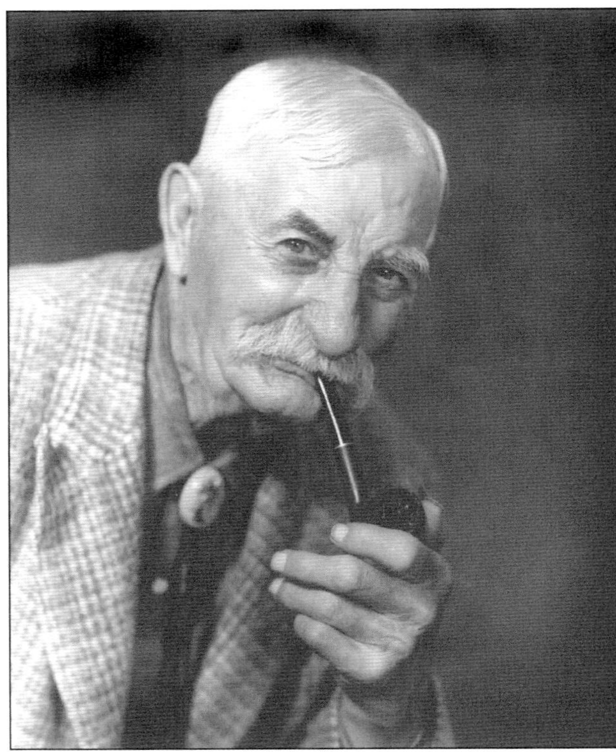

Smathers won many awards for her portraits, including a blue ribbon in 1962 for this image of Martin Price. At 91 years of age, Price was recognized as the oldest man in Douglas during Diamond Jubilee Days.

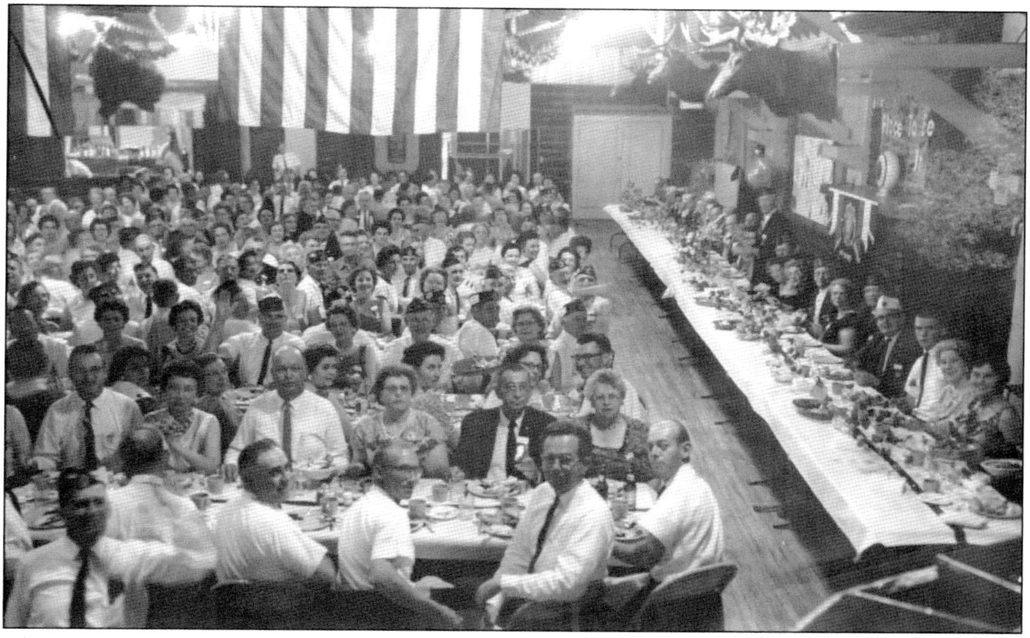

The American Legion was the town's primary gathering place for all types of events. In this image, legionnaires are celebrating the holidays. Attendance and participation was not a concern at any event held at the Legion. The legionnaires and their women's auxiliary were instrumental in providing services of all kinds to the community, and especially honored its veterans.

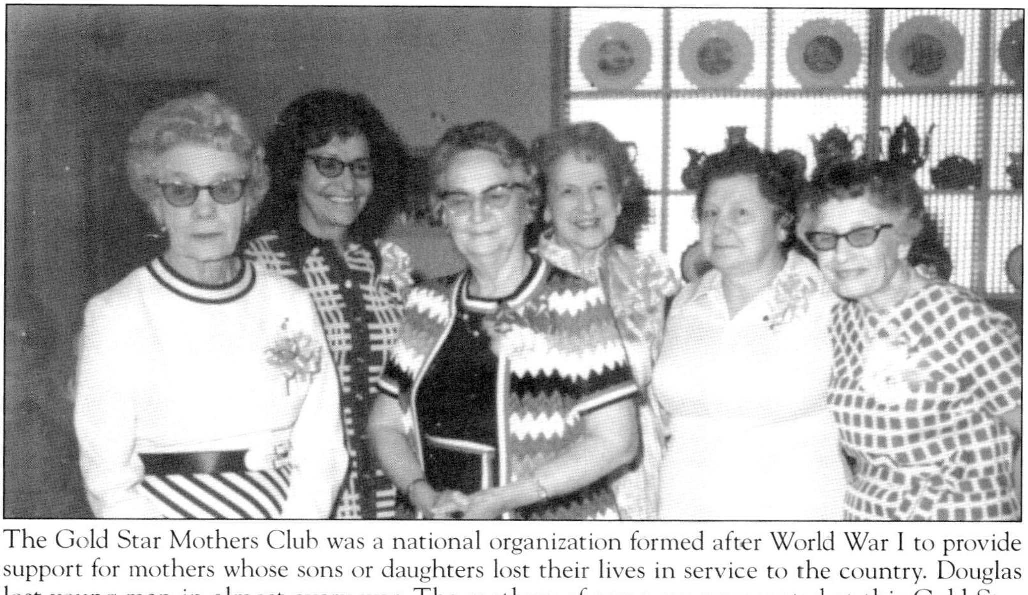

The Gold Star Mothers Club was a national organization formed after World War I to provide support for mothers whose sons or daughters lost their lives in service to the country. Douglas lost young men in almost every war. The mothers of some are represented at this Gold Star Mothers tea event held in their honor. They are, from left to right, Lucille Bower (Cpl. Maurice Jacque Rupe, World War II, U.S. Army); Georgia Graves (Capt. William B. Graves, U.S. Army, Vietnam); Rosie Septer (Sgt. Oren D. Septer, World War II, U.S. Marines); Eleanor Williams (Cpl. Jack Williams, World War II, U.S. Army); Bernice Hill (Spec. 4 Richard Hill, Vietnam), and Viola Cannon (Pfc. James O. Cannon, World War II, U.S. Army).

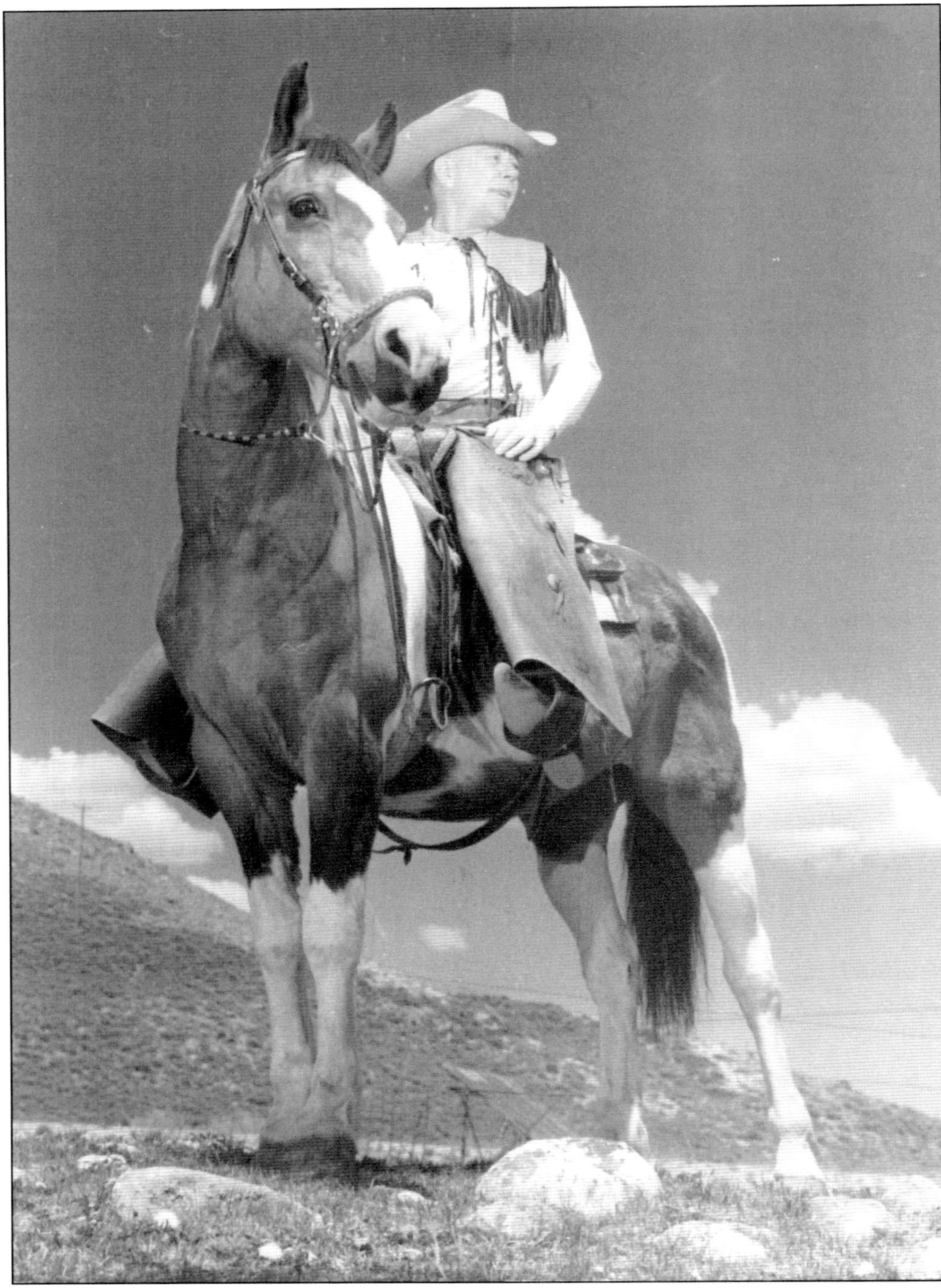

Red Fenwick was an author, historian, and humorist. He considered Douglas his "old hometown" and wrote often about his experiences here. He went on to become a well-respected columnist for the *Denver Post* and entertained readers with his stories about "ranchers in Wyoming, housewives in Kansas, and Native American life in New Mexico." Douglas honored him with Red Fenwick Day, and he was inducted (posthumously) into the Cheyenne Frontier Days Hall of Fame in 2006.

Eight

WHAT ONCE WAS . . .

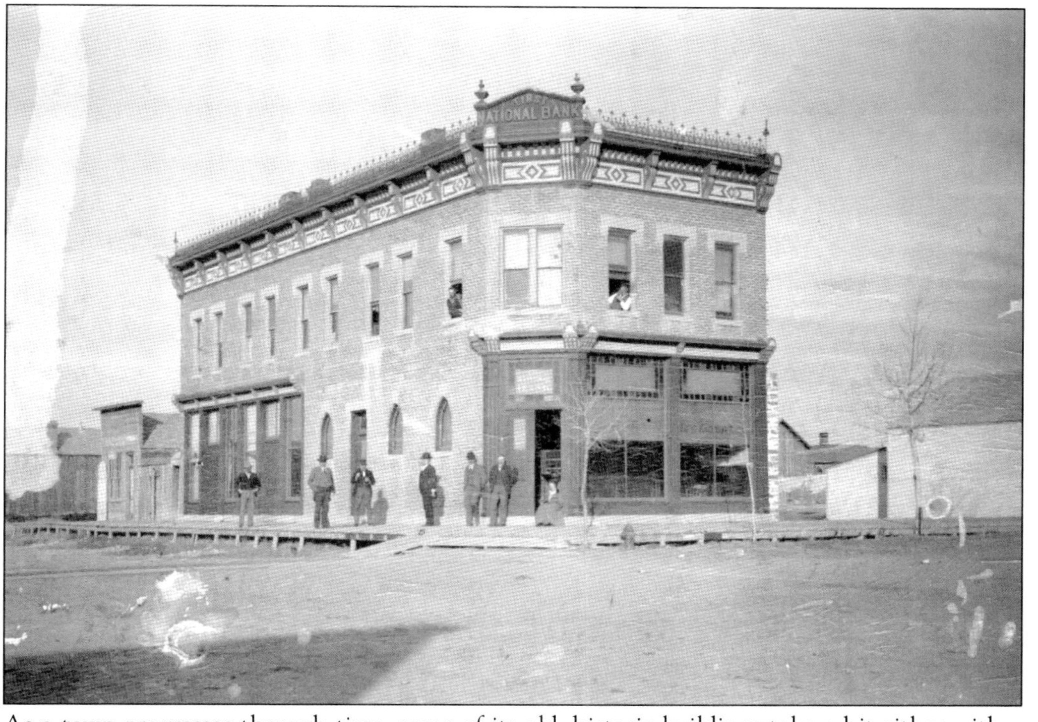

As a town progresses through time, some of its old, historic buildings take a hit either with a wrecking ball, fire, or extensive remodeling. In 1886, this fine example of architecture with its intricate details formed the First National Bank. The bank was the first brick building in town and was located on the corner of Third and Center Streets.

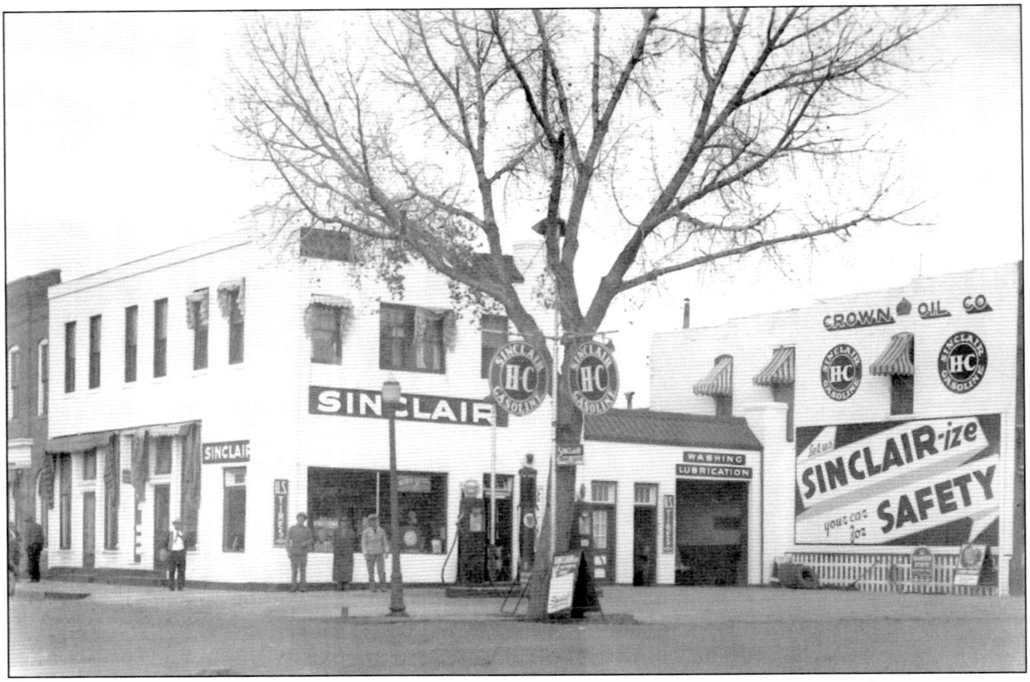

In later years, the First National Bank was remodeled extensively to become a Sinclair gas station. On the left are recognizable remnants of the old bank building.

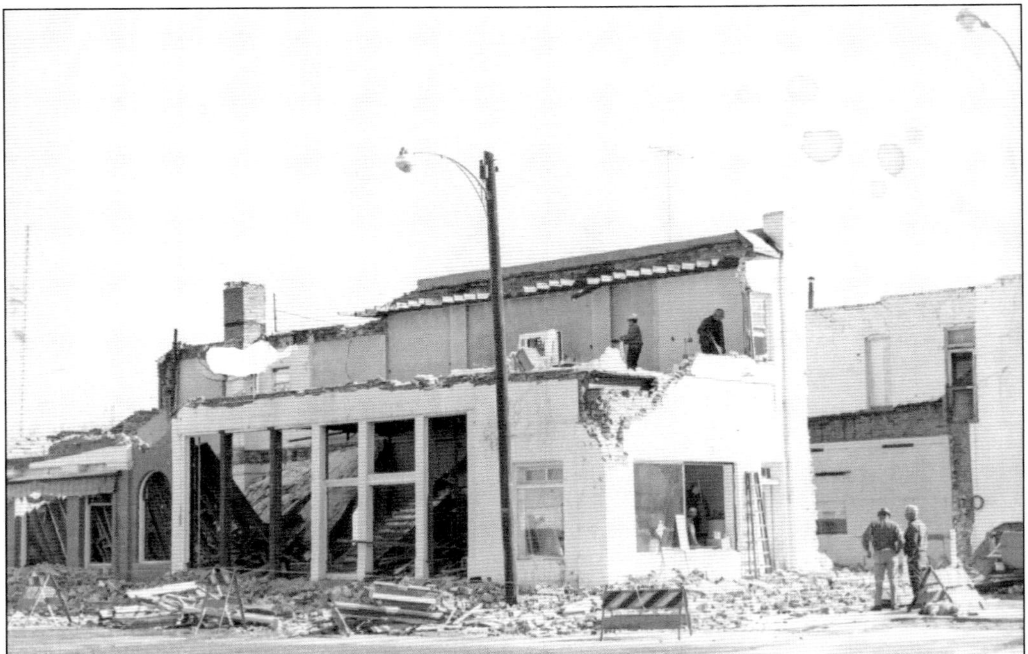

In the 1960s, the Sinclair station faced the same destiny as the bank. Workers took the structure down piece by piece to make way for a new hardware store. The site has seen many businesses come and go over the years; today Hometown Printed Apparel is located there.

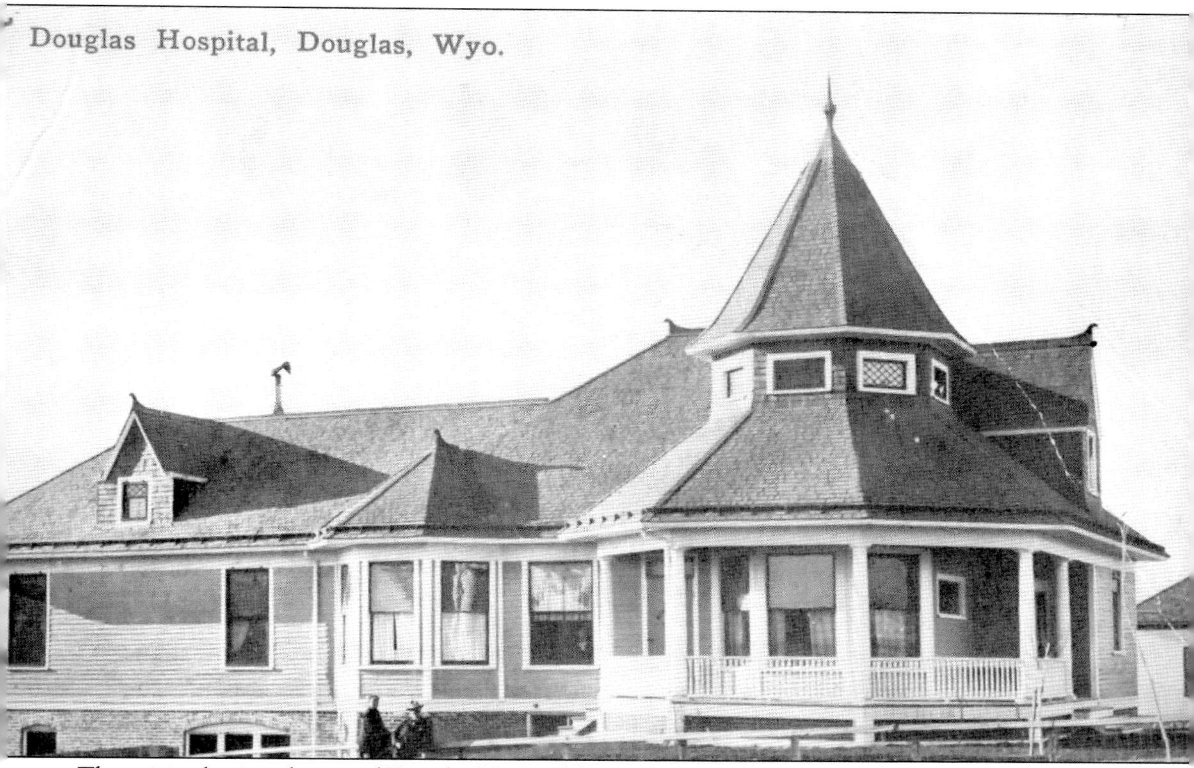

The original privately owned Douglas Hospital, located on North Sixth Street, fulfilled the needs of citizens from 1903 to 1946. Registered nurse Elizabeth Dickson hired a local construction company to build the hospital at a cost of $4,500. It contained a large parlor, spacious dining room, a three-bed ward, three private patient rooms, and a fully equipped operating room "illuminated by a large bay window facing the south." The second story was used by Dickson and her staff of nurses. The former hospital is now a private residence.

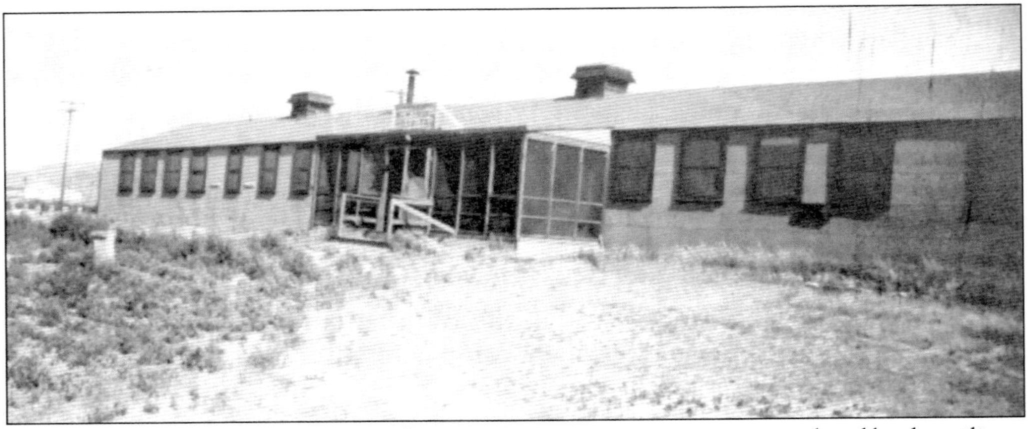

The Douglas Prisoner of War Camp, after serving its temporary purpose, was closed by the military in 1946, and all buildings were ordered sold. Its hospital building, consisting of five wards, two operating rooms, an emergency room, a large kitchen and dining area, and all existing equipment, was purchased by the county for $1. On October 17, 1946, more than 800 people attended an open house celebrating the acquisition of their new hospital.

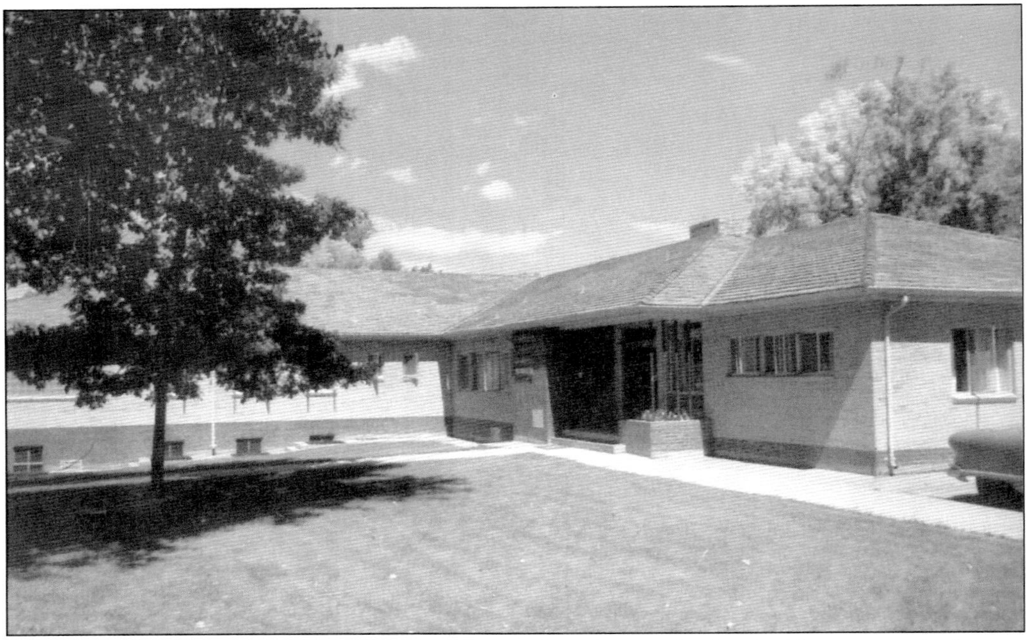

In 1951, the county abandoned the old prisoner of war hospital, after building a new facility on Oak Street. The new hospital was made possible through a bond issue of $200,000. At that time it became known as the Converse County Memorial Hospital. More than 1,400 people attended the open house in November 1951.

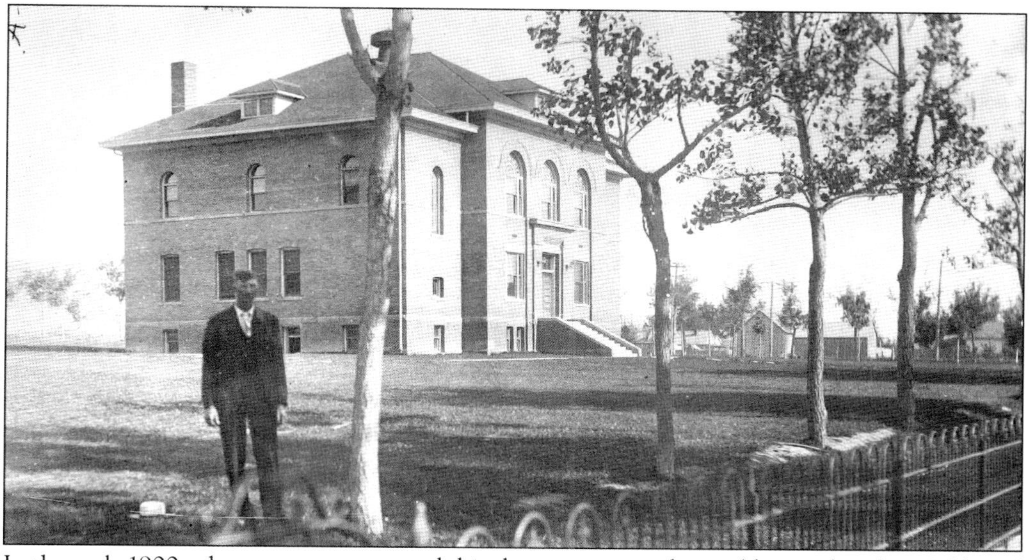

In the early 1900s, the county constructed this three-story courthouse (shown above) on Fifth and Center Streets. It is unknown as to why, just a few years later, in 1915, they chose to construct a "new" courthouse (shown below). The neo-Greek architecture is similar to a building one might find in Washington, D.C. The floors and stairs were of white marble. The woodwork and stair railings were made of beautiful cherry. As none of these commodities is produced in or near Douglas, one can only imagine that everything had to be shipped in on rail. (Notice the large crack in the building to the right side of the Portico. Could this have led to its demolition?) In 1916, the county built a new jail next to the courthouse.

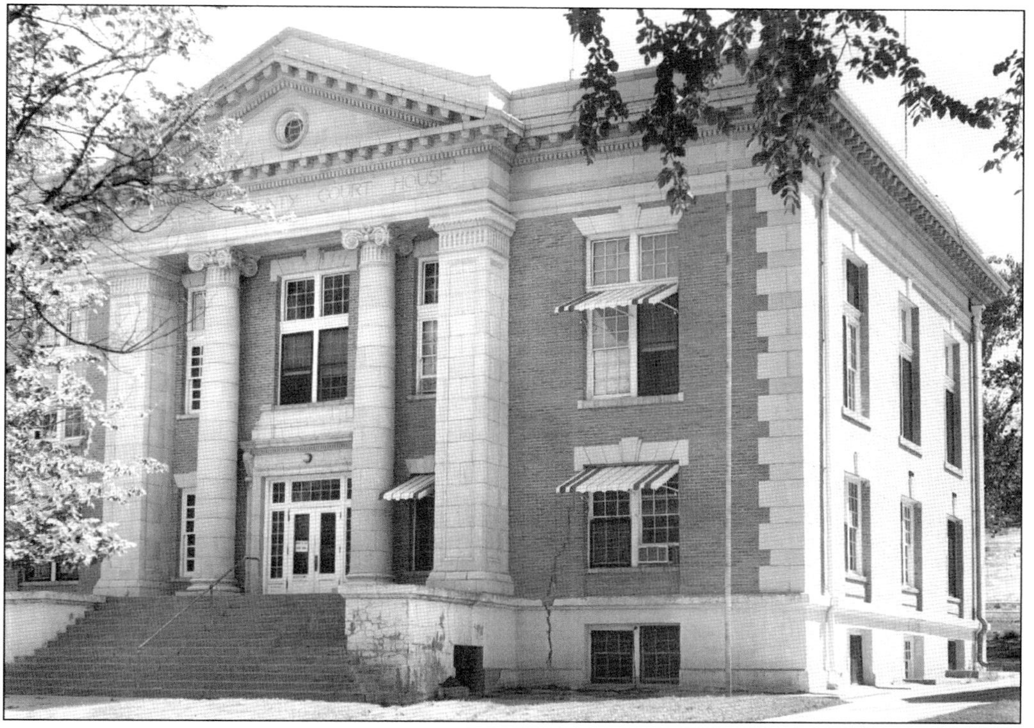

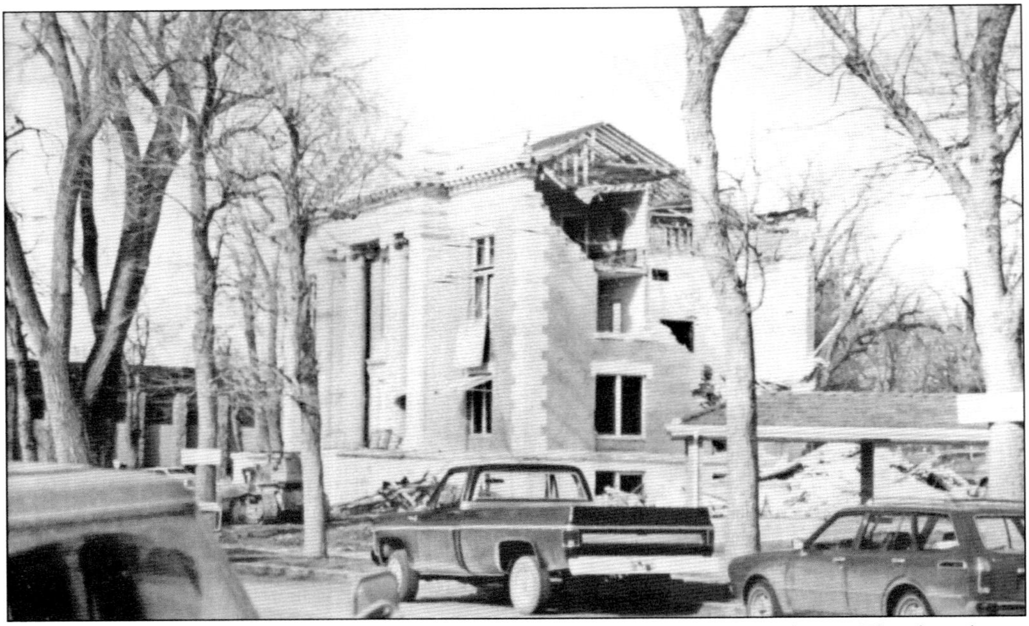

In the mid-1970s both the 1915 courthouse and the 1916 jail were torn down. The demolition of the courthouse is depicted here at various stages. The marble, bricks, and some of the wood were sold outright to anyone wanting them. The rest was taken to the local landfill. The new Memorial Hospital of Converse County now occupies the former location of Courthouse Square. A new courthouse was erected just north of the former location. It houses all the county offices, the sheriff's office, jail, and judicial courts.

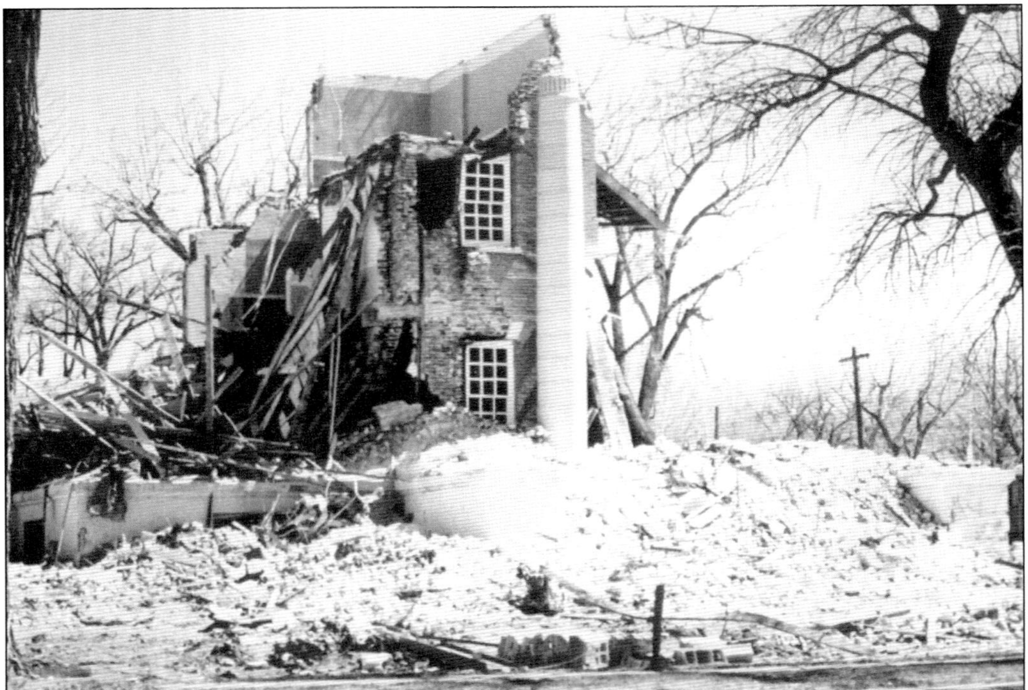

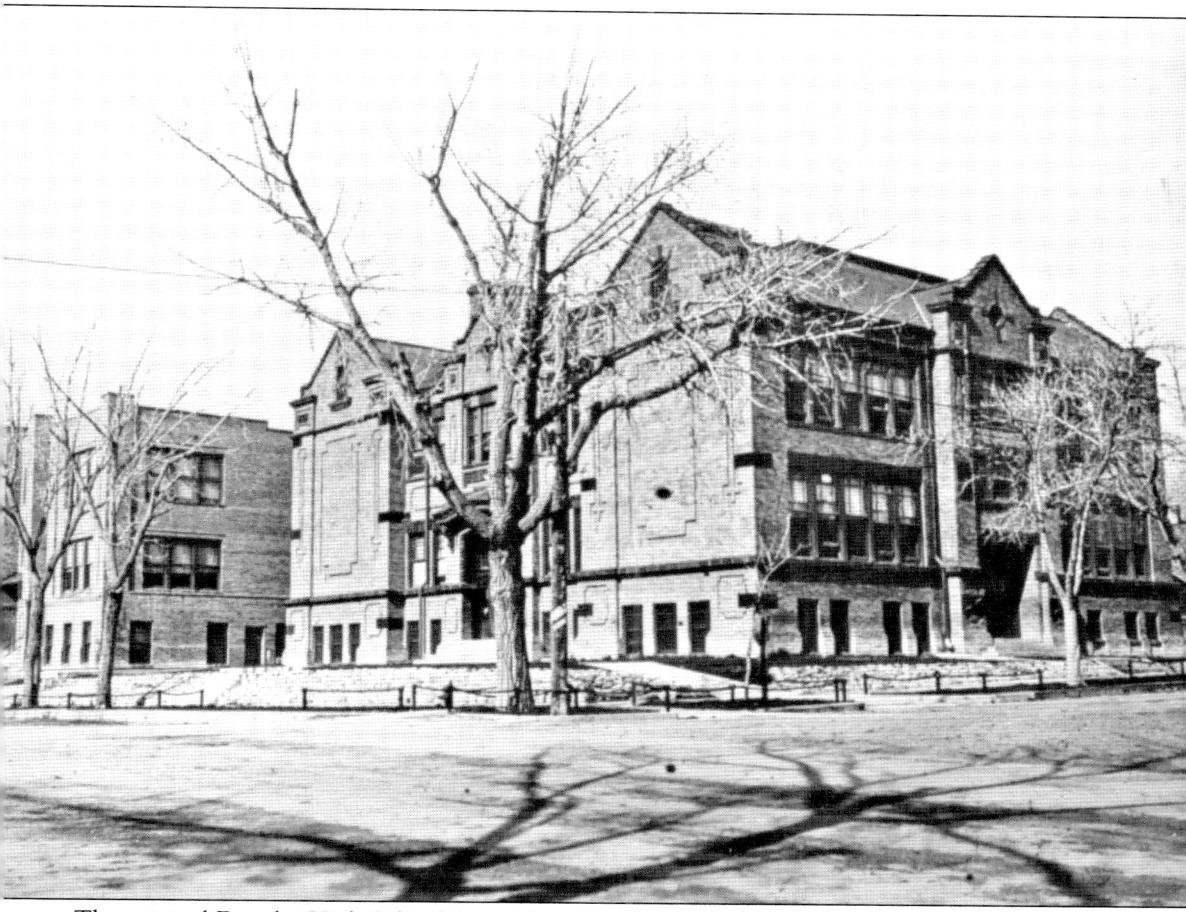

The original Douglas High School, located on Fourth Street, featured a state-of-the-art kitchen with a lunch program for students throughout the system. Elementary schoolchildren from South Grade and North Grade were bused there for lunch. After the high school was torn down, only the first floor of the annex remained, later used for many years as a very popular roller skating rink. Today the annex functions as a Boys and Girls Club. A new high school was constructed in the north part of town, serving the community for many years until it was abandoned in the late 1970s. The current high school, located at the east end of Hamilton Street, was built at that time and continues today as home of the Bearcats.

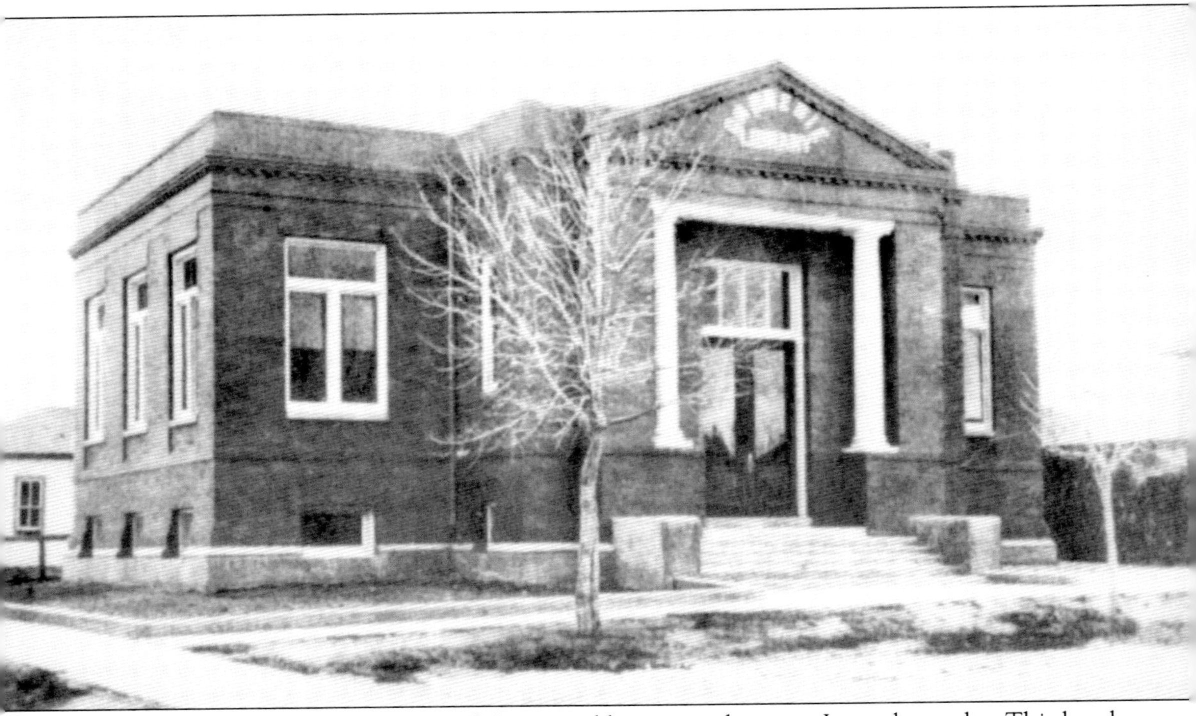

Douglas was home to one of several Carnegie libraries in the state. It was located at Third and Walnut Streets, just north of the existing federal post office. The building committee was made up of prominent Douglasites, including Edward T. David, chairman; Charles Maurer, secretary; A. B. Daniels, treasurer; J. DeForest Richards; and C. H. McWhinnie. Constructed in 1910 by architect J. C. Hadsall and contractor J. H. Esmay, the library served people of all ages. In the mid-1960s, the library was demolished, and a new building constructed on the same site.

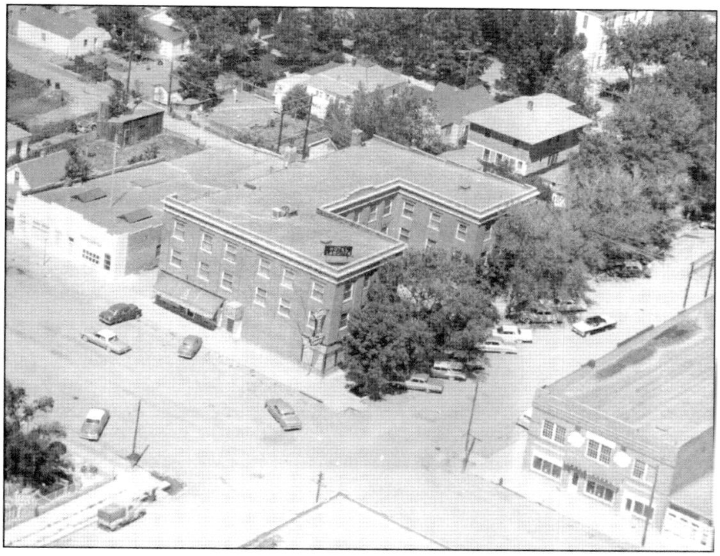

This aerial view shows the original courtyard of the LaBonte Hotel, one of the town's most prominent businesses. Today the courtyard has been enclosed to accommodate an expansion of the bar. To the south of the LaBonte Hotel, facing Second Street, is the old Studebaker Garage. In the 1960s it became Reeves Chevrolet. In the 1970s, along with several other buildings, it was demolished to make room for a parking lot.

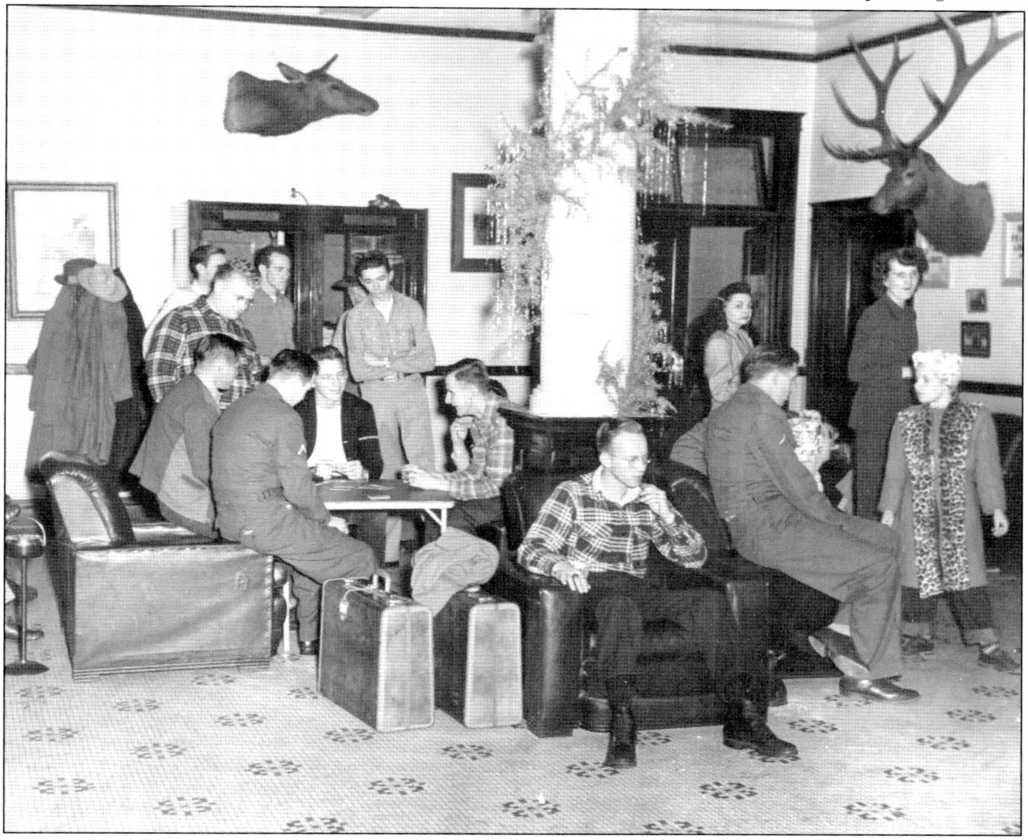

The LaBonte Hotel provided a wide variety of services, including a place for travelers to be picked up by the bus. The holiday travelers shown here are wiling away their time visiting and playing cards. While no longer a bus station, much of the original interior of the LaBonte Hotel is still in place, including the mosaic tiles.

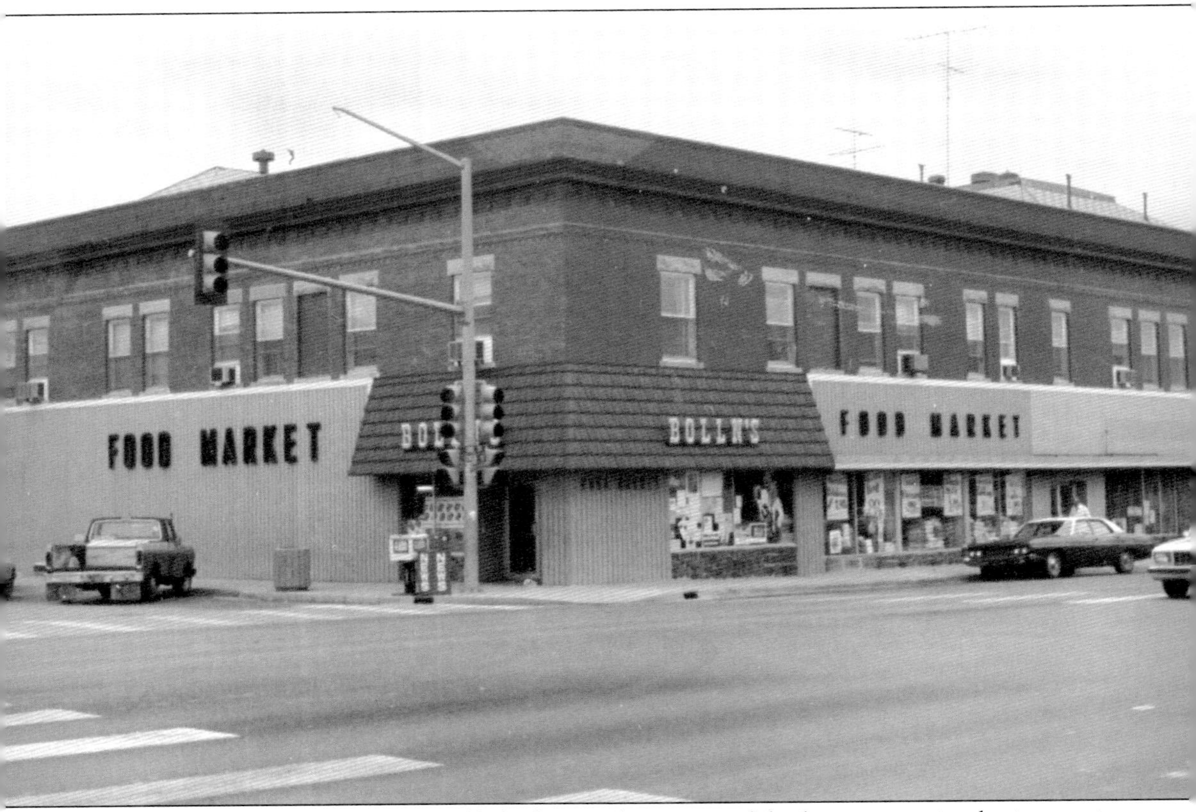

Peyton Bolln's Grocery Store, established in 1915, was one of the longest-running businesses in Douglas. Owned by Albert Peyton and Waldo Bolln, the store served the community for years. The boys applied for enlistment in the U.S. Army during World War I. Albert was accepted, but Waldo was rejected for health reasons. At that time, Waldo purchased Albert's interest in the store, retaining the name. In 1936, Waldo's son, Otto "Beef" Bolln, bought one-half interest, later buying the rest of the business in 1940. In 1970, Beef's son, Butch, bought into the store, buying out his father's interest in 1983. The store was located in the Temple Building on the corner of Third and Center Streets, where it remained until completely destroyed by a fire in the late 1980s. After the fire, the store reopened in a different location on Fourth Street. From the beginning, the owners had a firm commitment to their customers, letting ranchers run a tab and pay their bills at the end of the month, or when their livestock sold. During the Depression, they let people pay what they could, often bartering for services. One of their primary specialties was to make home deliveries, even putting the groceries away for their dedicated customers. In the mid-1990s, the store was sold and renamed Douglas Grocery. On the site today is Jackalope Square, offering townspeople a place to hold Farmers Markets, concerts, and other outdoor events.

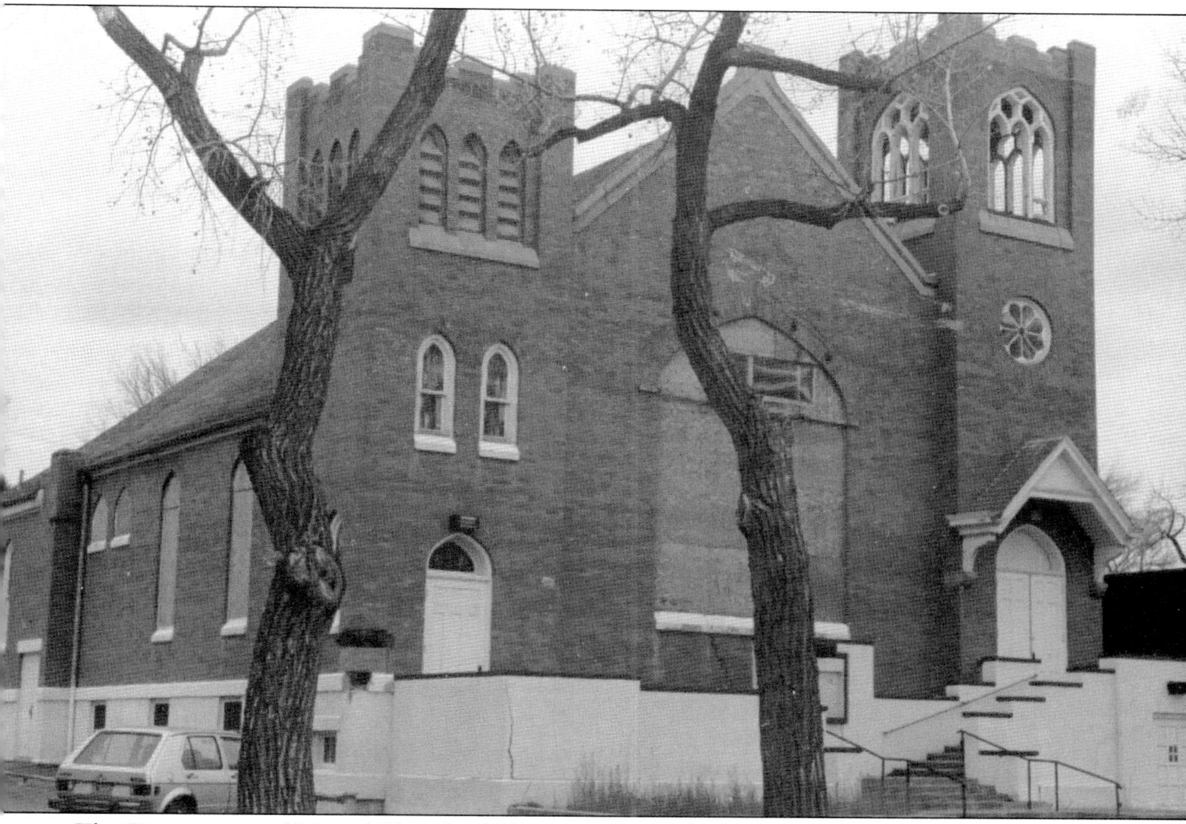

The Congregational United Church of Christ was established in 1886 at Fort Fetterman. In 1887 the first building committee was appointed, choosing a location on Center Street in the new town of Douglas for the church. In 1893, the congregation moved into its new church building on North Fourth between Center and Walnut. In 1916, after much growth, the congregation built this new brick church at the same location. The new building served their needs for more than six decades, including renovations in the 1970s that added new lighting, a new kitchen, a new roof, and a new brick front entrance. In the mid-1980s, this church was demolished. As of this time, nothing has been built in its place. A new Congregational church was built in 1985 at the end of North Sixth Street.

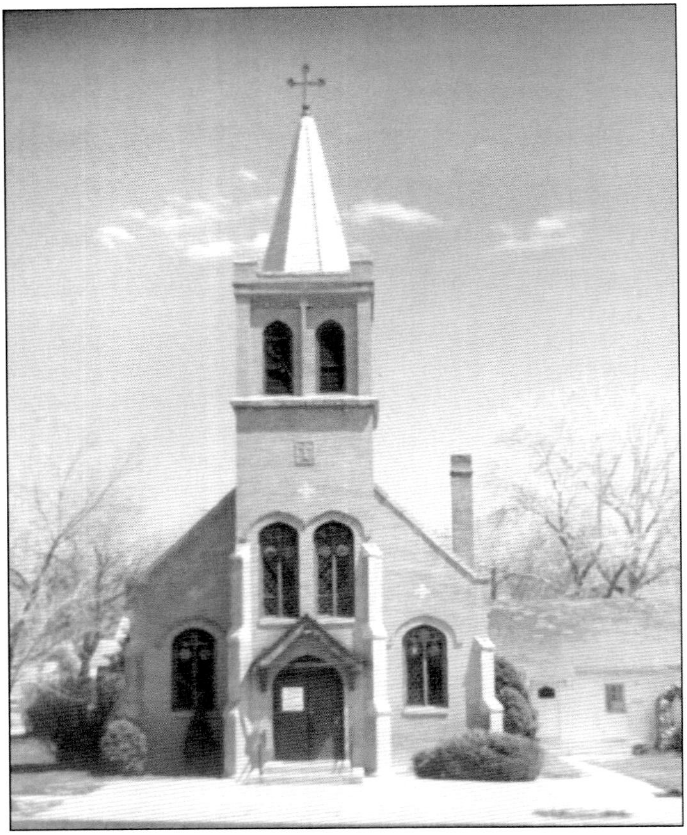

On Sunday, June 5, 1887, Fr. Patrick Brophy officiated at the first Roman Catholic Mass ever celebrated in Douglas, held in a public hall on the west side of town. In October of that year, the Territory of Wyoming became a diocese. Fr. James Keating of Casper came to Douglas regularly for services, building a small church at the corner of North Fifth Street. Toward the end of 1909, Fr. Ignatius Berna was the first Franciscan pastor at St. James Catholic Church. The cornerstone of the new church was laid on Sunday, July 14, 1912, at Fifth and Elm Streets. In 1979, it was evident that Douglas was bursting at the seams, and the church was no exception. An architect and contractor were hired, pledges were made, and the old church came crashing down.

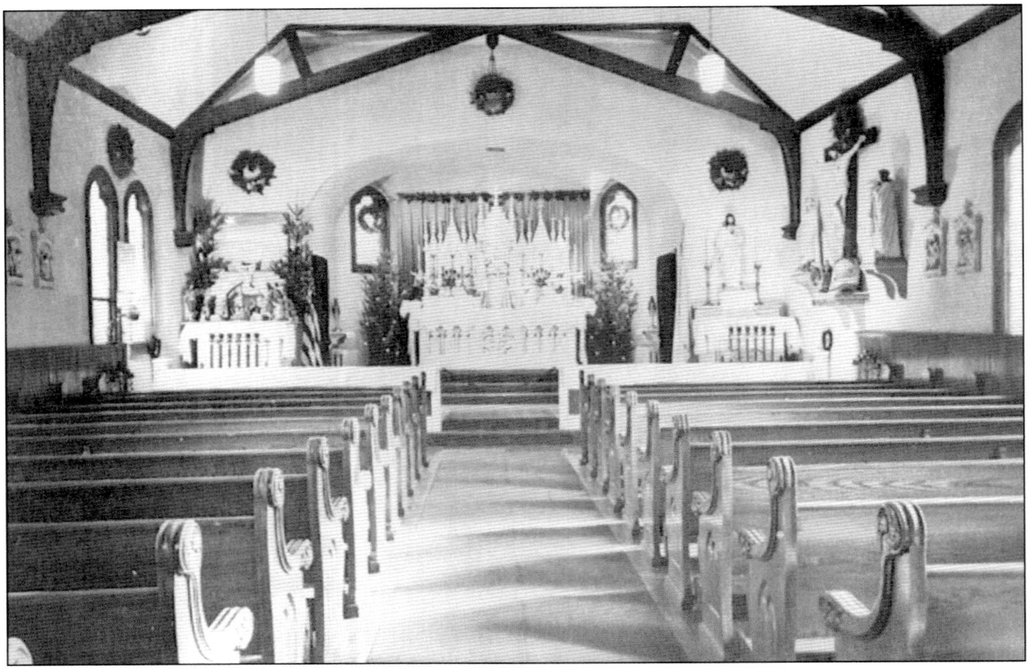

In 1934 the community organized a campaign to develop George Washington Memorial Park, 12 acres of land on the east side of town. Plans called for a 100-by-45-foot swimming pool, as well as a large community house. The local newspaper described the building as "40 by 60 feet, with a full basement and complete kitchen." The project was driven by the Works Progress Administration, an employment relief program initiated during the Great Depression under the administration of Pres. Franklin D. Roosevelt. Construction on the Washington Park Lodge began in earnest two years later, in 1936.

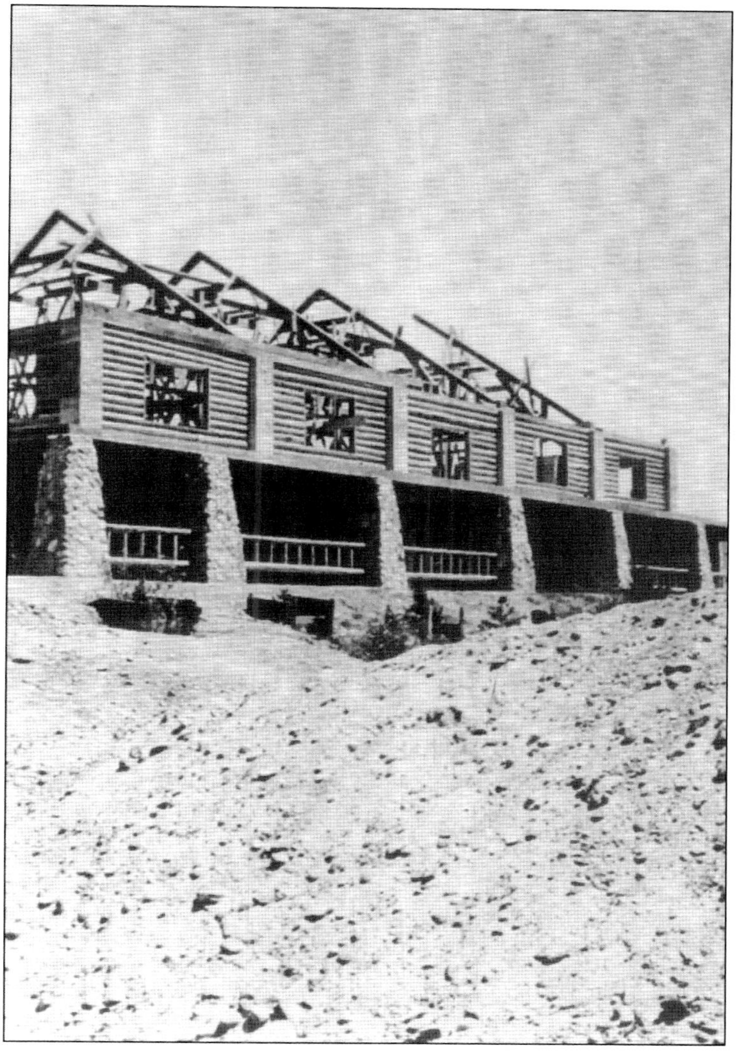

Opposite Page: The original St. James Catholic Church was beautifully decorated with rustic rafters, all the sacramentals, and wooden pews to accommodate up to 175 people. For more than 60 years, the church served the needs of its congregation, adding much to the community. Before the demolition, many of the church's statues and stained-glass windows were donated to other parishes throughout the state. It is common belief that some of the sacramental dishes and other religious objects were simply destroyed. After the church was demolished, a new, more modern structure was built on exactly the same location, where it remains today.

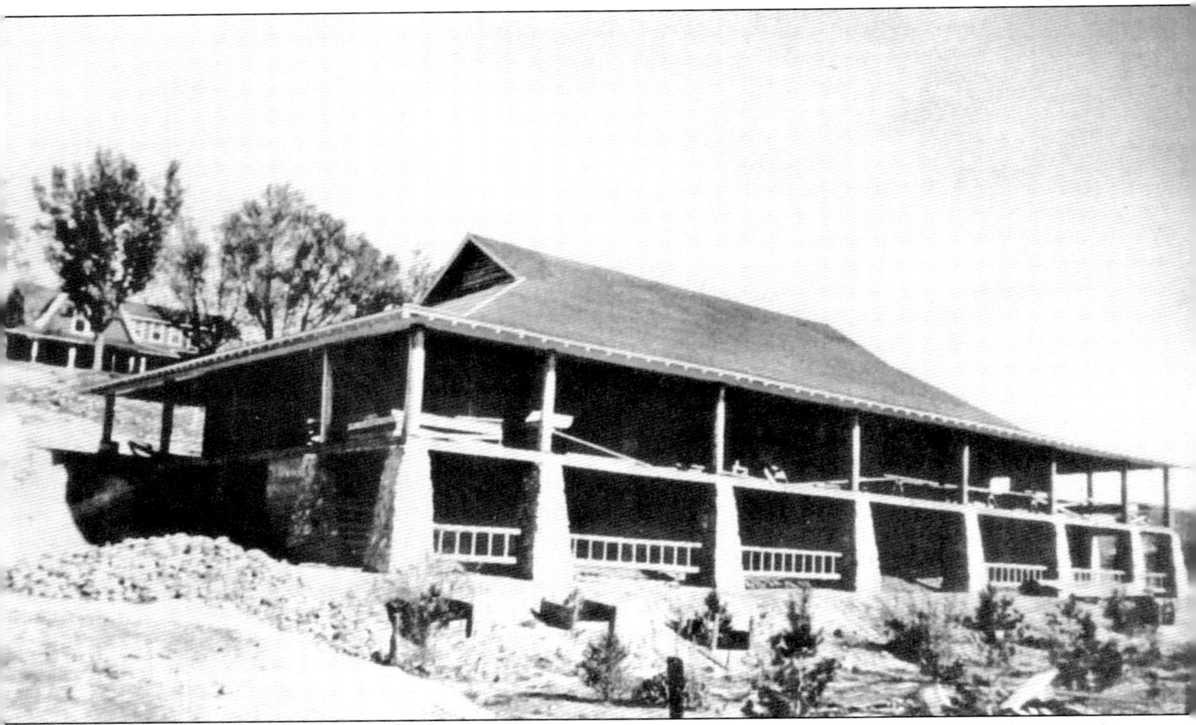

Logs for the community house were donated by Henry J. Bolln, and the cost of additional materials was estimated at $1,000. The logs, brought down from the mountains, were hauled by truck to town where workers peeled and trimmed them according to specifications. A total of $6,404 was allotted for construction of the log building, plans for which were drafted by local contractor J. H. "Pete" Esmay. The park improvements and construction projects were overseen by a group of local citizens called The Washington Memorial Park Board. Comprised mostly of members from several women's clubs, the board also saw to it that trees and shrubs were planted.

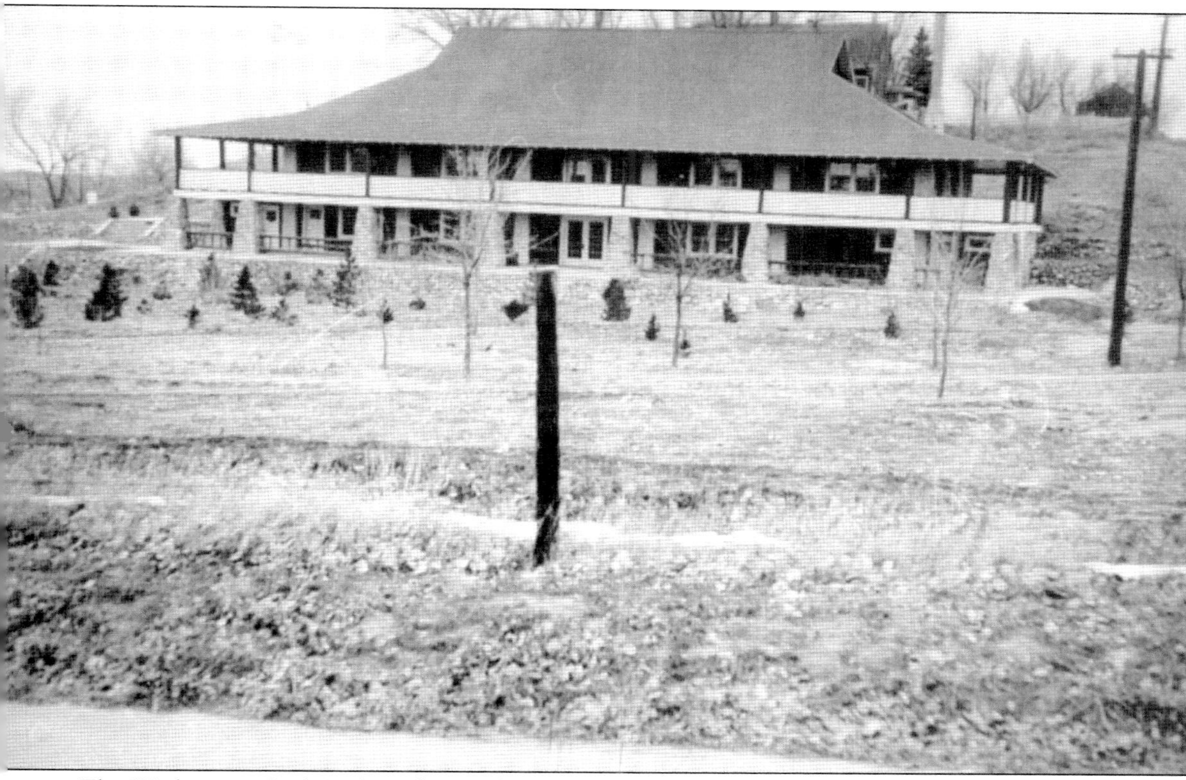

The Washington Park Lodge, of rustic design, featured an open porch running the entire length of the south side, and on the east and west fronts, with the roof extending over the porches. Two fireplaces, featuring rocks collected by the public, and some donated by American Legion Auxiliary departments from every state, were included in the successful effort of "adding to the attractiveness of the two pioneer heating units." The lodge was completed in 1937 and immediately became the heart and soul of the community.

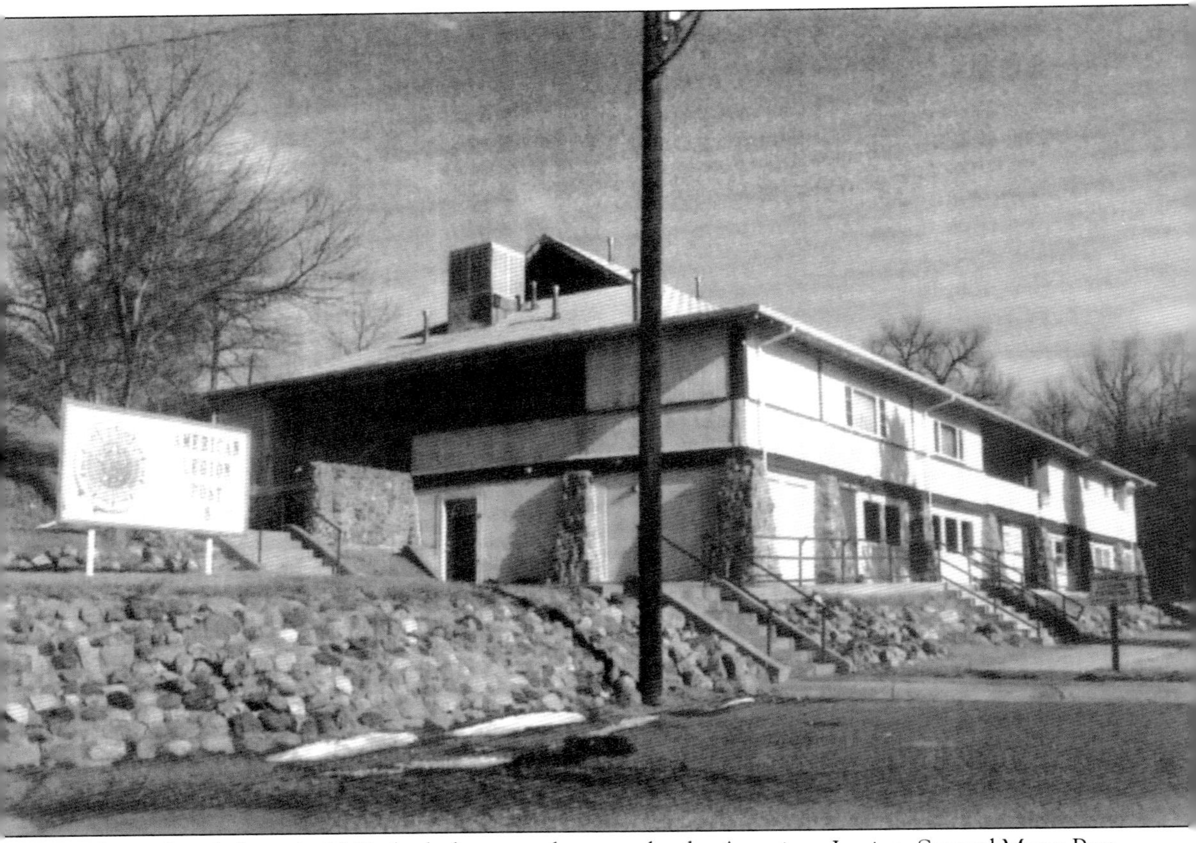

Just a decade later, in 1947, the lodge was taken over by the American Legion, Samuel Mares Post No. 8, which, to this day, uses it as their Post Home. The Samuel Mares Post No. 8 was organized by World War I veterans in 1919, and named for the first man from Converse County to be killed in action in that war. From the beginning to the present the lodge has been an important social institution in Douglas. Over the years, extensive remodeling has taken place, including enclosing the wraparound porches. While some of the building's rustic appearance has been compromised, the function of the facility remains the same: a centralized meeting place for wedding receptions, funeral dinners, dances, bingo, and, of course, a place for veterans to gather.

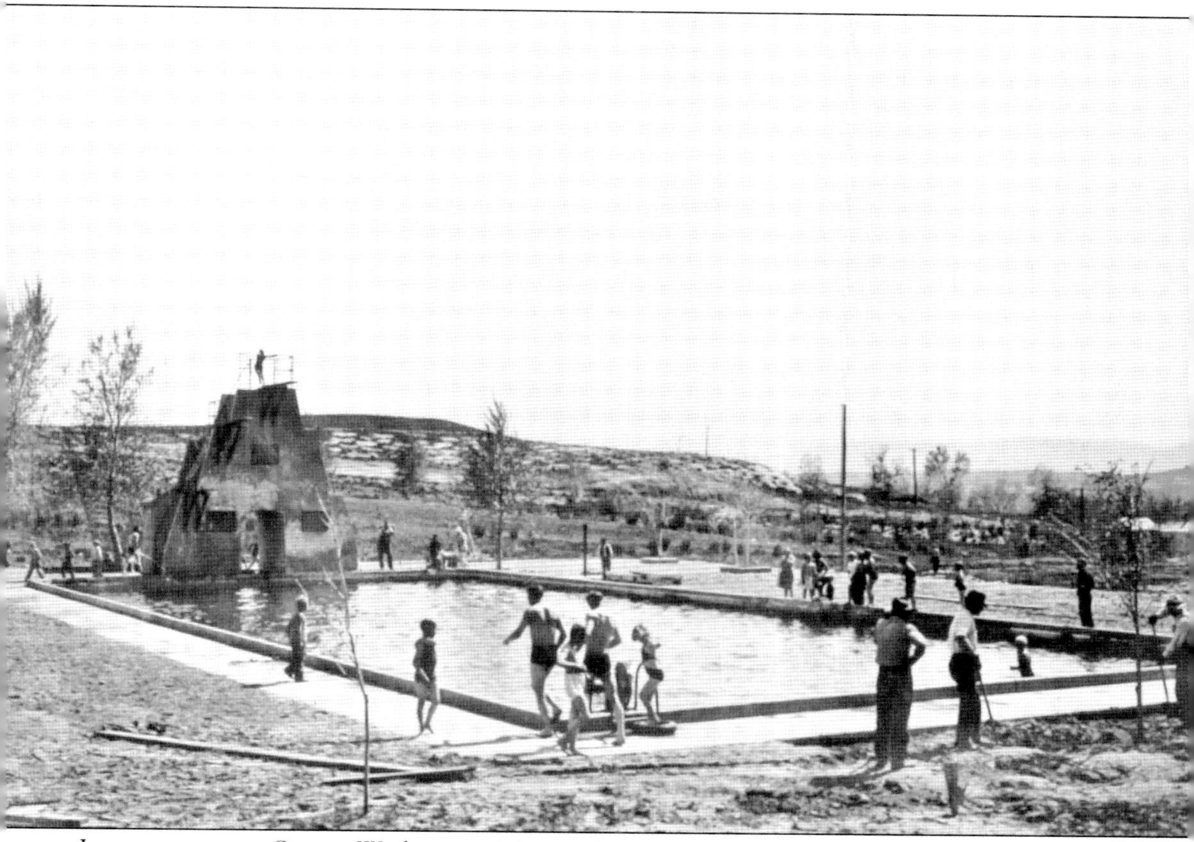

Improvements to George Washington Memorial Park included a swimming pool, shown here. The 100-by-45-foot pool included an enclosed stairway to the high diving board. Over the years, landscaping has been added, the area has been fenced, and the pool has been expanded. Today the original pool has been incorporated into a much larger water park. The pool, in all its variations, has been, and is, enjoyed by many.

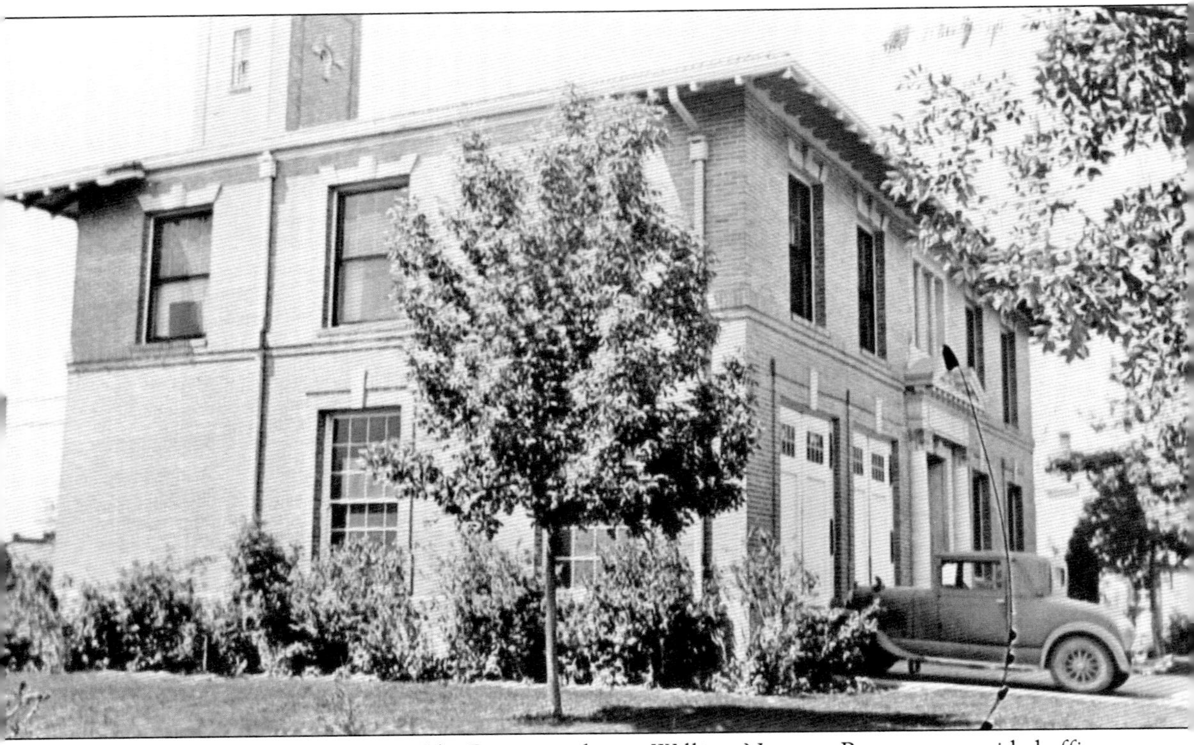

Douglas City Hall, built in 1915 by Denver architect William Norman Bowman, provided offices for employees, a municipal courtroom, police department, fire department, and jail. The familiar noon whistle was housed in the tower to the left. Still standing, the facility now houses the town's economic development agency. The building, a symbol of pride for the community, was nominated to the National Register of Historic Places in 1994. Functions for city hall are now administered out of a building at the corner of Fourth and Center Streets.

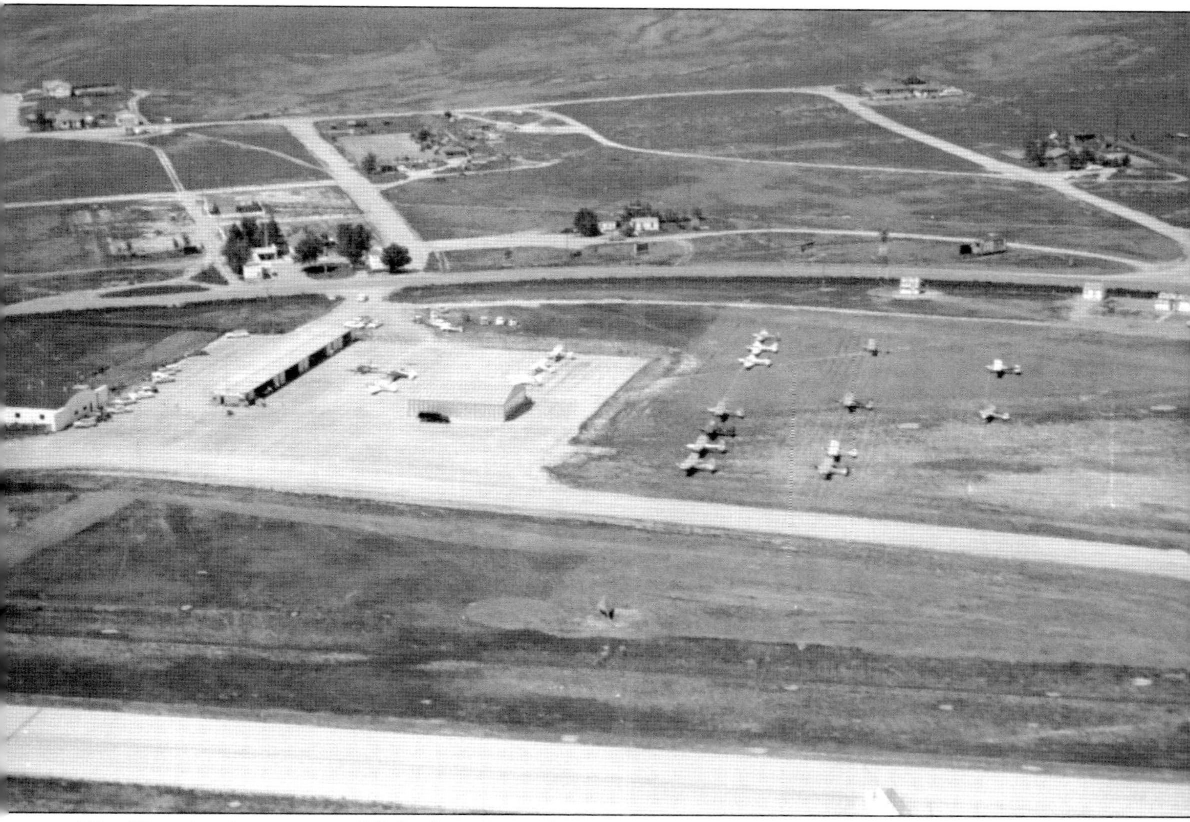

The Douglas Airport, established in the early 1920s, was located on the southern edge of town. The airport provided opportunities for smaller aircraft to fly in and out. Whenever anything big happened in town—like visiting dignitaries, or when a person had to be flown somewhere for medical reasons—the tarmac would fill with locals, there to get a glimpse of someone important or to wish someone well. During an expansion project in the late 1950s, one could enjoy an "inaugural flight" for only $2.50 a person. At that time the airport was maintained by Reeves and Good Aircraft. For a short time, during the energy boom in the 1970s, Frontier Airlines provided service. In the mid-1980s the town grew around the airport, causing officials to fear for the safety of Douglas citizens, and making a decision to move the airport to its present location north of town on Highway 59. Progressive citizens encouraged the development of a motor racetrack at the old location. Today, races at the track bring lots of families and tourists to town.

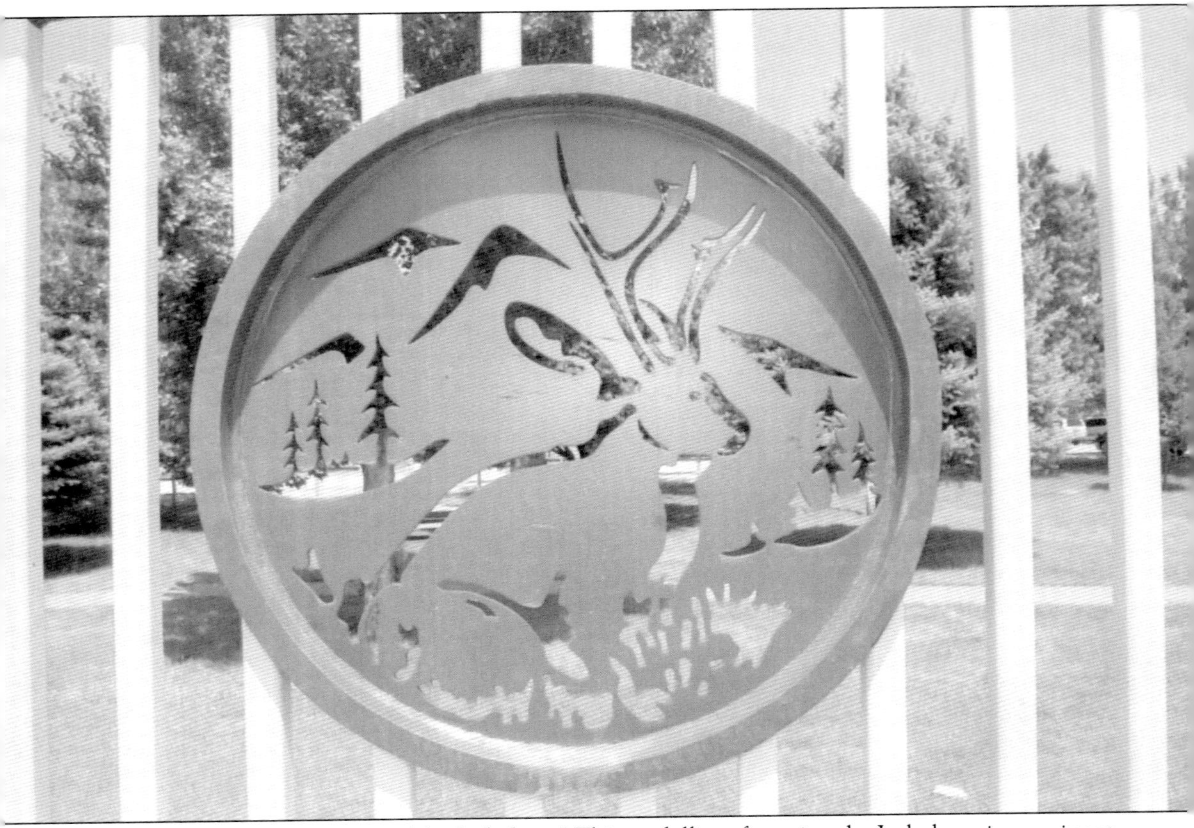

"Douglas, Wyoming – Home of the Jackalope." This medallion, featuring the Jackalope, is prominent on both sides of the brand-new bridge, further expressing the town's pride in its elusive mascot. (Courtesy Douglas Budget, Jourdan Corbitt.)

Bibliography

Barlow, Bill. *Bill Barlow's Budget*. Anniversary Edition, 1907.
Cles, Shirley L. *Heroes Among Us*. Self-published, 2002.
Douglas Budget. 75th Anniversary Edition, 1961.
Douglas Historic Preservation Commission. *Douglas Park Cemetery: A Walking Tour.*
———. *Historic Downtown Douglas: A Walking Tour.*
Leonard, Peggy Layton. *West of Yesteryear.* Boulder: Johnson Publishing Company, 1976.
Marmor, Jason. *Cultural Resource Survey of the American Legion Building*, 2000.
Office of the Area Engineer. U.S. Engineer Office: Douglas, WY, 2000.
Completion Report Douglas Internment Camp, 1943.
Pioneer People of Douglas and Converse County, Wyoming 1886, Douglas Diamond Jubilee Days. Self-published, 1962.
Roberts, Phil. *Wyoming Blue Books*, Volume 5. Cheyenne, WY: Wyoming State Archives, 2008.
The Midwest Review. Published by the Department of Industrial Relations, 1926.
Wyoming Pioneer Association. *Pages from Converse County's Past.* Casper, WY: Wyoming Historical Press, 1986.